CLOSING
THE
CIRCLE

Also by Richard Sandbrook

RICHARD SANDBROOK

CLOSING

THE

CIRCLE

Democratization and Development in Africa

Between the Lines
Toronto

Zed Books Ltd
London & New York

Closing the Circle

First published in Canada in 2000 by
Between the Lines
720 Bathurst Street, Suite #404
Toronto, Ontario
M5S 2R4

Published outside Canada by
Zed Books Ltd
7 Cynthia Street
London, England
N1 9JF
and
Room 400, 175 Fifth Avenue
New York, NY 10010
U.S.A.

Distributed in the U.S.A. exclusively by
St Martin's Press Inc.
175 Fifth Avenue, New York, NY 10010

Canadian Cataloguing in Publication Data
Sandbrook, Richard
          Closing the Circle : democratization and development in Africa
Includes bibliographical references and index.
ISBN 1-896357-37-7
1. Africa—Politics and government—1960- 2. Africa—Economic conditions—1960- 3. Democracy—Africa.
I. Title.
DT30.5.S36 2000   960.3'2   C00-931675-2

Zed Press edition (outside Canada)
ISBN 1 85649 827 1 hb
ISBN 1 85649 828 X pb

Cover and text design by Jennifer Tiberio, for Point of View

Printed in Canada by University of Toronto Press

Between the Lines gratefully acknowledges assistance for its publishing activities from the Canada Council for the Arts, the Ontario Arts Council, and the Government of Canada through the Book Publishing Industry Development Program.

THE CANADA COUNCIL | LE CONSEIL DES ARTS
FOR THE ARTS | DU CANADA
SINCE 1957 | DEPUIS 1957

Canadä

To Judith Barker Sandbrook, my partner in all things

do not imagine that the exploration
ends, that she has yielded all her mystery
or that the map you hold
cancels further discovery

Gwendolyn MacEwen, "The Discovery"

Contents

Tables

Acknowledgements

During the dozen years that I have worked on the themes of this book I have incurred many debts. The Social Sciences and Humanities Research Council of Canada provided funding at various points. I have benefited from the work of three exceptional research assistants: Susan Dicklitch, who now teaches at Franklin & Marshall College, Jay Oelbaum, and Jordi Diez-Mendez. These talented individuals will undoubtedly enjoy distinguished careers in political science. Cranford Pratt and Tim Brook, colleagues at the University of Toronto, were particularly helpful in sharpening my thinking on key issues. My editor, Robert Clarke, receives my respect and admiration for his assiduous attention to detail. At Between the Lines, Paul Eprile shepherded the manuscript through all its stages with tact and inexhaustible good will. As usual, my wife, Judith Barker Sandbrook, was my toughest and most constructive critic. Her impeccable sense of logic and diction enormously improved the manuscript.

This book represents the culmination of many years of reflection. Most chapters include revised and updated sections or versions of earlier published articles. Parts of chapter 2 appeared as "Transitions without Consolidation: Democratization in Six African Cases," *Third World Quarterly* 17:1 (1996). Chapter 3 draws heavily on work I conducted as part of a study group on the political economy of complex humanitarian emergencies between 1996 and 1998. This project was organized by the World Institute for Development Economics Research at the United Nations University, Helsinki. Chapter 4 bears a resemblance to "Democratization and the Implementation of Economic Reform in Africa," *Journal of International Development* 8:1 (1996). Chapter 5 is a modified version of an article I wrote with Jay Oelbaum: "Reforming Dysfunctional Institutions through Democratization? Reflections on Ghana," *Journal of Modern African Studies* 35:4 (1997).

AFRICA

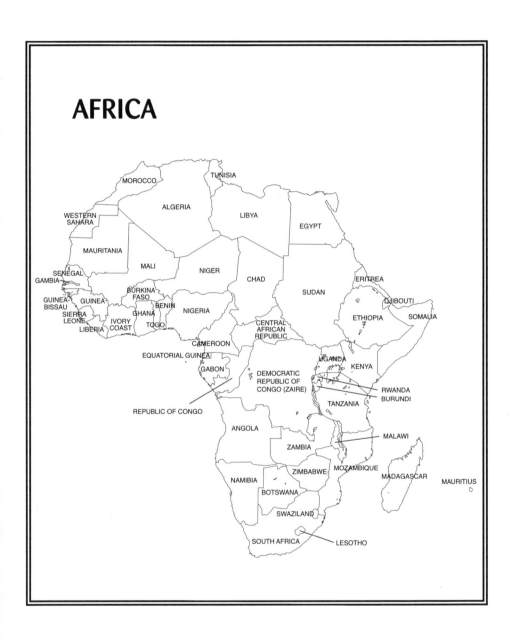

ONE

Patterns and Perspectives

S hould we be surprised that disorder, conflict and economic disarray mark the postcolonial histories of Africa's new states? State-building and nation-building have everywhere been violent and disorderly matters. In Europe through the sixteenth to the eighteenth century, monarchs, princes, lords, and parliaments fought to control and expand proto-states. Peasants and town-dwellers were embroiled in these labyrinthine wars, or independently rebelled against the exactions of ambitious and ruthless rulers. Politics then—and indeed well into the twentieth century in some regions—was a dismal tale of revolts, assassinations, pacification campaigns, and wars. Similarly, in Latin America the independence of most colonies about 1820 led to what novelist Gabriel Garcia Marquez (1970) ironically dubbed "One Hundred Years of Solitude"—a century or more of upheaval and violence as contenders vied to capture and fortify state power. Why should the history of Africa, since independence in the 1960s, be any different?

But Africa, in particular the forty-eight countries of the Sub-Saharan region, cannot afford one hundred years of turmoil. Its massive problems, afflicting a rapidly swelling population, will not be solved until order is created. Mass poverty, economic stagnation, and ecological degradation are obviously cause as well as effect of political disorder. Nevertheless, politics is primary: "getting the politics right" is a precondition of rising prosperity as well as of the liberty, security, and services for which all people yearn.

This dilemma explains the urgency of understanding the significance of the democratic wave that surged across Sub-Saharan Africa in the early 1990s. The earlier authoritarian governments that popular disgust swept away had largely failed to create order and tackle developmental challenges. Would democratic regimes do better? Specifically, do emergent democratic institutions aggravate or help to manage deep-seated ethnic, religious, and other divisions in these new states? Do democratic processes, such as they are, generate the policy and institutional reforms required by a thriving market economy? And what lessons can democracy movements draw from

1

the successes achieved in some democratic experiments? Broadly, these are the questions that have animated my research on development strategy since 1980.

My conclusions, briefly, are these. Democratization's impact varies markedly from country to country. What is remarkable is not that democracy has little substance in most countries—that is to be expected in light of the hostile conditions—but that it does exhibit vitality and promise in others. Also, democratic institutions can aid in averting deadly conflict: rebellions, civil wars, and the collapse of state structures. Although democratization has aggravated conflicts in some deeply divided societies, its institutions have helped manage conflict in others. Our existing knowledge suggests that certain institutional strategies are more likely than others to promote peace under particular conditions. New democracies, however, are only modestly successful in "getting the politics right" for market-based economic recovery. Creating the conditions for peace, order, and industry is the work of decades, not years. Nonetheless, proto-democratic regimes offer at least as much promise in forging the conditions for economic success as the discredited autocracies they replaced. But no African government can do much to change an external constraint on such success, namely the prevailing pattern of globalization. While democratic development—a "virtuous" and self-reinforcing circle of civil and political rights, growing prosperity, and state renovation—is rare, its attainment, I contend, would be eased by reforms of the global market economy. Closing this circle, in Africa and elsewhere, may therefore require a supportive social-democratic reform of globalization.

In support of these conclusions I start here by broadly sketching certain key trends, concepts, and arguments. I look at the authenticity of democratic transitions in Africa, emphasizing the *diversity* in experience (chapter 2). Then I explore how and under what conditions in divided societies democratic institutions foster social peace rather than deadly conflict (chapter 3) and attempt to show, in broadly comparative perspective, the modest contributions of democratic politics to the project of a market-led recovery (chapter 4). A "best-case" analysis (of Ghana), co-authored originally with Jay Oelbaum, illustrates how democratization influences the quest to build the institutional foundations for growth and security in a poor country (chapter 5). That the ascendant "pragmatic neo-liberal" strategy of democratic development has its shortcomings means, I would argue, that we must consider the practicality of instituting a supportive social-democratic globalization (chapter 6).

In all of this, certainly, we must step carefully, for debates about democracy, development, and globalization will surely lead us into an ideological minefield.

From Authoritarianism to Democracy

A strong authoritarian tendency emerged in the 1960s, the first decade of independence for most of the former colonies in Africa. The nationalist movements that had led their peoples to independence generally moved quickly to undermine or abolish the opposition parties. Control of the government gave the ruling group the patronage resources to co-opt opponents and extend and consolidate their support base. Control of the legal and coercive apparatus allowed government leaders to imprison opposition leaders (under preventive detention laws), limit the rights of assembly, free speech, and association, repress recalcitrant newspapers, and intimidate their opponents.

If the opposition did not "voluntarily" merge with the governing party (as in Kenya and Zimbabwe, for example), its parties were banned (as in Tanzania, Ghana, Guinea, and Niger, among others). Robert Fatton vividly describes the common pattern: "The single party became the unique voice of the people, and the unique voice became the exclusive voice of the ruling groups, and soon the voice of the ruling groups became the voice of a unique individual. The nation was the party but the party was the undisputed and unchallenged leader. Thus started the descent of the one party into the cruel hell of dictatorship, privilege, praetorianism, and injustice" (Fatton 1987: 26). As popular disgust with the venality and arbitrariness of single-party states grew, governments usually responded with increased coercion. This growing governmental dependence upon the military set the stage for the wave of coups and countercoups that punctuated political histories from the mid-1960s.

Democracy was soon in short supply. Of the original forty-seven[1] Sub-Saharan countries, only three—Mauritius, Botswana, and Gambia—retained multiparty democracy for twenty years or more. These three cases are atypical in their small populations (about one million inhabitants) and, with respect to the first two, economic prosperity.[2] Senegal, a larger (nine million people) and less prosperous West African country, began a phased return to competitive party politics in 1976 under its poet-president, Léopold Senghor, and maintained this system, albeit under strain, into the new millennium. The only other country that holds some claim to prolonged multiparty rule is Zimbabwe since its independence in 1980; but this is a case of a one-party dominant system in which the incumbent president, Robert Mugabe, has brooked little opposition, constitutional or not.

Circumstances changed dramatically in the late 1980s, ushering in a democratic wave in the early 1990s. Economic depression in the 1980s discredited authoritarian governments. Programs of macroeconomic stabilization and liberalization sponsored by the International Monetary Fund (IMF) and World Bank levied heavy costs on the strategically placed urban workers and middle class (as discussed in chapter 4), pushing them into opposition. Meanwhile, the joint pressures of economic contraction and stabilization programs shrank the patronage resources on which autocratic regimes had rested. Many countries were ripe for political change by the early 1990s. Urban demonstrations, riots, and strikes, and outbreaks of armed conflict or, in some cases, "terrorism," attested to the ferment in country after country. External developments gave impetus to domestic movements. The overthrow of Eastern European tyrants in 1989 encouraged democracy movements everywhere, and the new U.S. and British enthusiasm for democracy following the Cold War deprived "friendly" African dictators of their external supporters, leaving them vulnerable to opponents who espoused the principles of democracy.

The pace and geographical scope of democratization were remarkable. Of the forty-seven Sub-Saharan countries, twenty-nine staged a total of fifty-four elections in the period 1989–94. Election observers declared more than half of these elections free and fair. Voter turnout, moreover, was relatively high, averaging 64 per cent. In fourteen cases, elections initiated a peaceful transfer of power to a new president (Bratton 1998: 54–55). Political liberalization also blossomed in most of the countries that did not hold competitive elections, usually entailing the legalization of opposition parties, the launching of private newspapers, and the right of opposition parties to hold rallies (Joseph 1997: 368). By 1999 only a handful of countries had failed to convene competitive national elections. Holdouts such as Somalia, Sudan, and the Democratic Republic of the Congo (Kinshasa) had already succumbed to state collapse or civil war. Second sets of national elections began in 1995; but in ten of the sixteen countries that had held these campaigns by the end of 1997 the quality of the elections declined relative to the earlier set (Bratton 1998: 56). Opposition boycotts of elections were common.

Democratization, though, is a contested term, and calls for careful definition. I usually employ the formal or conventional usage, in which democratization is a process involving two phases. An *electoral transition* begins with a crack in, or breakdown of, an authoritarian regime. This phase ends with the holding of a "free and fair" election and the installation of a new government. To be free and fair, an electoral system must reflect certain core civil and political liberties: freedoms of movement, association, and expression and the right of all adult citizens to vote and hold office. The second, lengthier phase involves the *consolidation of democracy*: the growth of widespread support for the formal institutions of democratic competition and governance. Clearly, democracy will have little meaning if, between periodic electoral contests, rulers govern autocratically. The consolidation of democracy therefore involves the internalization of rules governing the exercise of power on a day-to-day basis, as well as of rules underpinning free and fair electoral contests. Political leaders, to achieve legitimacy, must come to accept horizontal accountability between elections—that they are answerable to the legislature, courts, oversight agencies (such as an auditor-general), and even the media, for their actions. Perhaps only Mauritius and Botswana approximate consolidated democracies in this broad sense, although opposition leaders in both countries would dispute this assertion.

I also employ a second, more informal sense of democratization. This refers to the activities of "popular" or grassroots movements to empower groups of citizens by asserting their rights or enhancing their control over their lives. The Greenbelt Movement in Kenya, for instance, mobilizes rural women for the seemingly prosaic task of planting trees; yet this particular organizational process has also shown broader implications for rural power relations. Although the term can be used to refer to both of these formal and informal processes, here, unless otherwise mentioned, democratization refers to the former.

How should we evaluate the authenticity of democratization in this formal sense? Skeptics contend that, whatever its theoretical merits, democracy in contemporary Africa is largely a sham. For critics on the left, Western-assisted democratization fosters only "low-intensity democracy" or "consensual domination," which functions merely to legitimize open-market economies (which is part of "structural adjustment") and divert the masses from a more radical democratization of social and economic life (Robinson 1996: 4, 6, 67).[3] "Polyarchy [Western-style formal democracy] in the emergent global society," according to W.I. Robinson, "has as little to do with democracy as 'socialism' in the former Soviet bloc had to do with socialism" (Robinson 1996: 384). Issa Shivji (1990), a foremost African critic of liberal democracy, also makes this general argument. Far from heralding major political reforms, he claims, multiparty democracy will, at best, merely widen the recruitment of political elites while the vast inequities and the old practices of cronyism and clientelism will continue as before. Western governments and agencies assist African democratization in order to reassert capitalist hegemony and encourage market-based development by disciplining capricious dictators. John Saul, another critic of liberal democracy and advocate of popular democracy, correctly argues that "much of the literature on 'Third World' democratization has come to turn on a very narrow reading of democratic possibility" (Saul 1997: 340). This reading is rooted, Saul suggests, in the notion of "polyarchy" (as popularized by Dahl 1971) in which democracy is reduced to a procedural exercise— periodic competitive elections in which organized groups vie for the popular vote in a context of protected civil liberties. Democracy is thus "thin," restricted to the political sphere and involving the replacement of one section of the elite by another. What is required instead is movement towards a "popular democracy." This notion is defined variously: by Saul (1997: 351) as synonymous with democratic empowerment, by Shivji as a political regime based on the expansion of popular participation via people's organizations, and by Robinson (1996: 57) as a "dispersal throughout society of political power" that can be used "to change unjust social and economic structures."

Albeit "thin" and elite-dominated, Africa's new democracies, I contend, are still experiments worth preserving and extending. It is inaccurate to characterize democratization as a foreign imposition, or even as solely an affair of the elites—unless that elite is construed to include such underprivileged elements as Ghana's famous "verandah boys," for example. Dictators have often yielded to genuine democracy movements, which sometimes draw upon a long tradition of struggle against oppression.[4] That Western powers have supported African democratization largely because it suits their own economic and strategic objectives is true, and their efforts to promote Western-style democratic governance may well bolster the hegemony of the emerging global political and economic order. But the story does not end there. Scholars often criticized the U.S. and other Western governments for supporting friendly dictators during the Cold War. Should we then fault these same governments when they have dumped dictators in favour of elections and due process—especially when this external support is avidly sought by Africa's democratic activists? Consider also the phenomenon of unintended consequences. Critics assume that Western governments can exercise considerable control over political processes in Africa. This proposition is dubious. Although outsiders may wish to promote market-friendly governments and divert radical grassroots tendencies, history suggests that they possess only limited leverage in achieving these goals.

Then too, just because African democracy can accurately be characterized as thin, it is not, therefore, a sham. Most mainstream evaluations also highlight the shortcomings of these experiments (see, for example, Diamond 1996; Bratton and van de Walle 1997; Joseph 1997; Chabal 1998; Osaghae 1999). In light of Africa's hostile structural and historical conditions, one would not expect otherwise. Yet if certain democratic regimes have decayed into "pseudo-democracy," others have not (see chapter 2); and new democracies are always a work in progress, not a final outcome. When regimes are in flux, it is premature to judge them definitively.

Even a low-intensity democracy may be preferable from the viewpoint of ordinary citizens to its practical alternative—which in Africa's conditions is probably renewed dictatorship. None of the critics offers more than the vaguest notion of what the more desirable alternative, popular democracy, would concretely entail, or how it might be achieved. Even Saul accepts that the prospects for popular democracy are bleak (Saul 1997: 351).

Democratization and Deadly Conflict

Democratization is potentially valuable not only as a defence against tyranny, but also as an institutional means of channelling and managing dangerous conflicts. Is this a merit of Africa's new democracies?

The weight of evidence—and it is, indeed, very weighty—suggests that democratic openings have often aggravated communal tensions in divided societies (see Conteh-Morgan 1997: ch.6). In the Africa of the 1960s and 1970s, the autocrats' strongest justification was that only a one-party state or military regime could safeguard national unity. Free, party-based competitive elections in heterogeneous societies, critics claimed, encourage leaders to manipulate latent regional, ethnic, or religious animosities as a way to mobilize electoral support. Since control of the state confers access to vast resources in societies with weak private sectors, this high premium on political power further aggravates the tensions surrounding electoral contests and all allocative decisions. Africa's recent democratic wave provides ample confirmation of these inherent dangers:

⦿   In **Congo (Brazzaville)**, Denis Sassou-Nguesso's party militia (the Cobras), backed by Angolan army units, overthrew elected President Pascal Lissouba in October 1997 in a five-month war that a U.S. reporter likened to "a high-tech urban gang war, the Crips and Bloods facing off with artillery and rockets" (*Washington Post*, Oct. 18, 1997). Sassou was a former military dictator, defeated by Lissouba in a rare multiparty election in 1992. Lissouba had miscalculated in June 1997 by trying to disarm Sassou's Cobras and other party militias in advance of a scheduled election. Because Lissouba drew his support from the south of the country and Sassou from the north, the conflict assumed an ethnic dimension. Vast stretches of Brazzaville were reduced to rubble, and ten to fifteen thousand people died in the conflict. Even a year later, much of the capital still lay in ruin. Violence erupted again in December 1998, as troops of the government and its Angolan ally cleared opposition strongholds in Brazzaville and elsewhere of their armed militias.

⦿   In the **Central African Republic**, too, a multiparty election in 1993, following several decades of authoritarian rule, set the stage for an ethnic-based civil war in 1996–97. The French, during a century of colonial rule before 1960, had relied principally on the Mbaka and Yakoma of the south for local administrators. Leaders of these groups continued to rule, under French tutelage, until 1993. The election of the northerner Ange-Félix Patasse to the presidency heightened ethnic tensions, because Yakomas still controlled the army. Non-payment of salaries in 1996 provoked Yakoma soldiers to mutiny, leading to fighting that was only halted a year later by an African peacekeeping force and an agreement to include the opposition in a government of national unity. Elections in November and December 1998 went ahead without a major incident, under the eyes of a United Nations peacekeeping force.

◉   In **Kenya**, ethnic clashes on the coast occurred in 1997 as supporters of the ruling KANU government of President Daniel arap Moi sought to "cleanse" the province of migrant opposition supporters prior to December's national elections. Ethnic cleansing had also preceded 1992 elections, which foreign donors had forced upon the authoritarian Moi government— though in this case the violence had occurred mainly in the Rift Valley stronghold of the governing party. In both cases the violence seemed to confirm the president's oft-repeated warnings that multiparty elections would aggravate ethnic animosities. But since the minority-based KANU was the main beneficiary of the ethnic cleansing and intimidation, these warnings sounded more like threats to opposition supporters than forecasts. The streets of Nairobi and other cities flowed with blood as insistent opposition demands for electoral reform were met with violence and divide-and-rule tactics.

These cases appear to confirm the skeptics' view that democratization, far from mitigating ethnic conflicts, may heighten them and even spawn civil wars (see, for example, Kabaya Katumbwa 1986; Sorensen 1996; Kohli 1997; Rapoport and Weinberg 1997). Marina Ottaway (1995: 235–36) succinctly identifies the critical dilemma: "Democratization . . . is a highly disruptive process in itself: it encourages the conflicts that exist in a collapsing state to manifest themselves freely, but without the restraint of the checks and balances, and of agreement on the basic rules, that regulate conflict . . . in a well-established democratic system. Democracy as a stable state is highly desirable, but democratization, or the process of getting to such stable democracy, can trigger highly undesirable side effects."

Yet the case against democratization is not quite so firm. Many authoritarian regimes too have had little success in dealing with ethnic rivalries. The endemic communal strife that pushed authoritarian Liberia, Sierra Leone, Chad, Zaire/Democratic Republic of the Congo, Uganda, Ethiopia, Somalia, and Sudan into civil war or state collapse cannot be blamed on democracy. On the contrary, democratization is looked to as a partial answer to these countries' deep-seated conflicts. Democratization has also apparently facilitated ethnic accommodation, political stability, and growing prosperity in certain African countries:

◉   **Mauritius**, a small yet exceedingly heterogeneous island country in the Indian Ocean, is divided by race (an Indian majority and Creole, African, and Chinese minorities), religion (52 per cent Hindu), and caste (within the Hindu Indian majority). But it has, since independence in 1968, steadily consolidated democracy. A pattern of shifting governmental coalitions has allowed all communities an opportunity to share power and gain access to public goods (Bowman 1991). This accommodative system has enhanced political stability, which in turn has reassured foreign and local investors. Good government, an effective response to a deteriorating economic situation in 1979, and an astute export-oriented industrialization policy have generated rapid economic growth and further dampened ethnic/religious/caste rivalries (Brautigam 1999).

◉   **Botswana**'s story is in some respects similar. Though equally as small as Mauritius, Botswana is less heterogeneous in that about 70 per cent of the population speaks Setswana. This cultural homogeneity does provide a basis for unity, yet, as the Somalian civil war so graphically illustrates, it fails to guarantee harmony. Indeed, the Batswana identify themselves as belonging to nine "tribes," and rivalry among these tribes is intense (Parson 1984: 52–53). Whereas the opposition parties garner their support from one or more of the tribes, the governing party, through seven elections after 1965, managed to gain backers from all or most of them through the strategy of "ethnic arithmetic" in the allocation of government posts. This political stability, together with sound administration and ample diamond and other mineral reserves, has fuelled steady growth and relative prosperity.

◉   **Mali** is another example of democratization promoting ethnic accommodation and recovery, though its circumstances differ markedly from those of Mauritius and Botswana. This country harbours among the most hostile conditions for democratization to be found anywhere. Mali is one of the world's poorest and least urbanized nations: life expectancy is only forty-six; and Malians have virtually no experience of democracy, inasmuch as the French manipulated political life before independence and authoritarian governments prevailed from 1960 until 1991. But the country has two assets: a history of ethnic harmony (excepting the Tuareg), which derives from the predominance of Islam and the role of Bambara as a lingua franca for 80 per cent of the population; and a popular basis for the democratic transition. Antigovernment protests in March 1991 precipitated a provisional government; this in turn led to a broadly based National Conference that drafted a constitution attuned to Malian circumstances. Although the Third Republic inaugurated in 1992 would have its share of problems, particularly frequent shifts in the coalitional basis of governments and election boycotts, it would also have its share of successes. These included ending the four-year rebellion of the northern-based Tuareg in 1996, fostering gradual economic improvement, and holding a second set of (admittedly controversial) elections in 1997 (Ramaro 1997).

Democratization, then, has seemingly contributed to forestalling vicious conflict in some societies, while it has exacerbated such conflict in others. Political liberalization is a gamble. However, since the alternative is probably not a benign, albeit authoritarian, developmental state but a predatory and weak autocracy, this gamble is worth taking. Under certain conditions and on the basis of certain institutional strategies, democratization can play a positive role in halting or reversing a society's downward slide into deadly violence. Hence, chapter 3, though accepting the well-documented case that democratization has often exacerbated ethnic conflicts, nonetheless endeavours to identify those efficacious conditions and democratic institutional forms that will reconcile rather than inflame communal cleavages and suspicions.

Democratization, Economic Reform, and the State

Some experts argue that democratization can also be valuable in fostering the policy and public-sector reforms required by market-led recovery. How valid is this argument?

That democracy leads to sound economic policy and growth is certainly not self-evident. During the era of state-led development in the 1960s and 1970s, scholarly opinion inclined towards the contrary view. Developing countries, as prominent development economist Jagdish Bhagwati (1966: 204) once phrased the dilemma, face "a cruel choice between rapid (self-sustained) expansion and democratic processes."[5] The reasoning behind this proposition was straightforward. According to Jack Donnelly (1984: 257):

> The exercise of civil and political rights may disrupt or threaten to destroy even the best-laid development plan, and must therefore be temporarily suspended. For example, elected officials are likely to support policies based on short-run political expediency rather than to insist on politically unpopular but economically essential sacrifices. Freedoms of speech, press, and assembly may be exercised so as to create or inflame social division, which an already fragile polity may be unable to endure; free trade unions often merely seek additional special benefits for a labor aristocracy; elaborate and punctilious legal systems on the Western model may seem to be extravagant anachronisms; and so forth.

Yet in the 1980s a major shift occurred in development thinking with respect to both the proper balance between state and market and the merits of democracy in promoting economic reform. The market-led approach of neo-liberal models came to dominate development thinking about Africa, and the reasons for this ascendency are complex.[6] Economic trends were important, especially the failures of state-led development in Western countries as well as in Africa and Latin America in the 1970s and 1980s. Political trends played a major role: the emergence of neo-conservative political leaders such as Margaret Thatcher and Ronald Reagan, and the discrediting of the socialist alternative with the collapse of the Soviet bloc.

In Africa most governments have had little option but to adopt structural adjustment (market-oriented reforms). All but a handful of Sub-Saharan countries fell into steep economic decline in the late 1970s or early 1980s— manifest in a rise in inflation (outside the franc zone) and a drastic fall in output, export revenues, and private capital inflows. Their desperate need for foreign credit pushed African governments into the arms of the IMF and World Bank. The IMF had long been a bastion of neo-liberal thinking; the World Bank became a convert in the early 1980s. Both organizations, and the bilateral donors whose generosity to particular recipients depended on an IMF seal of approval, negotiated policy and institutional conditions with African governments in exchange for loans and credits. Thus a massive experiment in social engineering began in the early 1980s.

Underlying neo-liberal or neo-classical analysis is the assumption that market exchange is the universal or natural form of economic behaviour. Market forces are always present, waiting to be released from their fetters. A major fetter is a monopolistic and interventionist state, which in various ways prevents the expression of economically rational behaviour. The aim of economic reform, therefore, is to remove such fetters so that the economy can assume its natural state. This approach will allow for increased efficiency, sustained growth, and eventual prosperity.

The neo-liberal model has not, however, remained static. The World Bank has had a preponderant influence in shaping both development strategy and its intellectual foundations. Successive official Bank reports reveal shifts in the mainstream view of the market-state relationship and the role of politics in the adoption and success of neo-liberal reforms.

The initial formulation of the Bank's adjustment thinking reflected a fairly pure neo-classical perspective. An overextended state is the principal factor accounting for economic stagnation, according to *Accelerated Development in Sub-Saharan Africa* (World Bank 1981). The solution is, therefore, to pare down the size and responsibilities of the state, augment its capacity to fulfil its minimal economic role, and correct a variety of "domestic policy deficiencies" that waste resources and suffocate market forces. The report places a high priority on these policy reforms, especially the removal of biases against agricultural production in the form of overvalued exchange rates, high direct and indirect taxes on primary commodities, and low producer prices. Such structural reform, the World Bank confidently expected, would produce results within several years.

However, Sub-Saharan Africa's intractable conditions soon impelled the Bank to adopt a more broad-gauged, complex, and long-term approach. One important dimension of this shift was a recognition of the centrality of political factors in Africa's economic decline and recovery. *Sub-Saharan Africa: From Crisis to Sustainable Growth* (World Bank 1989) still treated the state as a major part of the problem of economic decline; but now, it said, the state also needed to be a major part of the solution. On the one hand, this report contended, the policies and practices of increasingly predatory states were stifling entrepreneurship and investment. State-interventionist policies and instability favoured "rent-seeking" behaviour[7] and encouraged waste, speculative investments, and capital flight. Incompetent and unpredictable management of the public sector magnified these problems. Legal systems that failed to safeguard property rights or enforce contracts further discouraged potential investors. On the other hand, if it was to play certain essential roles in economic recovery, the state had to be reoriented and rejuvenated. Improved governance, said the report, is essential to economic recovery; indeed, the economic crisis was largely a "crisis of governance." Government had to possess the technical capacity to engage in complex negotiations with donors and to design or at least implement complex reform programs. More fundamentally, this report acknowledged, states needed to create a facilitative "enabling environment" for the private sector. If certain institutional conditions for the efficient operation of markets were absent, downsizing overextended governments and removing constraints on market forces would not suffice Markets could not work their magic in the absence of social peace and political stability, a range of reliable physical and social infrastructure, a disciplined and expert Weberian-type bureaucracy, functioning financial institutions, the rule of law, and a predictable and non-confiscatory tax system. If these conditions did not exist, the state must create them.

The reorientation and rebuilding of African states thus assumed a high priority in World Bank and donor assistance after 1989. One set of programs aimed to enhance the governments' administrative and technical capacities. Actually, the Bank's concern to promote superior public-sector management dates from 1983, as its *World Development Report* (World Bank 1983) of that year attests. However, these "public-sector assistance programs" were extremely narrow in scope; they focused on reducing the civil service, devising appropriate salaries policies, and implanting better financial management. After 1990 the World Bank deepened its commitment to augmenting the capacity of African state apparatuses. For example, the body established a Capacity-Building and Implementation Division in its Washington headquarters and, with the United Nations Development Programme (UNDP), an Africa Capacity-Building Foundation in Harare, Zimbabwe. This Foundation aims to augment the critical mass of well-qualified policy analysts and managers in Africa's public and private sectors.

Improvement of governance constitutes a second programmatic response to the weak and predatory nature of many African states. Implicit in this notion is the idea that "getting the politics right" for capitalist development is as essential as getting the prices right. But what is good governance, and how is it to be promoted? The term remains vague. In its *Governance and Development* report the World Bank (1992) equated good governance with "sound development management." This improvement was to flow from enhanced accountability within the public sector, transparency and openness in decision-making, the rule of law, and more efficient public management. More concrete is identification of better governance with democratization and the protection of human rights, especially freedom of expression. Bilateral aid donors have felt far less inhibited than the international financial institutions (IFIs) in linking democracy to better governance. To explicitly support "democratic governance," the U.S. Agency for International Development, for instance, merged the concepts of governance and democracy in 1992. The IFIs and the donors, after 1990, sought to promote better governance through a combination of political conditionalities and financial support for particular projects.[8] The financial support ranged from bureaucratic capacity-building programs through projects aimed at rejuvenating moribund judiciaries or underfunded national assemblies to assistance to human-rights organizations and non-governmental organizations.

If economic recovery demands a structural adjustment of politics as well as economies, then, forward-thinking neo-liberals hope, democratization might be the vehicle of such an adjustment.[9] Democratization should re-establish the rule of law, open up policy debates, reduce governmental waste and capriciousness through enhanced accountability, and empower coalitions supporting market-based reforms.

Many outside the neo-liberal camp, however, reject this case for democratization in Africa. The adjustment viewpoint is highly instrumental, even technocratic: recovery requires market reforms, but these reforms will neither be properly implemented nor, if implemented, work their magic, unless African governance improves. And democratization remains the best way to reform capricious, interventionist, and predatory government and empower pro-market forces. Hence, according to this viewpoint, political liberalization, in addition to its intrinsic merits, is a means to an important goal: to return an economy to its "natural," or unconstrained, state—that is, to a self-regulating market economy. But skeptics who do not regard free-market solutions as self-evidently correct find this instrumental logic unpersuasive.

Is there, then, a case for structural adjustment that might prove persuasive even to those who do not subscribe to the neo-liberal faith? We obviously have to establish such a case, if we are validly to assess African democratization from the viewpoint of its efficacy in fostering market reform. I believe that such a case exists, but it does not rest on the contention that adjustment has, to date, demonstrated its economic and social prowess.

Unfortunately, no methodology exists to forge a consensus on the efficacy of the market-led development model in Sub-Saharan Africa. Whereas the World Bank in its periodic reports paints a rosy picture of early and intensive adjusters achieving superior economic performance, critics vociferously disagree. The methodological problems are several.[10] Analysts with different political values will select different measures of success and failure. They will also differ in their estimation of how quickly a country should show positive results, and how extensively a particular country has implemented economic and political reforms. Since, moreover, many other factors, including international conditions, are also changing, isolating the impact of any particular policies on overall prosperity is challenging. And a judgement ultimately hangs on the analyst's evaluation of alternatives: their coherence, likely efficacy, and political feasibility. Even the vaunted "counterfactual" method, which supporters of adjustment tend to favour, is of dubious validity. In that method the analyst evaluates success by comparing a reforming country's performance to the counterfactual, that is, to what would have happened if that country had not adjusted. But critics contest such judgements because of the speculative assumptions that constitute the counterfactual. Are we to believe that countries with imploding economies would have continued with the same failed approaches?

Despite the methodological uncertainties, most observers would probably agree that economic progress after more than a decade and a half of adjustment has been modest. A thumbnail assessment would read something like this. Governments have restored realistic exchange rates, decreased taxes on agriculture, reduced or removed subsidies and controls on prices, interest rates, and foreign exchange, lowered tariff and non-tariff barriers, restricted the growth of public-sector employment, sold or liquidated some money-losing parastatals, and rehabilitated some physical infrastructure. These reforms have often restored a precarious macroeconomic stability, manifest in the lowering of inflation rates. (See, for example, Killick 1995; Harvey 1996; Mair 1996: 176–77). Yet even Ghana, flagged by the World Bank as a success story, saw its inflation rate again accelerate in 1993, reaching 60 per cent in 1995 before sliding back to about 28 per cent in 1997. As well, many economies continue to record substantial deficits in their current accounts and government budgets, if grants are excluded (see Table 1.1). Furthermore, aggregate savings and investment rates (as Table 1.1 also shows) have not improved since the early 1980s; the region thus remains heavily dependent on official development assistance. What foreign private investment there was flowed mainly into mines and natural resources. Finally, Africa remained dependent on the export of traditional primary commodities whose world prices notoriously fluctuate.

The second, or institutional, phase of adjustment, which has followed policy reform, has generally not progressed far. The first phase of adjustment (1981–90) naively assumed that policy reforms, especially those pruning the

TABLE 1.1
SELECTED MACROECONOMIC INDICATORS FOR SUB-SAHARAN AFRICA

Year	GNP per Capita ($US)	Current Account Balance (% of GDP)[a]	Overall Fiscal Balance (% of GDP)[b]	Exports (% of GDP)	Gross Domestic Savings[c] (% of GDP)	Gross Domestic Investment (% of GDP)	ODA[d] (% of GDP)
1980	590	—	—	19	23	23	3.4
1981	580	—	—	—	—	—	—
1982	550	—	—	—	19	20	—
1983	550	—	—	19.7	18	14	1.5
1984	530	—	—	22	13	13	6.2
1985	400	—	—	21	22	23	—
1986	370	-4.9	-6.6	19	14	16	8.3
1987	330	-5.9	-9.6	14.7	12	15	8.8
1988	330	-7.2	-8.2	—	13	15	7.9
1989	340	-5.7	-6.2	—	16	16	9.6
1990	340	-4.6	-5.2	28	16	16	10
1991	350	-7.5	-6.2	26	15	16	—
1992	530	-9.4	-7.0	—	—	16	—
1993	520	-8.6	-9.7	27	16	16	11.5
1994	460	-8.4	-7.0	28	16	17	16.3
1995	490	-11.2	-4.8	—	—	19	—
1996	500	-6.7	-4.6	—	—	—	5.3
1997	500	-6.6	-1.8	20	18	18	—

[a] Refers to the balance of payments on current accounts as percentage of GDP, excluding grants, where + refers to a surplus and - to a deficit.
[b] Of the central government, excluding grants.
[c] Refers to the difference between GDP and total consumption.
[d] Official Development Assistance.

Source: World Bank (*World Development Report*, various issues); IMF African Department; World Economic Outlook.

state's economic role, would suffice to reignite growth by releasing market forces. By about 1990, however, development agencies had recognized that the required adjustments included institutions as well as policies. If the ancillary political, legal, administrative, and financial institutions did not exist, markets could not work efficiently. Hence, the adjustment agenda broadened. Institutions requiring extensive reform included the civil service, decision-making bodies, the regulatory and monitoring agencies, the tax administration, essential services, the agencies charged with managing the social safety net, the armed forces, and the judicial system. Where state-owned corporations drained public resources, their privatization would need to be accelerated. The financial sector, too, would generally require widespread restructuring and upgrading. Whereas the earlier changes in foreign exchange rates, interest rates, prices, and tariffs could be achieved by a "stroke of the pen," none of these institutional changes would succeed without the co-operation of diverse constituencies within the public and private sectors. Creating social peace and mobilizing such support posed major political challenges for reformers.

Overall, sustained growth remained elusive in the late 1990s. Conditions did improve in 1995–98, as real GDP in Sub-Saharan Africa grew at an average annual rate of more than 4 per cent—four times the average during the preceding four years. Also, the average rate of inflation declined from its peak of 47 per cent in 1994 to about 10 per cent in 1998, while domestic and external financial imbalances also fell (Calamitsis 1999: 7). Even if these relatively favourable trends had continued, however, they would not have reduced absolute poverty much (owing to the rapid population increase). But the Asian economic crisis in 1997–99 halted this shortlived recovery, as world demand for Africa's key commodities shrank. Prices of non-petroleum commodities fell 16 per cent in 1998 and another 8 per cent in 1999 (*Financial Times* [London], April 8, 1999). Sub-Saharan Africa, with three-quarters of its export revenues deriving from commodities, bore the brunt of these lower prices. The UNDP's annual human development reports starkly reveal the human consequences of this continuing economic depression. In 1998, twenty-nine of the bottom thirty-four countries ranked according to a Human Development Index were Sub-Saharan; the bottom fifteen were all from the region (UNDP 1998: Table 1).[11]

Despite these disappointing results, it would be a mistake to dismiss the neo-liberal model out of hand. For one thing, many African governments did not consistently implement market reforms (Hibou 1999). Also, the developmental challenges in many African countries are probably insoluble except in the longer term—which means decades rather than years. An important task, therefore, is to "unpack" the adjustment packages by separating those measures that address real problems from those that derive more from liberal faith than reasoned argument. On the one hand, it is generally true, as neo-liberals hold, that heavily state-led development in most African countries has proved disastrous. There is, in the World Bank's words, a "crisis of governance," though this crisis is actually more profound than that phrase implies. Hence, much of structural adjustment makes good sense as a long-term program. Even skeptics support certain policies designed to reduce inflation and budget deficits: an increased reliance on market forces; a reduced state role in economic management; an expanded role in social provisioning for decentralized communities and voluntary organizations; a focus on democratic governance; and a concern for institutional capacity-building in the private and public spheres. On the other hand, the neo-liberal model links these adjustments to Africa's deeper integration into the prevailing global market economy. It assumes that all participants in self-regulating global markets will eventually benefit. But globalization has already proved unfavourable to African economies in various ways. The rapid and unilateral liberalization of imports has devastated local manufacturing enterprises; the promotion of output of Africa's traditional commodity exports has led to declining prices in the face of stagnant world demand; and the focus on the domestic roots of economic problems has underestimated the importance of external debt, technology gaps, limited financial and investment inflows, and poor terms of trade to Africa's predicament. *Africa's tragedy is that onerous external as well as internal constraints operate—and that both require attention.* Hence, development and democracy in Africa must involve a struggle to reform the existing pattern of economic globalization, as well as to reform domestic policies and governance.[12]

Concerning the latter, a "crisis of governance" does not adequately characterize the sense of "state failure" referred to by many analysts. What had widely emerged by the 1970s was *not* a mismanaged capitalist economy, as many economic analysts assume, but rather an alternative, integrated system operating according to the principle of "redistribution" (to use Karl Polanyi's [1944] term) rather than market exchange. Max Weber provides a key to understanding the logic and consequences of this system.[13] He analyzed the historical development of "patrimonial" rule and "political" or "booty" or "patrimonial" capitalism in early-modern Europe, Asia, and Africa. Weber's main point is that patrimonial rule, though compatible with the expansion of trade, hinders "production-oriented modern capitalism, based on the rational enterprise, the division of labor and fixed capital" (Weber 1968: 1091 and, more generally, 1091–99). This result occurs for various reasons,[14] but principally owing to its arbitrariness and exploitation by political insiders of state-supported monopolies and sinecures, which discourage long-term investments.

An analogous system of *political capitalism* and *neo-patrimonial rule* had emerged in many African countries by the 1970s—and not only in Africa; Hernando de Soto's (1989) famous exposé of mercantilism in modern Peru bears a strong resemblance to Weber's political capitalism. In this system, a central political elite captures resources from economic actors, and redistributes them to individuals and groups on the basis of political allegiance. The reasons for the emergence of this neo-patrimonial rule are rather obvious: historical and material conditions in many Sub-Saharan countries favoured such an outcome. Rulers are faced with the task of governing weakly integrated, poor, and largely peasant societies. Land and labour in the rural areas have as yet been only partially converted into commodities for sale on the market. Business classes and urban middle classes are politically weak, as they are small in numbers, dependent on government, and poorly organized in representative associations. Patrimonial traditions often remain deeply embedded in the culture (Bayart 1993). The normative basis of central authority is weak or non-existent. In these difficult circumstances, how do rulers consolidate state power and retain their own positions? One option is to promote economic development and the provision of important public services to all citizens; but this is a long-term approach, whereas leaders face immediate and insistent demands and dangers. Hence, the rulers' desire both to integrate a heterogeneous and divided society and to cement personal power and privilege pushes them in the direction of subordinating economic considerations (investment, efficiency) to short-term political expediency.

Unless restrained, a patrimonial system becomes economically destructive (Price 1984). The resources channelled to political ends derive from several sources: appointments to the public sector; taxes and royalties on agricultural producers, exporters of natural resources, and importers; the operations of state corporations; foreign loans and aid; and foreign investors. Production suffers as rulers invest the resources under their control to realize non-economic objectives. Moreover, officials are constantly under pressure to expand the public sector as they try to capture new resources to service and extend clientele networks. This system may maintain a precarious unity, but only at a high economic price. Potential entrepreneurs respond to perverse incentives by pursuing state-derived "rents" or engaging in speculative activities, rather than creating new wealth in risky independent investments. The system also diverts scarce resources from public investments in high-quality roads, schools, and health facilities in order to favour cronies and their own clienteles. And finally, uncertainty and indiscipline, nurtured by patronage appointments to the civil service, unpunished corruption and fraud, and the insider manipulation of public resource allocations, taxes, licences, imports, and so on, further raise the risks to potential investors (including rent-seekers with disposable income). This political-economic system consequently fosters economic stagnation or, at best, very modest growth.

Political capitalism would appear to deter development, a judgement that provides grounds for supporting a market-led strategy. Structural adjustment is, in essence, a political alliance in which external forces (the IFIs, the donors) join with domestic groups, especially the market-friendly sectors of business and middle classes, to engineer institutional changes that disembed economic activities from patrimonial relations. Democratization may provide a way of taming the neo-patrimonial state and re-establishing legitimacy based on representation and the equitable provision of important public services. Of course, this strategy is not ensured of success. Elites who have prospered under neo-patrimonial rule have often manipulated market reforms and the accompanying inflows of aid to maintain their factions and further enrich themselves. One such defensive strategy is for governmental leaders to privatize state corporations into their cronies' hands (Hibou 1999). Yet democratization can invigorate reformist impulses, in part by empowering a host of non-governmental organizations to press their interests against a recalcitrant government.

This line of argument justifies our focus here on the relationship between democratization and market reform (see chapters 4 and 5). The question can be addressed in general terms. Does the comparative evidence suggest that political liberalization fosters the implementation of neo-liberal reforms? The findings (chapter 4) are not encouraging. The best-case analysis of whether democratization actually assists in reforming the institutions of patrimonial capitalism in Ghana (chapter 5) offers another insight. Institutional change is case-specific, which means that a focus on political struggles in a particular historical and cultural milieu is important, and Ghana may be regarded as one of the potentially more promising African cases.

On the one hand, Ghana is similar to other West African countries, having suffered from authoritarian rule and political instability throughout most of the period 1960–85. The country's economy also followed a trajectory similar to that of many other Sub-Saharan countries: economic decline after the mid-1960s, leading to virtual economic collapse by the early 1980s. On the other hand, Ghana enjoys certain advantages in making democracy work. It boasts a relatively long experience in the late-colonial and post-colonial era of responsible and representative government. The country also entered into independent statehood with a comparatively large educated class, a prosperous, if dependent, economy based on smallholder cocoa production and gold, and a relatively advanced infrastructure. Ghana also benefited after 1983 from unusually large inflows of loans and grants from the international financial institutions and bilateral donors. Finally, of the sixteen Sub-Saharan countries holding second national elections in 1995–97, Ghana was one of only two in which the quality of elections improved on the second occasion (Bratton 1998: 63). What then can be achieved in the way of reforming neo-patrimonial institutions under relatively favourable circumstances?

The Future: Democracy, Development, and Globalization

Let's return to the central question: does democratization matter? The answer, of course, varies from country to country. But even in the more positive cases, democracy has limitations. Elections usually lack policy content and are subject to subtle manipulation. Between elections presidents evade accountability by undermining opposition parties, the independent media, oversight agencies, and assertive watchdog associations. The life-chances of most people improve but little. Democracy may assist in managing conflicts in certain countries and improving governance for effective market reforms in others, but change is modest.

How can democratization come to matter more? A common aspiration animates many African intellectuals, whether proponents of popular democracy or liberal democracy: that democratization, prosperity, and state strengthening will proceed in tandem, thus substituting a virtuous circle of development for a destructive downward spiral. But how is this circle of democratic development to be achieved? All may agree that the strategy requires democratizing, or deepening, democracy: institutional reforms to render democracy more meaningful to ordinary people; measures aimed at eliminating mass poverty and achieving equity; and programs to rehabilitate state structures so that they can reliably deliver security and other services to citizens.[15] Still, opinion divides regarding the specific extent and nature of reform.

A neo-liberal version of democratic development—what I refer to as a "pragmatic neo-liberal" strategy—can be inferred from the reports of the World Bank and other proponents. The efficacy of self-regulating market systems is a given. Within this context, the strategy is to buttress liberal-democratic institutions, build the capacity of state organizations, and support safety nets to cater for the destitute and those who lose out in competitive markets.

Whether these measures will sustain democratic development is questionable. Most African countries fall into the category of the world's poorest countries, with destitution widespread. And "poverty is a trap," as Adam Przeworski and his colleagues confirmed in a crossnational study of 135 countries: "Poverty breeds poverty and dictatorship" (Przeworski et al. 1996: 49). The lower the level of economic growth, and hence the higher the vulnerability to economic setbacks, the more fragile is democracy. How will democracy survive in countries whose rates of output growth barely exceed population growth, particularly when Western donors have sharply cut back aid budgets?

Beating the poverty trap and bolstering a virtuous circle of development will probably require complementary reforms in the operation of the global market economy. A social-democratic "grand bargain" (Castaneda 1993) on a North-South basis would facilitate sustainable and democratic development worldwide. Furthermore, a reform of neo-liberal globalization into a social-democratic globalization is not as unrealistic as it may first appear. Markets—both domestic and global—are needed to create wealth, but they need to be governed by human needs and social values. Democratic processes offer a way of determining these needs and values, and, I would argue, they provide a legitimate way of doing so in contemporary Africa.

The Real World of
African Democracy

As Africa's "Second Liberation" swept the continent in the early 1990s, observers warned that hostile socio-economic and historical conditions threatened these fragile democratic experiments (for example, Decalo 1992; Lemarchand 1992). New democracies had to contend with a low level of economic development, mass poverty and illiteracy, stagnant or modest economic growth following the "lost decade" of the 1980s, and, frequently, deep ethnic and/or religious cleavages. Historical legacies were also often burdensome. Not only did the precolonial political traditions of many societies bolster authoritarian rather than democratic institutions (Simiyu 1987), but democratization occurred in countries with resilient neo-patrimonial practices (Bratton and van de Walle 1997) and a limited experience of multiparty democracy. To make matters worse, the ubiquitous structural adjustment programs raised political tensions (see chapter 4). Adjustment policies, unfortunately, exact a high price from precisely those organized urban groups—university students, professionals, civil servants, and workers—who spearheaded the pro-democracy movements. To thwart the aspirations of such influential groups was to court disaster.

Inevitably, these onerous conditions have damaged democratization. They have not prevented reasonably fair electoral contests, arranged even in desperately poor countries plagued by ethnic/regional tensions, rampant clientelism, and limited democratic experience. However, the hostile environment warps emergent democracies in characteristic patterns. Following the initial elections, the democrats' eagerly anticipated "second transition"—the phase of consolidation in which all major actors accept the rules of the democratic game—rarely comes to pass. If a few countries exhibit this felicitous institutionalization of a new regime, most undergo a hollowing out of formal institutions as the early democratic promise fades. The result is either a reversion to an authoritarian regime, in the form of a military junta or one-party state, or the emergence of pseudo-democracy.

Table 2.1
Basic Data, Sample Countries

	Colonial Power	Year of Independence	Population (in millions) 1997	GNP/capita (U.S.$) 1997	Economic Growth Rate (average annual % change in GNP) 1976–86	Economic Growth Rate (average annual % change in GNP) 1987–97	External Debt (% of GDP) 1997	Current Budget Balance (as % of GDP)* 1986	Current Budget Balance (as % of GDP)* 1997
Mali	France	1960	10	260	0.9	3.1	116.3	0.8	3.8
Niger	France	1960	9.7	200	0.4	1.2	88.6	-0.2	-0.3
Ghana	Britain	1957	18	370	-0.1	4.5	93.9	1.7	1.1
Zambia	Britain	1964	9.4	380	-0.1	0.1	168.4	-22.3	2.0
Tanzania	Britain	1961	31.3	210	—	4.4	126.7	-4.3	1.1
Madagascar	France	1960	14.1	250	-0.7	1.4	121.3	1.9	0.7

* Excluding grants.
Source: World Bank.

A pseudo-democracy is the sort of political regime that occupies the hazy terrain between genuine representative or multiparty democracy, on the one hand, and authoritarianism, on the other.[1] Multiparty democracy, as classically defined by Robert Dahl (1971: 3) as "polyarchy," includes three elements: regular contests among organized groups for political power; the right of virtually all adults to participate in these contests; and protected freedoms of personal security, movement, expression, association, and assembly. Other theorists expand the notion of democracy beyond electoral contests to encompass the practice of power between elections (Diamond 1996). Democracy, after all, is of limited value if elected presidents act as virtual dictators most of the time, or if privileged elites (the military, bureaucrats, oligarchs) reserve the right to act unilaterally and with impunity to protect their institutional interests or their notions of the national interest. So accountability of rulers to the ruled on a day-to-day basis is also a key feature of a genuine multiparty democracy. Typically, opposition parties, legislatures, courts and oversight agencies, the independent media, and civil associations monitor, publicize, or enforce the rules governing the exercise of power. Pseudo-democracies mimic representative democracies inasmuch as they tolerate opposition parties and periodic elections; but they diverge from representative democracies in distinctive ways. Their electoral contests, at the worst, are merely a façade, behind which a government intimidates and harasses opponents, enforces legal restrictions on the opposition, and rigs the vote. Key institutions that should channel mass participation, resolve conflicts, and enforce accountability, such as party systems and legislatures, are weak and fragmented. Parties, for example, evolve into factions engaged in personalistic or ethnic power struggles. The state in a pseudo-democracy also affords limited protection of civil and political liberties: governments repress oppositional groups, undermine the critical organs of the independent media, and manipulate the judiciary.

Democracy therefore varies in its authenticity in Sub-Saharan Africa. Although many, perhaps most, purportedly democratic regimes resemble pseudo-democracies, a minority manifest a less shallow embrace of democracy: some combination of fair elections, a vibrant press, an independent judiciary, and the emergence of vital civil associations such as human rights organizations. This variation springs from two sources: the uneven severity of the objective and cultural conditions facing democratic reformers; and the ingenuity and actual commitments of political leaders and movements. Finally, blatant reversions to military or one-party authoritarianism are still rare. Not only is democracy widely perceived as the only legitimate form of government, but also external donors and creditors can be expected to react antagonistically to such reversals.

In the following pages I use the experience of six countries—Ghana, Mali, Niger, Zambia, Tanzania, and Madagascar—to illustrate the variability of democratization. (See Table 2.1 for background data.) This sample may fall short of validly mirroring Sub-Saharan Africa's emergent democracies, but nonetheless it reflects the experience of the many low-income countries that suffered the implosion of their economies in the early 1980s, pursued structural adjustment programs in the 1980s and 1990s, and underwent electoral transitions in the early 1990s. The sample, moreover, is geographically diverse, with cases drawn from West, South-Central, and Eastern Africa, and it includes both former French colonies (Mali, Niger, and Madagascar) and former British colonies or trust territories (Ghana, Zambia, and Tanzania). Using these countries, the analysis deals in turn with the conduct of elections, the nature of the emergent party systems, the existence of basic freedoms—especially the freedom of expression—and the role of independent media.

Elections: How Free and Fair?

Authoritarian governments acceded to competitive elections after strong domestic protests and pressure from donor countries. Domestic mobilization against authoritarian rule forced the hand of autocratic rulers in Mali, Niger, Madagascar, and Zambia. In Mali a series of urban protests, involving students and workers in particular, led to the deaths of forty demonstrators in March 1991. This violence in turn prompted a coup by progressive officers, who instituted important changes. They constituted a provisional government; reinstated civil and political rights; convened a representative National Conference to draft a constitution, electoral code, and party law; and eventually presided over national elections. A similar pattern (though without an overt military takeover) emerged in Niger and Madagascar about the same time. There, major urban protests and demonstrations led to a paralysis of government, followed by the installation of a provisional government, the deliberations of a representative national conference, and the holding of free elections. In Zambia President Kenneth Kaunda and the ruling United National Independence Party (UNIP) retained greater control over the transition to multiparty elections than did the one-party governments in Mali, Niger, and Madagascar. Kaunda, too, confronted widespread protests in 1990 by his erstwhile supporters in the Copperbelt and major cities, as continuing economic decline and austerity measures assaulted their living standards. The emergence of a united opposition movement, the Movement for Multiparty Democracy (MMD), afforded Kaunda little option but to capitulate. However, UNIP managed to control the transition in that only minor modifications to the existing constitution preceded the election in October 1991. Although Kaunda and UNIP still lost the election, the incoming MMD government inherited a range of repressive powers from the former one-party state (Bratton 1994).

In Ghana and Tanzania, donor pressures—or anticipation of such pressures—together with the example of democratic openings in nearby countries, weighed more heavily than protests and riots. Neither country experienced mass demonstrations against the governments in the period leading up to the democratic openings. In Ghana, Flt.-Lt. Jerry Rawlings, who had formerly denounced multiparty politics in favour of a localized "no-party" system, reversed course in April 1991, rapidly stage-managing an electoral transition in late 1992. Rawlings' belated embrace of party politics apparently owed more to his need to placate donors than to his sudden conversion to liberal democracy (which he continued to denounce from time to time). The Chama Cha Mapinduzi (CCM-Revolutionary Party) government in Tanzania undertook a similar strategic manoeuvre. Between 1990 and 1992, demands for an opening up of the one-party state emanated mainly from the pages of newly established independent newspapers—and these demands were politely worded and rational arguments from the pens of academics and lawyers. More significantly, in 1990 former president Julius Nyerere criticized the CCM, charging that it had "gone to sleep" (Baregu 1993). The party needed, he proclaimed, the stimulus of an organized opposition to rejuvenate itself. Although a presidential commission on a future political system reported in January 1992 that only about one-fifth of those consulted had favoured a multiparty system, President Ali Mwinyi nevertheless announced a transition to multiparty politics in June 1992. He may have calculated that a small and fragmented opposition would not pose a threat to the ruling party, as proved to be the case in the chaotic election of October 1995.

The electoral systems in the six countries vary widely. Generally, the former French colonies (especially Niger and Madagascar) adopted some version of the French system of a strong and independent presidency and a national assembly elected by proportional representation. Zambia, Ghana, and Tanzania preferred some form of plurality voting within individual constituencies, with a separate contest for a president with strong executive powers. Each system exhibits its own peculiarities and its own problems. One problem common to Niger, Mali, and Madagascar, for instance, is the precise division of powers between the president and the national assembly. Some ingenious compromises emerged from the national conferences convened to negotiate *inter alia* the rules of contestation. In Mali, for example, the constitution requires proportional representation in the election of councillors to the country's nineteen urban commune councils. For the national assembly, however, the electoral code provides for a majority system of electing deputies within fifty-five electoral districts. The code allocates from one to six deputies per district in proportion to its population. Voters then cast ballots for party lists of deputies within each district, and the list securing a majority in the first or second round of voting takes all the district seats. This finely crafted compromise thus reassures the small parties that they will gain a measure of representation, while seeking to avoid a national assembly subject to unstable ruling coalitions of splinter parties (Kanté et al. 1994).

Irrespective of the precise electoral arrangements, donors and others assisted in planning, executing, and monitoring the initial and several of the subsequent national elections. Although the details of this assistance and the roles of the various external agencies varied, the external interventions were extensive everywhere. International consulting agencies, foundations for the promotion of democracy, international human rights groups, and bilateral donors worked, usually in concert, to promote a fair electoral outcome. Each country received advice on, and/or contributions to, some combination of a number of services:

- programs to build an effective and independent electoral commission to manage the elections;
- programs to recruit and train those who register voters and/or those who eventually administer the conduct of the vote at the polling stations and the higher levels at which the votes are counted;
- voter education programs, which inform voters about how to register and/or cast a ballot;
- programs to verify the eligibility of prospective voters, either voter identification cards (usually too expensive) or voter registers combined with the use of indelible ink to mark the thumbs of voters;
- development of a data-processing capacity on the part of electoral commissions, to produce voter lists, allow for their easy updating, and compute the final vote tallies;
- programs to train the major parties' agents, who will monitor the vote at the polling stations and elsewhere; and
- the provision of international teams to monitor the conduct of the election campaign (usually only the final few days) and the vote itself.[2]

How fair were the transitional national elections? Teams of international observers declared each of them "free and fair," though usually their reports noted certain "irregularities" or registered only conditional approval (Geisler 1993). Given that elections in Zambia (1991), Mali (1992), Niger (1993), and Madagascar (1993) brought new governments to power, the electoral contests in those cases would appear to be reasonably fair. National (constitutional) conferences and provisional governments in Mali, Niger, and Madagascar provided some assurance of a neutral electoral process. The presumption of fairness finds further grounds in the case of Niger, where fresh elections for a deadlocked Parliament in January 1995 reconfirmed the opposition alliance's majority hold. (Ironically, Niger's opposition parties complained of electoral fraud before election day, and the president's alliance made precisely the same charge afterwards.) In Zambia the opposition MMD did not dispute the fairness of an election awarding it a landslide victory.

The most problematical transitional elections occurred in Ghana and Tanzania. In Ghana the opposition parties declared the 1992 presidential elections (won by the incumbent dictator, Rawlings) to be fraudulent, and they refused to participate in the subsequent parliamentary elections. The New Patriotic Party, the main opposition group, issued a report detailing hundreds of alleged irregularities (New Patriotic Party 1993). Tanzania's elections in October–November 1995 were chaotic affairs (see Cranenburgh 1996). On the islands of Zanzibar and Pemba, which together with the mainland form the United Republic of Tanzania, the incumbent CCM won both the presidential and parliamentary elections of October 1995 and the local elections of March 1996, in the face of widespread popular support for the Civic United Front (CUF). (The Zanzibari government exercises some legislative autonomy within Tanzania.) Both foreign human rights organizations and local observers alleged that intimidation and rigging of the elections played a significant role (Amnesty International 1997). Indeed, the opposition boycotted the 1996 elections in protest. Extensive repression directed against protesting opposition supporters and the press followed these votes. In mainland Tanzania the elections of October–November 1995 were marred by disorganization and inadequate preparations rather than systematic intimidation or rigging. So numerous were the irregularities surrounding the voting in the capital city, Dar es Salaam, that the electoral commissioner declared the October elections null and void and convened a special election in November. The CCM handily won both the presidential election (in which Benjamin Mkapa replaced Ali Mwinyi) and the parliamentary election (with 214 of the 275 seats).

Even if the correct procedures for validating voters and recording and tallying votes were rigorously observed, earlier irregularities and the incumbents' unfair advantages may still have shaped the results. Commonly, governments took repressive actions: denying opposition parties access to the publicly owned mass media; restricting opposition rallies by requiring permits for public meetings; using public resources to subsidize the governing party's campaign; deploying militias and police to intimidate opponents; and channelling patronage only to supportive constituencies (see Wiseman 1992).

The Ghanaian and Zambian cases illustrate the abuses and errors that creep in when an authoritarian government oversees a democratic transition. Although a Commonwealth Observer Team pronounced Ghana's presidential election "free and fair," this verdict ignored a pre-election warning from an expert team placed in the field by the Washington-based International Foundation for Electoral Systems. The team stated that it was "imperative" that Ghana's Electoral Commission conduct "a complete re-registration of all voters" because the shortcomings of the current register "directly affect the success of the transition" (Cooper, Hayward, and Lee 1992: 45). These alleged faults included multiple entries of the same voter, inconsistent name order, failures to record corrections, "ghost" entries, and failure to list about 5 per cent of the eligible voters. An estimated 1 million of the 8.4 million entries were erroneous. And there was a further, virtually inevitable, electoral bias: Rawlings and his newly minted National Democratic Congress (NDC) took full advantage of incumbency in the election campaign. The government ingratiated itself with civil servants by awarding them a major pay raise just before the election, even though this action pushed the budget into deficit. Rawlings liberally dispensed patronage in the form of electricity extensions, water supplies, and roads to wavering rural supporters, and NDC campaigners liberally utilized state property in their campaigns, especially government vehicles and public radio and television. By delaying the granting of permits to hold rallies, Rawlings' administration confounded the opposition parties (Rothchild 1993; Haynes 1993). The 1996 elections, in contrast, exhibited far fewer irregularities (see chapter 5).

Some of the same errors and abuses characterized the 1991 election campaign in Zambia. There too the electoral register was outdated. It had last been systematically updated in 1987 (although the registers were open to correction for three weeks in 1990). Because younger voters were thought to favour the opposition MMD, this oversight may have benefited UNIP. UNIP also endeavoured to take advantage of its control of the governmental machinery, although a better-organized opposition and a more independent judiciary (in 1991–92) than in Ghana often frustrated the party's efforts. Regulations associated with Zambia's State of Emergency, such as restrictions on movements after dark and the need to obtain permits to hold public meetings, limited the MMD's activities. A highly partisan state administration dissuaded citizens who needed to obtain licences or public services from openly supporting MMD. Meanwhile, UNIP candidates had access to government vehicles and office equipment in carrying out their campaigns, as well as unequal access to the government-owned media (two daily newspapers, radio, and television).[3]

Despite the shortcomings in these campaigns, this comparative analysis is encouraging. Reasonably free and fair transitional elections were mounted in some of the world's poorest countries. If a provisional government held sway during the run-up to the elections, the chances of a fair outcome increased. Where authoritarian governments managed the process, uncorrected errors, irregularities, and the partisan use of state resources occurred. Even then, however, a united opposition could triumph, as the Zambian example attests. Foreign assistance to the electoral process often facilitated free elections.

Subsequent national elections would reveal whether democratic consolidation was underway. A prime indicator would be peaceful alternation in power. According to this criterion, among the five countries that have held second elections only Madagascar passed the test. Elections in Madagascar tend to be chaotic, with allegations of malfeasance emanating from all the various party alliances (Ratsimbaharison 1997). Nonetheless, the country's electoral record is impressive. Fair presidential elections in 1992 brought a leader of the democracy movement, Albert Zafy, to power, while rancorous but apparently free National Assembly elections in 1993 installed deputies from an array of parties, with the former governing party in a minority position. In 1995 the country witnessed both successful local elections and a referendum that amended the constitution to authorize the president to appoint the prime minister. When Zafy then overstepped his powers by trying to name his political allies to key cabinet posts, he was impeached by the National Assembly and removed from office in September 1996. Former dictator Didier Ratsiraka won a slim majority in a subsequent two-stage election, which returned him to the presidency in early 1997 (see Rajoelisoa 1997: 50–58). The new president's party, however, won only 11 of the National Assembly's 150 seats in March 1998 elections. After six years the Third Republic could boast of two peaceful transfers of power and an enhanced status for deputies who had successfully impeached a president, both notable achievements. On the debit side, Zafy's persistent refusal to accept Ratsiraka's 1996 victory, even when the Constitutional High Court recognized its validity, and President Ratsiraka's intention to amend the constitution to expand the president's powers threatened democratic continuity. The other country with an equally promising electoral record is Ghana. Although President Rawlings maintained control of the presidency and of Parliament in late 1996, his National Democratic Congress encountered vigorous opposition in the elections. Reasonably free elections led to a strong presence of the opposition in the National Assembly and a more vibrant national debate (see Lyons 1997).

Second elections in Mali, Zambia, and Niger were marred in several ways: boycotts, heated allegations of electoral malpractice by the party in power, and, in two cases, serious repression of critics and opposition supporters.[4] In Mali, President Alpha Konaré won an astounding 95.9 per cent of the vote in May 1997 when major opposition parties boycotted the presidential elections on the grounds that the electoral commission was biased. The subsequent parliamentary elections were again boycotted by seven parties, allowing the governing party to garner 128 of the 147 seats. Violence and low voter turnout further marred these elections (*The Economist*, July 26, 1997: 39).

Even more problematic was the situation in Zambia, where UNIP and other parties boycotted the presidential elections of November 1996. The boycott extended to the parliamentary elections, which yielded 131 of the

158 seats to the governing MMD. The opposition protested various irregularities and grievances: a faulty registration of voters, government control of
appointments to the National Electoral Commission, the incumbent MMD's
unequal access to the state-owned media, and above all MMD leader
Frederick Chiluba's constitutional amendment that disqualified former
president Kaunda as a presidential candidate on the basis of his foreign
birth. Following the boycotts and protests, the government cracked down
on the opposition and the critical media (Baylies and Szeftel 1997). Violence,
including bomb blasts and assassination attempts, marred Zambia's political
life after the elections.

Niger suffered an outright reversion to authoritarian rule. A paralyzing
deadlock between the president and the prime minister in 1995 precipitated
a January 1996 coup, which temporarily terminated the democratic
experiment (see Ibrahim and Niandou-Souley 1996). Col. Ibrahim Bare
Mainassara, who led the coup, then sought to legitimate his hold on power
by means of a presidential election in July 1996. Characterized by "gross
irregularities" (Amnesty International 1997), including the jailing of the
colonel's rivals, this election returned Mainassara with 52 per cent of the
vote. (The displaced former president allegedly received only 20 per cent of
the votes.) In protest the major parties boycotted the subsequent elections
for the national assembly. Street demonstrations, military mutinies, and
widespread strikes followed, leading to the assassination of the president by
his own bodyguards in April 1999 and the formation of a junta.

On the basis of the electoral evidence, Niger (prior to the junta),
Zambia, and the island of Zanzibar in Tanzania most closely fit the model of
a pseudo-democracy. Ghana and Madagascar boast far more promising
records of consolidating electoral democracy. A close look at the countries'
party systems and human rights records confirms this assessment.

Party Systems or Factional Systems?

With the legalization of opposition parties in the early 1990s, aspirant political leaders hastened to register their own parties. Some of the parties
emerged from political clubs or civic-minded organizations that had led a
shadowy existence under authoritarian rule: the Movement for Freedom
and Justice in Ghana, the Movement for Multiparty Democracy in Zambia,
the National Convention for Constitutional Reform and the Civil and Legal
Rights Movement in Tanzania, and the Alliance pour la Démocratie au
Mali. Others were the reincarnation of substantial parties whose lives had
been cut short, sometimes more than once, by a coup d'état or one-party
regime. Ghana's New Patriotic Party traces its lineage to the country's first
major anticolonial party, the United Gold Coast Convention. Mali's Union
Soudanais-Rassemblement Démocratique Africain (US-RDA) is the latest

incarnation of one of West Africa's oldest parties. Several of Madagascar's major parties have survived since colonial times, as the authoritarian Second Republic (1975–91) permitted parties to operate that adhered to the Front National pour la Défence de la Révolution Socialiste Malgache and its vague socialist principles.

Parties constitute the central intermediary structure in a representative democracy. Democratic consolidation, therefore, implies the institutionalization of a stable party system. Strong parties augment both governmental responsiveness and the resolution of conflict by articulating and aggregating the demands of diverse constituencies in the form of public policies. For new democracies to survive—given the current context of extreme deprivation and the resource shifts inherent in structural adjustment—party systems must be able to mediate the many inevitable tensions. In addition, parties broaden political participation, at a minimum by disseminating political information and opinions and by mobilizing voters in elections. Finally, opposition parties are valuable to the extent that they enhance governmental accountability via their role as a "loyal opposition"—by exposing counterproductive policies and abuses of power. It is commonly supposed that a two-party or stable coalition or parties organized on a left-right basis is most propitious for durable and effective democratic governance.[5] If, however, the party system fragments into a plethora of factions animated by personal and/or communal ambitions, political parties will not perform these important functions. Party competition will instead inspire mutual distrust or cynicism, together with a reluctance on the part of political actors to honour the normative rules of democratic contestation—abjuring communal appeals, bribery of voters, and the intimidation of opponents. Unfortunately, many of Africa's party systems resemble factional systems.[6] Perhaps only Ghana among the six cases is developing a stable two-party system. Tanzania exhibits a one-party dominant system in which the opposition parties (on the mainland) are weak and divided. Zambia appears to fit the model of a two-party system, with the governing MMD facing a defeated UNIP, but the reality is somewhat different. The party systems of Niger, Mali, and Madagascar exhibit fragmentation, unstable coalitions, and factional manoeuvring.

In Tanzania, the Chama Cha Mapinduzi relinquished its status as the sole legal party only in July 1992. Within two years factionalism had emerged within the CCM, with a Group of 55 within the one-party Parliament adopting some controversial positions. It denounced official corruption and supported the separation of Tanganyika (mainland Tanzania) from Zanzibar (West et al. 1994: 104). A dozen registered opposition parties, some of them led by prominent dissenters from the 1960s, also appeared. The opposition parties, however, did not establish themselves as a major threat to the ruling party, except in Zanzibar and Pemba (Cranenburgh 1996). They operated under a legal regime that vested considerable authority over the registration and regulation of parties in the hands of the administration. None of the five main opposition parties commanded sufficient resources to mount effective election campaigns in 1995, even with government supplements. And in the 1990s none of them developed a policy stance or ideological viewpoint that differentiated it from the CCM. The Civic United Front had a strong political base, especially in Zanzibar, which derived partly from its implicit identification as a Muslim party. All parties accepted market-oriented adjustment thinking, and all condemned official corruption; indeed, corruption was the main election issue in 1995. Symptomatic of the opposition's weakness was its failure to win any of the three by-elections contested in 1992–94 (see, for example, Mmuya and Chaligha 1993). The CCM handily won the October 1995 elections on the mainland, though it is widely believed that only electoral fraud prevented the CUF from assuming control of the Zanzibari government.

Although Zambia appears to fit the two-party model, it is actually closer to an unstable, factional model. In the October 1991 election, the opposition Movement for Multiparty Democracy defeated President Kaunda and returned 125 candidates to the National Assembly to UNIP's 25. Yet the MMD has not succeeded in transforming itself from a movement to overthrow UNIP's authoritarian government into a party with a unity of purpose and policy (Ihonvbere 1995). The MMD emerged in 1990 around the nationwide organizational framework of the Zambian Congress of Trade Unions. Although the party selected a trade unionist, Frederick Chiluba, as its leader, the movement was actually a coalition of all the forces disillusioned by Zambia's economic decline and UNIP's mismanagement. These forces included professionals, intellectuals, and business people, as well as organized labour. The movement managed also to establish itself in the rural areas (save Eastern Province) and ethnic groups (Bratton 1994: 124). But as soon as the MMD formed the government, its unity vanished. The party was racked by factional struggles, and by July 1994 no fewer than thirteen cabinet ministers had already departed. Some were sacked for alleged corruption and incompetence, while others had resigned in disgust. As many as thirty opposition parties were formed, though few gained much credibility. UNIP, the former governing party, remained the strongest opposition party. The National Party, registered in 1993 and led by some of MMD's founding members, was also well organized, and it polled second to the MMD in the 1996 parliamentary elections (boycotted by UNIP and some other parties). Whether the MMD's glue would hold long enough to fight future national elections remained in doubt.

The factional tendencies discernible in Zambia are fully realized in Niger, Mali, and Madagascar. All three countries display a fragmented party system. In Niger, thirty parties emerged after the legalization of opposition parties in late 1990. Some of the smaller parties soon disappeared; yet ten parties still held seats in the National Assembly following elections—

boycotted by the main opposition parties—concluded in January 1997. Some forty-seven parties registered in Mali in 1991–92, though only three (ADEMA, US-RDA, and CNID) boasted any broad national appeal. Even those parties suffered debilitating splits and factional struggles (Vengroff 1993). As a result, ten parties won seats in the National Assembly in July–August 1997, while another seven parties (including two of the most substantial) boycotted the elections. With Madagascar's political opening in 1990, parties proliferated. In the 1993 national elections, 122 parties and special-interest organizations contested the 138 parliamentary seats. Some twenty-six of them won seats. In the second Parliament, elected in March 1998, there was an impressive change: only nine parties gained seats.

Personal and ethnic/regional, not ideological, allegiances also constitute the basis of most parties. In Niger the former monopolistic party, the Mouvement National pour la Société de Développement (MNSD), maintained a broad appeal before the 1999 coup, although it was based in the Songhai/Zarma people. The remaining parties were all regionally oriented (Ibrahim 1994). Similarly, no clear policy issues distinguish Mali's personality-based and regionally based parties. In Madagascar, most of the parties are vehicles for individual politicians. Parties and alliances reflect the strong regional loyalties that exist on the island, especially the suspicions harboured by coastal peoples towards their traditional masters in the central plateau, the Merina (Allen 1995: ch.4). A related trait of the factional syndrome is the parties' reliance upon patron-client relationships to forge alliances and followings. Parties in governing coalitions operate largely as patronage machines. Most have a minuscule organizational presence in the rural areas between elections, and they do little to promote political participation other than periodic voting (Charlick et al. 1994: 109; Kanté et al. 1994: 114; Fox and Covell 1994: 24).

Unstable governing coalitions complete the factional model. In Niger an Alliance des Forces de Change (AFC) united nine parties in 1993 with the sole common purpose of defeating the former single party, the MNSD. Despite winning the presidency and a legislative majority, the alliance soon splintered. New elections returned an opposition alliance built around the MNSD with a parliamentary majority in January 1995. This situation precipitated a political crisis as the president and the assembly's majority struggled for control. A coup ended the stalemate, ushering in a repressive pseudo-democracy, which in turn succumbed to outright military rule in 1999. Mali, too, has suffered from governmental instability. One two-year period there saw the installation of four governments. Shifting alliances have little to do with policy differences, but much to do with the distribution of governmental positions and resources. Madagascar has witnessed the same tendency towards unstable and ineffective government. The original governing alliance ("Forces Vives"), formed to deny electoral victory to former autocratic president Didier Ratsiraka in 1993, soon shattered when that goal was achieved. After 1994 governments came and went on the basis of shifting alliances among the National Assembly's many parties.

Ghana is closest to a stable two- or three-party system. Although the opposition's boycott of the Fourth Republic's first parliamentary elections permitted President Rawlings' NDC to dominate the legislature, the 1996 elections restored some balance between the NDC and the most popular opposition party, the New Patriotic Party.

A brief comparison of the contrasting cases of Ghana, on the one hand, and Niger and Mali, on the other, accounts for this propitious trend. The deeper consolidation of a functioning party system in Ghana may derive partly from its more favourable socioeconomic conditions compared to the other two (see Table 2.1; World Bank 1995a). While Ghana is a low-income developing country, its per capita income ($370 in 1997) and literacy rate (60 per cent) are far higher than the corresponding figures in its two West African neighbours (Niger: $200 and 28 per cent; Mali: $260 and 32 per cent), and well above the Sub-Saharan averages. More to the point, Ghana undertook its latest democratic transition when real, if modest, economic progress—with real per capita annual growth at 1.2 per cent in 1985–92—was underway. Niger and Mali, in contrast, embarked on multiparty politics when per capita growth had been negative for years, and they have attempted to consolidate democracy in the context of stagnant or declining real per capita incomes. These economic problems, by deflating the high expectations associated with democratization, probably weakened the legitimacy of democracy itself. Worse yet, structural adjustment policies have exacted high costs from precisely those urban groups—students, civil servants, and workers—who had fomented the protests and demonstrations that deposed the autocrats. These influential groups have been alienated by several trends: higher tuition fees and reduced educational grants, shrinking employment prospects, redundancies, and increasing prices for goods and services. Fledgling democracies face a major challenge in contending with urban unrest in the form of general strikes, demonstrations, and riots (see, for example, Fay 1995). Ghana has not been as subject to these urban tensions, because macroeconomic stabilization had exacted most of its heavy costs prior to 1993, and sporadic recovery continues. Still, the introduction of a value-added tax (VAT) in early 1995 prompted the first massive urban demonstrations in many years and forced the government to retreat from its imposition of the new tax.

Ethnic tensions also impede adherence to the normative rules of compromise, peaceful competition, and majority rule, especially in Niger. Ghana is far from free of ethnic tensions: indeed, warfare erupted between the Konkomba and the Dagomba of the Northern Region in February 1994, leading to a declaration of a State of Emergency in the affected area. Yet the division between Ghana's conservative Danquah-Busia tradition and the populist Nkrumahist tendency is not fundamentally an ethnic/regional one. The Ashantis and Brongs tend to support the Danquah-Busia parties, and the Ewes and Northerners the Nkrumahist parties. But both traditions have always garnered support from a wide regional spectrum. Mali shares Ghana's tradition of relative ethnic harmony, aided by its 90 per cent Muslim population and its lingua franca (Bambara). In Niger, though, political struggles before the democratic transition manifested a pronounced ethnic dimension. The Songhai/Zarma managed to dominate the authoritarian governments of the First and Second Republics, despite their minority status (Ibrahim 1994); and both Niger and Mali were racked by rebellions of the Tuareg in their northern regions until the mid-1990s. Where parties reflect ethnic loyalties, peaceful competition easily degenerates into a free-for-all.

Contrasting historical legacies also work to foster differing patterns of democratization. Ghana has gained more extensive experience with multi-party politics than has either Niger or Mali. Rapid constitutional progress since 1946 led Ghana (then the Gold Coast) to three national elections during the colonial era (in 1951, 1954, and 1956). Then, three democratic interludes in the postcolonial period—1957–59, 1969–72, and 1979–81—augmented Ghana's experience. Niger and Mali, by contrast, were virtual democratic neophytes before 1992. French colonial administrations manipulated and coerced incipient parties and party leaders in accordance with French policy prior to 1960. From independence until the early 1990s, one-party or military governments held sway.[7] All three countries' legacy of personalistic and clientelist politics—a legacy with roots in the precolonial period (Owusu 1970: *passim*; Charlick 1991: ch.2; and Amselle 1992)—constrains democratic politics. The perpetuation of such practices impede the institutionalization of healthy, issue-based parties. In Ghana, although Rawlings' PNDC regime (1982–92) suppressed state-oriented clientelist networks and the corruption spawned by those networks, such practices have since resurfaced.

Finally, the design of electoral systems has greatly influenced the emerging party systems. Proportional representation, though ensuring even small groups of some representation, nonetheless encourages the proliferation of parties. This proliferation, in turn, sets the stage for unstable governing coalitions. Niger, with its system of proportional representation, has been more likely to manifest this ill than is Ghana, with its plurality voting within individual constituencies.

With both countries ranking among the world's least likely democratic prospects, it is surprising that even a truncated multiparty politics has survived in Mali, and Niger until 1999. Their party systems, however, have been deformed by violence, election boycotts, and military mutinies. Like Zambia and Tanzania since their last parliamentary elections, Mali now exhibits a one-party dominance in which a monopolistic governing party confronts a host of small or defanged opposition parties. Ghana's prospects of institutionalizing an efficacious party system are brighter, partly because of the opposition's resurgence. Madagascar may be edging towards a less fragmented and unstable party system. But even the last two experiments remain fragile and vulnerable to reversal.

Civil and Political Rights: How Protected?

In representative democracies, civil and political rights are not only ends in themselves; they are also instrumental to the conduct of free elections and the ability of legislatures, courts, press, and civil associations to hold leaders accountable between elections. Consolidated representative democracies are those in which the normative rules of the game entailed in these rights— security of the person, free movement, association and expression, and peaceful assembly—command widespread support and protection. Such consolidation is, however, rare. More commonly, civil liberties receive only limited protection. Governments permit opposition parties to exist, and they hold regular elections; but incumbents repress strong oppositional groups, manipulate elections, influence the judiciary, and undermine the independent media. Although not overtly authoritarian, such governments are more aptly designated pseudo-democracies than democracies.

Many African regimes, though not military juntas or one-party dictatorships, more closely resemble pseudo-democracies than representative democracies, as demonstrated by the following brief review of politicalrights observance in 1996 and 1997.[8] In some cases the abuses were minor—Ghana, Mali, and Madagascar—and in others—Tanzania (especially Zanzibar), Zambia, and Niger—more serious.[9]

⊛   **Ghana.** To protect themselves from charges of human-rights abuses, government leaders took legal actions to block investigations by the Commission on Human Rights and Administrative Justice into state malfeasance and to overrule certain of the Council's rulings. The right to personal security remained weakly established, as seven political prisoners convicted by a partisan Public Tribunal in the early 1980s remained in prison without the right of appeal to an independent court. In addition, a few individuals, mainly opposition supporters, were detained for varying lengths of time without due process of law. Journalists continued to be subject to harassment. Occasional allegations of police brutality and the use of torture were made, especially by the government's political opponents. The police killed four people during protests and riots in 1997.

⊛   **Mali.** Most of the reported abuses of individual liberties arose from protests against the government's alleged manipulation of the electoral process in 1997. In May and June these protests turned violent, leading to dozens of arrests and rough treatment of opposition leaders and supporters. In August police arrested further dissidents during the boycott of the parliamentary elections by opposition parties. There were scattered allegations of torture and police brutality throughout 1997. Journalists and the press were unimpeded in reporting the news, with two notable lapses in 1997.

⦿   **Madagascar.** Despite a series of strikes and urban demonstrations instigated by the standoff between President Zafy and his opponents in the National Assembly in 1996, few allegations of police brutality and no reports of political prisoners or extrajudicial killings surfaced. Occasional instances of arbitrary arrest and detention occurred. Traditional village vigilantes (the *dina*) meted out summary justice, including executions, in the face of rising rural banditry.

⦿   **Tanzania.** In Zanzibar the CCM government instituted a wave of repression against protesting opponents following the rigged elections of 1995 and 1996. Dissidents were detained without charge beyond the forty-eight hours allowed by law. The government laid charges of sedition and treason against critics. The police and the Anti-Smuggling Unit tortured and mistreated scores of opposition supporters during 1996 (Amnesty International 1997). Journalists required licences, and those denied a licence were banned from practising their trade. In contrast, many fewer abuses were reported on the mainland. The worst instance involved the forcible return home of about 500,000 Rwandese refugees and a smaller number of Burundi refugees in 1996 and 1997. Some journalists were harassed, for instance by the laying of criminal charges.

⦿   **Zambia.** In the aftermath of the boycotted November 1996 elections and an abortive coup in October 1997, the MMD government escalated its attacks on its opponents and the press. The security services often resorted to excessive force. They broke up opposition rallies that were held without permits (such as the Ndola rally of February 1997). Several people were shot and killed without apparent justification. Police shot UNIP leader Kenneth Kaunda and his deputy in August 1997 while they were driving towards an unauthorized party rally in Kabwe, and then dispersed the crowd using live ammunition. The government intimidated the press by laying criminal charges of defamation and revealing state secrets against journalists and editors, and sought new legal powers to curb journalistic freedom. A state of emergency, proclaimed by President Chiluba following the coup attempt of October 1997, unleashed further repression. (Chiluba lifted the state of emergency in March 1998, following pressure from Western donors.) More than ninety suspects were indefinitely detained and held incommunicado, some allegedly subjected to torture. Kaunda was placed under house arrest until June 1998. Finally, a prominent Rwandese refugee was returned to Rwanda without due process in 1997. On the positive side, the Supreme Court demonstrated its independence by ruling against the government in several key cases, and the press continued its critical reportage.

◉   **Niger.** A state of emergency following the coup of January 1996 prohibited all forms of political activity and led to severe abuses of human rights. Scores of opposition supporters were arrested and detained for up to three months, both in January–February 1996 and in the aftermath of the fraudulent election of July 1996. Some detainees, including former government ministers, were tortured—beaten, humiliated, or subjected to mock executions. The government also detained and mistreated journalists in these two periods. The repression continued in 1997. The security forces reportedly engaged in further acts of torture as well as in extrajudicial killings. Mass protests in Niamey in January 1997 led to the arrest of the three main opposition leaders and the detention of about one hundred others. Activists and journalists who criticized the government faced arrest on the charge of criticizing the president. In this repressive context, a guerrilla group—Front démocratique révolutionnaire—opened an armed conflict with the government in the east of Niger. Mutinies, protests, and strikes convulsed political life in the following year.

Clearly, the extent to which regimes respected individual liberties widely varied. Ghana and Madagascar had a relatively good record in 1996–97, whereas Niger and Zambia engaged in a variety of abuses. The other two cases balance between these two extremes. In all of these cases, the role of the independent mass media provides a key to an assessment of freedom of expression. Print and electronic journalism is arguably of prime importance in securing accountability when elections are far apart and manipulated and party systems and legislatures weak. The media may not only inform their audiences about policy alternatives and the norms of democratic politics, but also act as watchdogs by publicizing corrupt and abusive practices and inept public programs and policies.

Africa's independent media, though, are highly circumscribed, even in formally democratic countries. Governments regard print and electronic journalists with suspicion—perceiving them as partisan rather than unbiased chroniclers of political struggles—and try to neutralize them. Their tactics include a reluctance to surrender the state's monopoly of broadcasting outlets, the intimidation of reporters, editors, and owners of printing presses, the application of stringent libel and media laws, delays or cutoffs in the allocation of imported newsprint, and the withdrawal of governmental advertising from critical newspapers. In addition, the private media must contend with the limitations imposed by small markets. Newspapers and television cater mainly to an urban and middle-class audience, whereas the bulk of the population is poor and lives in the rural areas. Due to widespread poverty, few outside the elite can afford to purchase a newspaper regularly, let alone own a television set. In any event, at least half the population is typically illiterate, and poor infrastructure impedes the distribution of newspapers and magazines outside the cities and larger towns.[10] Only radio can reach the rural masses; for this reason, governments have only reluctantly relaxed their grip on broadcasting.

Limited print runs and a paucity of advertising revenues result in the undercapitalization of the press. Critical newspapers confront not only a dearth of governmental advertising but also sparse private revenues, as local firms fear public association with what the government regards as an anti-government vehicle. Constricted revenues translate into low salaries for journalists which, along with intimidation, discourage qualified professionals from pursuing journalistic careers. Limited journalistic training, combined with the meagre resources available for investigative reporting and the reluctance of public officials to provide information, produces reportage that sometimes relies on rumour and hunch rather than substantiated fact. The consequent muckraking style inflames a government's indignation and perpetuates the cycle of recrimination and harassment.

Despite these severe impediments, the private media have played a valuable role in newly installed democracies. Courageous journalism has not arisen in a vacuum: newspapers in many countries have inherited a tradition of protest with its roots in the early anticolonial struggles. Among our six cases, the Gold Coast (Ghana) developed the most vibrant and independent press. Ghana's oldest surviving private newspaper, the Kumasi-based *Pioneer*, opened for business in 1939, distinguishing itself as a critic of colonial policies and officials. Kwame Nkrumah and other nationalist leaders later established their own newspapers as a means of mobilizing popular support against colonialism and their political opponents.

With the end of colonial rule, the new governments typically adopted an intolerant attitude towards the independent press (see Ansah 1991). The new rulers used several strategies to quell press criticism: banning some newspapers and buying or controlling others; harassing and detaining recalcitrant journalists and publishers; and domesticating any remaining private newspapers by draconian press laws and threats to their advertising revenues and access to newsprint and printing presses. In 1980, about 90 per cent of Sub-Saharan Africa's ninety daily newspapers were owned by governments or governing parties in single-party states (Wilcox 1982: 209). Radio and television broadcasting was the exclusive preserve of the state.

Yet the degree of repression varied. A subdued but obliquely critical press survived here and there—not in Niger, Mali, or Madagascar between 1975 and 1989, but in Zambia, for instance. Even UNIP-controlled newspapers (the *Zambian Daily Mail* and the *Times of Zambia*) criticized government policies and corruption in the 1970s and 1980s, although they never dared to directly criticize President Kaunda. In Ghana the hardy *Pioneer* survived even Rawlings' repressive "culture of silence" in the 1980s, but only by means of judicious self-censorship. A tribute in *West Africa* magazine to the *Pioneer* in 1989 reveals much about the tribulations of independent newspapers under autocratic governance: "It had been censored, its editors brutalized or jailed without trial, banned, intimidated or, some of the time when tolerated, starved of inputs. None of its peer secular papers, nor any other founded within three decades after it, survives today. It stands alone: a shadow of the heyday of independent journalism, ironically, in the 1930s–50s, and a troubled symbol of an uncertain future of freedom of the private press" (*West Africa*, Oct. 2–8, 1989).

A critical journalistic tradition also endured in Ghana's *Free Press* (though its editor, publisher, and journalists were detained from time to time in the 1980s) and *Catholic Standard* (until the Rawlings government cancelled its licence). The church press retained an equally critical edge in other post-colonial countries, too.

Although the political openings of the early 1990s owed little to the domestic media, the freer atmosphere rejuvenated the private press. The international mass media helped crystallize opposition to authoritarian and often inept governments (Randall 1993: 634–38). The growth of short-wave radio, satellite television, and fax machines had undermined the governments' monopoly of information and opinion. Radio France Internationale, the BBC World Service, and the Voice of America conveyed to their many African listeners the downfall of Eastern European autocrats and the grievances and successes of democracy movements in African countries, including their own. Such reportage prompted a bandwagon effect for political change, and, as popular interest in politics waxed, a reborn national press chronicled and agitated for a transition to democracy.

Even in countries lacking a critical journalistic tradition, private newspapers and magazines soon appeared. In Niger, twelve independent newspapers and four party-run newspapers published on a weekly, biweekly, or monthly basis in the period 1991–93 (Charlick et al. 1994: 111). More significantly, in that overwhelmingly rural and illiterate country, the first privately owned radio station received a licence in the early 1990s. In Mali the political opening occurred earlier, and two Bamako-based newspapers denounced the autocratic regime of Moussa Traoré in 1988–89 after three decades of journalistic silence. Dozens of newspapers emerged (and dozens quickly vanished) after the overthrow of the Traoré government in 1991 (Kanté et al. 1994: 114). In 1997 Malians were served by four dailies and thirty-five weeklies. In Madagascar, as in Mali, the rising opposition to the long-time authoritarian ruler President Ratsiraka compelled the government in 1989 to lift censorship and tolerate an independent press. Many newspapers took advantage of their first taste of freedom since 1975 to excoriate the government. The country's first independent, though illegal, radio station also broadcast in 1991 (Radio des Forces Vives). As part of its phased political liberalization, in 1988 the Tanzanian government allowed the first independent newspapers to publish since the mid-1960s. The privately owned *Business Times*, *Family Mirror*, and *Fahari* (Bull) quickly established themselves as the opposition press. They became a forum for moderate criticism of the government and CCM, especially of political corruption, and for debates about the pros and cons of multiparty democracy. A proliferation of the Kiswahili and English press (thirty-eight newspapers circulated in mid-1997) and a growing independence of view in the state-owned newspapers and the organs of the formerly CCM-dominated mass organizations characterized the 1990s.

Both Zambia and Ghana, with their more highly developed tradition of critical journalism, also experienced a flowering of press freedom after 1990. Newspapers emerged to represent the major political tendencies; others avoided partisanship by focusing on sports and gossip. Both Kaunda and Rawlings tried to deny opposition forces access to publicly owned broadcasting in the run-ups to the transitional elections in 1991 and 1992, but court orders allowed opposition voices access to the airwaves. In Ghana twelve newspapers regularly appeared in 1997, but the only two national dailies (*Daily Graphic* and *Ghanaian Times*) were still government-controlled. Government ownership of the press continued in Zambia too, alongside several privately owned newspapers. *The Post*, an independent launched in 1991, became the MMD government's most zealous critic. But *The Post* suffered from the same debilitating conditions that afflicted the other privately owned newspapers from the mid-1990s on—the escalating cost of newsprint, falling revenues, and shrinking circulation.

Albeit reluctantly, governments also permitted the operation of privately owned radio and television stations. Mali, for instance, boasted fifty-two independent radio stations in 1997, some of them commercially run and others operated by non-governmental organizations. Even the far-flung rural areas were well-served by their own regional stations. Licences for privately owned television stations were issued in 1998. Niger had several private radio stations (though no private television) before the repression that followed the coup of January 1996. But Niger's government, even before that event, had acted arbitrarily—for example, by refusing to allow human-rights groups and women's associations to air their views on public radio concerning a controversial Family Code in 1994. Of Madagascar's six private radio stations in 1994, three catered to regional audiences and two had a clear political affiliation. Public broadcasters, moreover, did not noticeably favour the government in their presentation of local news, offering air time to non-governmental organizations (Fox and Covell 1994: 54–55).

In the early 1990s, governments in Tanzania, Zambia, and Ghana resisted demands for private broadcasting. But eventually all three countries gave way. In Tanzania a privately owned television station started broadcasting in 1994, though only in Dar es Salaam. By late 1997 five television stations and eight radio stations were reaching about a quarter of the country's population. Independent outlets also appeared in Zambia in the mid-1990s. In Ghana the Rawlings government procrastinated on granting private broadcasting licences. In 1994 some frustrated broadcasters took matters into their own hands by establishing a pirate radio station, Radio Eye. The government soon closed it down, but that action created such a furore (including demonstrations in Accra) that the administration formed a special committee of Parliament to devise guidelines for the allocation of frequencies (Sharfstein 1995: 45). By 1997 fifteen private stations were broadcasting in the urban areas of Ghana, although the government's Ghana Broadcasting Corporation was the only broadcaster to reach all of the country's ten million radios. The government's monopoly of television ended only as the millennium dawned.

Despite these advances in most of the countries, government leaders continue to denounce the press for its "misrepresentations," "falsehoods," and "irresponsibility." Yet newspapers, except in Niger, persist in featuring stories that allege corruption, malfeasance, incompetence, and sexual indiscretions on the part of prominent politicians. Both sides have grounds for complaint. Newspapers, shackled by poorly paid and inexperienced journalists and paltry investigative resources, often mix unsubstantiated charges with hard news. Governments, for their part, usually harbour ministers and even presidents with a lot to hide. When opposition parties fracture and lack the capacity for policy analysis and communication with the grassroots, journalists assume by default a major responsibility for holding public officials accountable between elections. This role inevitably creates tensions.

Although the record in the six countries is quite variable, these tensions have frequently precipitated repressive acts.[11]

◉   In **Mali** in 1997 journalists were generally functioning without fear of reprisals. But two notable abuses of state power emerged: the arrest and beating of fifteen journalists covering an opposition press conference; and the censorship of a private radio station. Although the press law was draconian, it was seldom applied.

◉   In **Ghana** the independent press remained vociferous in its criticism of the activities and policies of public figures. Journalists were, however, harassed. The government's favourite tool in intimidating journalists, editors, and publishers was Section 185 of the penal code, which makes libel a criminal offence. The government strongly warned the press in 1996 by charging three prominent editors and publishers with publishing a report "likely to injure the reputation of Ghana or the Government"—a charge that carried a maximum of ten years in prison. This case dragged on into 1998. Meanwhile, in 1997, another four journalists were arrested on charges of criminal libel.

⦿   In **Madagascar** the government continued to respect freedom of expression or, when it did move against journalists, the courts protected this freedom. In 1997 independent journalists in print, radio, and television reported on the horrendous prison conditions, but without reprisals. The last recorded major abuse occurred in 1994, when a radio journalist who had revealed a sapphire smuggling ring was beaten to death (United States, Department of State 1996, 1997).

⦿   In **Tanzania** in 1997 the independent media confronted not only severe financial pressures, but also active hostility from government, especially in Zanzibar. The government in Dar es Salaam was highly selective in allocating broadcast licences, ensuring that broadcasters offered largely pro-government positions (Committee to Protect Journalists 1997). Both the mainland and Zanzibar governments were applying a number of outdated and repressive laws to detain and charge journalists and ban publications (see Peter 1997). Even journalists who reported on the inadequate police response to a mine disaster in Arusha were detained, along with their colleagues who alleged an overreaction on the part of the police to a riot in Dar es Salaam. Zanzibar acted even more repressively by requiring all journalists to carry revocable licences. Those practising without a licence could be jailed for up to five years.

⦿   In **Zambia**, following the boycotted elections of November 1996, President Chiluba's government undertook a "persistent campaign against the independent press, specifically targeting individual editors and journalists," and there were "more court cases pending against journalists . . . than anywhere else in Africa, the state's intention being to financially incapacitate the independent press" (Committee to Protect Journalists 1997). *The Post* alone was served with more than one hundred writs concerning criminal defamation and other charges. The police detained editors and journalists in overcrowded jails. The government introduced a harsh media law that would have required the registration of all journalists, but withdrew it in the face of widespread protest. The state of emergency following the abortive coup in October awarded the police sweeping powers of arrest; this action placed further pressure on journalists.

⦿   In **Niger**, the state had again asserted tight control over broadcasting and the press. Some six months after Col. Ibrahim Bare Mainassara's January 1996 coup, he imposed himself as president in elections widely regarded as fraudulent. A wave of arbitrary arrests then intimidated the press as well as opposition politicians. In June a repressive press law mandated the licensing of all journalists and reinstated insults of the president as a criminal offence. The government's Upper Communications Council would exercise extensive regulatory powers over the mass media. Finally, uniformed men ransacked privately owned Radio Anfani and forced it off the air. The culprits were not apprehended.

Journalists, editors, and publishers clearly live precarious lives in most countries. Limited markets, precarious finances, and the intimidating power of government to reward friends and punish enemies impel some newspapers and broadcasters to temporize with the politically powerful. Certain journalists are bought off. Some publishers placate the government in order to escape libel actions, avoid unsettling threats and harassment, and buttress advertising revenues from firms fearing association with an oppositional newspaper. Some newspapers bypass political controversies by transforming themselves into tabloids devoted to sports and scandals. Yet a surprising number of print and electronic journalists still play a key democratic role by criticizing policies and publicizing abuses of power. They will continue to attract the attention of political leaders who resent stories embarrassing to the powerful.

The Practice and Promise of Democratization

What these six country studies reveal is not the shallowness of democratization in some African countries but its resilience in others. Mass poverty, limited economic development, ethnic/religious divisions, and weak pluralist traditions—the prevailing conditions in all six cases—present the most unpropitious environment for democratic institutions imaginable. That Niger and Zambia have succumbed to pseudo-democracy or outright authoritarianism is therefore unsurprising. That Tanzania, and especially Zanzibar, have made little progress towards consolidated representative democracy since the transitional elections of 1995 is also unremarkable. But what is surprising is the vitality of democratic institutions in Madagascar, Ghana, and, to some extent, Mali.

Pseudo-democracies, such as those in Niger (1992–99), Zambia, and perhaps Tanzania, exhibit certain distinctive traits. Incumbent regimes resort to restrictive laws, intimidation, and even rigging to win elections, though they continue to tolerate the existence of weak opposition parties. Democratic institutions other than electoral systems also decay. For instance, such key institutions as political parties degenerate into factions built around individuals, and/or they can come to reflect ethnic/regional/religious cleavages. Civil and political rights become more formal than real, as human-rights abuses proliferate and the judiciary and the independent media are intimidated into inaction. At the worst, as in Niger, an authoritarian regime simply hides behind a façade of elections and due process.

But in Madagascar, Ghana, and perhaps Mali, the situation is not so bleak. All three have maintained a relatively good human-rights record in recent years. Madagascar and Ghana, though not Mali, have navigated through stormy and flawed, but nonetheless essentially fair, second sets of national elections. Mali's major opposition parties boycotted the 1997 elections because they believed that the playing field between government and opposition was not level; but at least the system allowed them to protest peacefully and survive to fight future campaigns. None of these emergent democracies has institutionalized a strong party system, though Ghana has come closest to this goal. Although one cannot yet speak of consolidated representative democracies in these countries, the democratic experiments continue.

Obviously, the consolidation of these democracies will take decades rather than years in such hostile circumstances—if it occurs at all. For democracy as a learned practice to survive, people need time to internalize the new rules of the political game. India, a democracy that, despite many shortcomings, has endured for over fifty years in conditions as unpropitious as Africa's, teaches this lesson (Brown 1985: 364). Still, democracy may well be overthrown in one or more of our promising countries before such an institutionalization has occurred. Democratization, under prevailing conditions, will probably be an intermittent experience.

Yet democratization holds a great promise: to link rulers to ruled through representative institutions that provide benefits to citizens and hence command their allegiance. Such a structure of legitimate authority will provide governments with the means to deal effectively with the pressing problems of development, and especially the challenges of violent conflict, market reforms, and state rehabilitation.

THREE
3 Democratization and Deadly Conflict

Although deadly conflicts have afflicted most continents since 1980, no part of the world has been more badly hit than Africa. Bosnia, Kosovo, and Tajikistan in Europe, Sri Lanka, Cambodia, and Afghanistan in Asia, and Peru, Colombia, Haiti, and El Salvador in South and Central America have all borne the extensive human costs of prolonged, violent conflict. In Africa, the list of political emergencies is even more extensive.

Since 1980 more than half of Sub-Saharan Africa's forty-eight countries have been buffeted by countrywide or regional civil wars or wars with neighbours, and often a combination of both (see Table 3.1). In West Africa, deadly conflicts in Liberia, Sierra Leone, Equatorial Guinea, Guinea-Bissau, and Senegal (Casamance) have interacted in a mutually destabilizing pattern. The devastating internal wars in Liberia and Sierra Leone drew in peacekeeping forces from several members of the Economic Community of West African States, principally Nigeria. Similarly, civil wars have linked countries together from Central to East and Southern Africa. Some eight contiguous states in these regions endured rebellions or civil wars in the middle and late 1990s. Armed interventions by neighbouring states intensified the turmoil. Uganda supported the Rwandan Tutsi forces in 1990–94; Uganda along with Rwanda, Burundi, and Angola assisted Laurent Kabila in his overthrow of Zaire's Mobutu in 1996–97; Rwanda, Burundi, and Uganda then backed rebel forces against Kabila in 1998–2000, while Angola, Zimbabwe, Namibia, and Chad buttressed Kabila's army; and wartorn Angola intervened in Congo (Brazzaville) against President Lissouba and his forces in 1997 and 1998. The defeated combatants of three decades of civil wars were scattered in exile throughout this region, and they heightened insecurity by hiring out as mercenaries. Central African conflicts have, in turn, spilled over to exacerbate civil wars and insurrections in the Horn of Africa and East Africa, mainly in Sudan, Uganda, and Somalia. In 1998–2000 a bloody border war pitted two erstwhile allies in the Sudanese conflict, Ethiopia and Eritrea, against each other.

Table 3.1
Conflict in African Countries, 1990-97

LEVEL OF CONFLICT	TYPE OF REGIME*	
	Authoritarian	Democratic/Semi-Democratic
High (countrywide insurrections, civil wars, and/or genocides)	Algeria (1992–) Angola** (1975–96) Burundi** (periodic) Chad** (periodic) Ethiopia** (1974–91) Liberia** (1989–98) Mozambique** (1976–92) Sierra Leone** (1991–) Somalia** (1977–) South Africa (1984–94) Sudan** (1983–) Togo (1991) Zaire/Congo** (1996–)	Central African Republic (1996–97) Congo (Brazzaville) (1993–97) Rwanda** (1994–)
Medium (regional or periodic insurrections & civil wars that do not threaten the centre)	Djibouti (1991–) Egypt (1992–) Mali (1990–95) Niger (1985–) Nigeria (periodic since end of civil war in 1970) Uganda (1986–)	Ghana (1994–95) Kenya (1991–92, 1996) Senegal (1990–)
Low (absence of organized political violence)	Burkina Faso Cameroon Gabon Guinea Guinea-Bissau Lesotho Mauritania Morocco Tunisia	Benin Botswana Côte d'Ivoire Madagascar Malawi Mauritius Namibia Tanzania Zambia Zimbabwe

* at time when violent conflict began
** complex humanitarian emergencies

Sources: author's files; International Peace Research Institute 1997.

Other countries, though avoiding state collapse, civil war, or interstate conflicts, have nevertheless contended with isolated rebellions or sporadic political violence. Nigeria, with the continent's largest population (110 million), is a case in point. This country is remarkably diverse, with an estimated 250 ethnic groups and a religious composition (47 per cent Muslim, 35 per cent Christian, 18 per cent "traditional") largely reinforcing ethnic cleavages. Nigeria constantly teeters on the brink of disaster, propelled by many problems: long-standing misrule; economic contraction; collapsing health and educational services; insurrection in the oil-rich Niger delta; periodic ethnic/religious clashes; and the contagion of successful insurgencies nearby.

Can democratic institutions serve as an antidote to violent conflict in Africa? At first glance, it seems unlikely: democratization often heightens, rather than mitigates, ethnic conflicts. A cross-national study discovered that democratization, in combination with low levels of socio-economic development and ethnic fragmentation, augments the likelihood of civil war (Jakobsen 1996). In Africa, new democracies and semi-democracies have, indeed, been associated with high and medium intensities of internal war (see Table 3.1). But (as Table 3.1 also indicates) some new democracies achieve a relatively peaceful politics. Mauritius, Botswana, and South Africa after the end of apartheid are examples of plural societies in which democratization has been associated with enhanced peace and prosperity. If democratization is far from a panacea for deadly conflict, it may, nonetheless, be a worthwhile gamble.

The Complex Political Emergency Syndrome

"Complex humanitarian emergencies," "complex political emergencies," or just plain "complex emergencies": the term varies, but the nub of the malady is deadly conflict that rips a society asunder. Civil wars, insurrections, and state collapse exact an enormous human toll (see Vayrynen 1999; Cliffe and Luckham 1999). In 1990–95, major armed conflicts around the world left 5.5 million people dead and displaced 40 million people (International Peace Research Institute 1997: 24, 26). Warfare also feeds upon, and further magnifies, mutual fear and distrust along ethnic, religious, or racial lines. It accelerates economic decline through the destruction of social and economic infrastructures, the exodus of skilled refugees, capital flight and disinvestment, and the channelling of government revenues towards the war effort. Warfare, compounded by drought and environmental scarcity, leads to famines and accompanying epidemics that the weakened state is either unwilling or unable to counteract.

Because of this multidimensionality, it is impossible to isolate a single pathology of this vaguely delineated malady. Complex emergencies share only a family resemblance, though they all feature civil wars or state collapse. To extend the medical metaphor, several strains of this disease exist, as with hepatitis with its A, B, and C variants. The particular strain of political emergency found widely in Africa manifests four mutually reinforcing symptoms: growing ethnic/communal tensions in a plural society; an increasingly predatory and incapacitated state; a stagnant and declining economy with a concomitant increase in absolute poverty; and a deteriorating environment that heightens scarcities and threatens livelihoods. A downward spiral involving these four interconnected processes fosters a pervasive sense of insecurity, fear, and mistrust that the government is either unwilling or unable to assuage, or actively aggravates through its discriminatory, oppressive, and corrupt practices. To regain a sense of security and power, people, therefore, identify with their primary community (ethnic group, clan, race, religion). A dramatic event—a political assassination, a severe famine, the violent suppression of a demonstration, a military mutiny, a collapse of living standards—eventually precipitates violence that escalates into civil war or state collapse.

These mutually reinforcing processes form a complex political emergency (CPE) syndrome.

1. Rising ethnic tensions. Ethnic tensions endure in many countries *without* leading to armed conflict. "Ethnicity," defined broadly as encompassing "tribes," "races," and "nationalities," refers to an inclusive group identity "based on some notion of common origin, recruited primarily through kinship, and typically manifesting some measure of cultural distinctiveness" (Diamond and Plattner 1994: xvii). Ethnic tensions arise neither from this cultural distinctiveness per se nor generally from a primordial hostility. Africa's polyethnic societies were produced through the creation of artificial colonial borders, and in many of them ethnicity manifests only a moderate political saliency, as in Ghana. Crosscutting or narrower identities stemming from class, religion, gender, clan, and patron-clientship also shape political behaviour. In other societies (such as Rwanda and Burundi) ethnic cleavages are rigid, persistent, and decisive in determining political allegiances.

Differential ethnic access to state power, public goods, and/or economic opportunities sharpens ethnic hostilities (see Holsti 1999). When, in this context, a state's authority withers to the point that it cannot guarantee law, order, and basic services, or a regime openly exploits ethnic differences, the stage is set for ethnic tensions to escalate into armed combat. Ethnic bosses are tempted to manipulate the prevailing insecurity, fear, and alienation to mobilize support among their communities by offering protection and other services. Civil wars develop as regional/ethnic movements are emboldened by state decay to challenge the central authorities or a perceived ethnic enemy.

2. An increasingly predatory and incapacitated state. A predatory state is one in which office-holders and their clients prey upon society by extracting wealth, through legal and illegal means, without offering any useful services. Such a state is the most degraded form of neo-patrimonialism. Governments may even resemble an organized crime syndicate, in that office-holders engage in drug-running, money-laundering, fraud, and other scams (Hibou 1999). State capacity erodes as rent-seeking, corruption, and arbitrary governance eviscerate political authority, public revenues, and the integrity of the civil service. Nonetheless, a decaying state, in retaining a capacity to act repressively, remains a threat to its own people.

"Warlord politics" (Reno 1998b), in countries such as Liberia, Sierra Leone, Chad, Congo/Zaire, and Somalia, has followed such a process of political decay. Warlords, usually dissident soldiers or lieutenants of government leaders, abandon their allegiance to central authorities in order to "freelance." They build their power on the grievances of clans, ethnic groups, or regions, and the distribution to followers of booty and the revenue obtained from foreign firms who export local natural resources: diamonds, gold, rubber, or tropical timber. Civil society weakens, as professionals emigrate, associational membership dwindles, and repression grows. As the government increasingly resembles a criminal gang, new warlords emerge, demanding their share of the national wealth. The resultant economic collapse alienates the large cohort of semi-employed and unemployed young men, creating a fertile soil for warlords to recruit warriors to their private militias.

3. A declining economy and growing absolute poverty. The causes of Africa's economic decline, which began in the 1970s or even earlier in some countries, are complex and disputed.[1] The World Bank and the IMF, both highly influential, have attributed the decline largely to domestic failings in Africa: poor policies and governance that distorted market signals and raised the risks of investment. Many other experts, including in the 1980s the Ethiopia-based Economic Commission for Africa, have rejected this internalist explanation in favour of one that stresses onerous external constraints: droughts, terms of trade, technological gaps, and commercial rules favouring advanced-country interests, for example. Undoubtedly, the timing of Africa's economic crisis (beginning in the early 1980s) owed much to international trends. A deep recession in the West, two increases in the price of oil (1973 and 1979), and exceptionally high interest rates damaged poor, oil-importing, and commodity-exporting African economies. Both external and domestic constraints are important.

Regardless of the precise causes, economic well-being deteriorated markedly in many African countries in the 1980s (see Table 1.1). Already abysmal per capita incomes dropped (to an average U.S.$330 in 1987–88). A modest growth in incomes per capita of 1.4 per cent in the 1960s plummeted to 0.2 per cent in the 1970s and -2.8 per cent in the 1980s. More than half of the African population has subsisted in absolute poverty since the early 1980s. The peoples of Nigeria, Liberia, and Niger, among others, suffered a decline in real incomes of 25–50 per cent (World Bank 1990). Even in the unlikely event that the region had attained an annual increase in output of 4 per cent in the 1990s, Sub-Saharan Africa's poor would still have grown by 85 million. While Asia's share of the world's absolute poor has declined, Africa's share has steadily expanded, according to World Bank statistics.

Drastic reductions in social expenditures after 1980 accentuated the crisis. In the 1960s and 1970s, basic health indicators, including life expectancy and infant mortality rates, markedly improved. During that period, school enrolments grew faster than in any other region: the primary school population nearly doubled. But budgetary cutbacks and declining incomes lowered rates of primary school enrolment, caused life expectancy and infant mortality rates to stagnate, and worsened nutritional levels.

The record was not uniformly bleak. Consistently high economic performers include Botswana and Mauritius; and Côte d'Ivoire, Gabon, Kenya, Malawi, Mali, Senegal, Tanzania, Lesotho, and Zimbabwe experienced either high growth in the early years or long stretches of modest growth. Ghana, Tanzania, and Uganda have achieved periods of high growth under structural adjustment. Also, some of the poorer countries, such as Tanzania, rank higher on the human development scale than many countries with higher per capita incomes (UNDP 1998: Table 1). Nonetheless, by the early 1990s most Africans were as poor or poorer than at independence.

Economic decline, state decay, and ethnic antagonisms may become locked in a mutually reinforcing, vicious circle, often aggravated by environmental scarcities.

4. Environmental degradation and scarcities. Whether environmental degradation is a cause or an effect of deadly conflicts is debatable. Most accurately, perhaps, it is both (Kibreab 1999). Internal wars have certainly contributed to environmental decline and resource scarcities in many cases, including in the Sudan, as we will see. But the converse is also true. Competition over scarce resources combines with ethnic, political, and economic tensions to fuel violent conflicts.

Consider famine, the most striking manifestation of environmental deterioration and scarcity in Africa, with twenty-seven countries "at risk" (Watts 1991: 13). Civil war is often associated with the emergence of famines. In addition, national and international development patterns play a significant role in fostering droughts that then lead to famines: "greenhouse" gas emissions in industrial countries produce climatic change of which the now-frequent African droughts are a likely by-product; transnational logging companies engage in unrestricted logging with negative impacts on soil erosion and microclimates; and megaprojects displace people onto marginal land, where fragile soils swiftly deteriorate. Also, concentrated land ownership, as in countries of South-Central and Eastern Africa, squeeze poor peasants onto small landholdings, which they may overexploit in order to survive. Then too, increasing populations in the countryside lead to growing scarcity of land, which in turn can generate farming and grazing practices that degrade the soil—as, strikingly, in strife-torn Rwanda and Burundi.

Famine, moreover, combines with other factors in a mutually destructive manner. Economic decline raises the risk of famine in several ways: lowering public revenues and hence expenditures on infrastructure, health services, and measures to prevent further environmental destruction or restore degraded areas; declining employment and purchasing power renders households more vulnerable when drought strikes; and reduced import capacity owing to falling export revenues limits the government's capacity to import food during periods of drought (Watts 1991: 13). Drought and famine, in turn, can reinforce economic decline by lowering agricultural productivity, cutting export revenues, and draining scarce resources on food imports and relief.

Environmental scarcities also contribute to the growing ineffectiveness of the state by eroding a regime's legitimacy and revenues (Homer-Dixon 1994: 25). Droughts and famines—or even the impoverishment attendant upon growing populations on decreasingly productive land—heighten demands upon government at the same time as export receipts and revenues are probably falling. The inability of the state to respond adequately to the hardships of citizens aggravates popular grievances, while shrinking revenues and demoralization undermine administrative capacity.

Famine will tend to heighten civil strife, especially civil wars. Growing economic hardships and weakening central authority will encourage aggrieved groups or warlords to challenge the government or settle scores with ethnic rivals. Also, drought and the associated deforestation and desertification spur population movements, as people leave their homes in search of refuge in the cities, other regions, or other countries. Such migration often engenders ethnic conflict. Migrants place burdens on the people of the host area: food prices rise, excess labour depresses wages, and increasingly scarce common property resources engender competition over water, forests, and grazing areas. Insecurity in both migrant and host communities can solidify group identities and provoke violent conflict (Swain 1996; Homer-Dixon 1994: 20–23). Conversely, civil wars make populations vastly more vulnerable to famine. They displace farmers, destroy crops, impair roads, railways, and health facilities, and lead combatants to manipulate famine relief for partisan advantage (Watts 1991: 14).

Deadly Conflict in the Sudan

Sudan provides an apt case to illuminate the roots of Africa's political emergencies. Not only has Sudan suffered Africa's longest-running emergency—more than four decades of periodic civil war—but also this emergency may well be the most destructive of any on the continent. The fighting grew ever more fierce and widespread after the resumption of fighting in 1983, as the fault lines multiplied. War deaths between 1983 and 1998 numbered about two million, according to the U.S. Committee on Refugees—and this in a country of only twenty-seven million. Population displacements were massive (the U.S. Committee on Refugees estimated the number at five million in 1998), including at least a million southerners who sought refuge around Khartoum and Omdurman. Cattle raids, displacement of farmers, drought, and famine devastated the pastoral economy of the south. Malnutrition and disease became rife in the war zones, which came to include large areas in the east (along the Ethiopian border) and west (near the border with Chad), as well as the south. Even slavery reappeared in the 1980s, as the Baggara and others raided the Dinka for slaves as well as cattle and grain (Keen 1994: 101).

The civil war did not originate as the culmination of a downward spiral featuring the CPE syndrome. It began with a mutiny of the Torit garrison in the south in the final days of the colonial Anglo-Egyptian Condominium. During a two-week rampage in Equatoria Province in 1955, southern soldiers murdered northern civilians and officials. This atrocity led to reprisals by northerners, establishing a legacy of fear and vengeance (Ali and Matthews 1998a). Resentment in the Christian-animist south lay behind the revolt: the transfer of power to an Arabized, Islamic, northern elite, principally through rapid indigenization of the civil service and central restrictions on missionary education, fed southern fears that independence would entrench educational and other regional inequities.

Neither two parliamentary regimes (1956–58 and 1964–69) nor the military regime of General Ibrahim Abboud (1958–64) terminated the civil war. Indeed, the failure of reconciliation during the second civilian regime led to a renewed war in the south, which spread beyond its epicentre in Equatoria. At the heart of the problem was the domination of all three regimes by one or more of the sectarian Islamic parties—the Umma, Democratic Union Party, and Muslim Brotherhood—which had loyal constituencies in the north. Southern leaders believed that all three advocated a policy of Arabization and Islamization of the Sudan (Khalid 1990: 15 and *passim*). Only an autocrat, General Gaafar Nimeiri, who assumed power through a coup in 1969, could negotiate a settlement of the war in 1972; and he achieved this feat only because he needed southern support to compensate for his alienation of the northern sectarian movements (Keen 1994: 64).

Although the CPE syndrome was not evident at the outbreak of war, it would grow increasingly salient. Fighting resumed in 1983 as Nimeiri squandered his opportunity to remove the inequalities and discriminatory policies that underlay the conflict. Instead, he searched for an accommodation with the northern sectarian parties, which advocated an Islamic state and opposed regional autonomy in the south. His government's increasingly strident Islamist tone and aggressive moves to undo the earlier settlement precipitated a civil war that grew ever more violent. Neither a parliamentary regime dominated by the Umma Party (1985–89) nor the following repressive Islamist military regime was able to halt a downward spiral of ethnic conflict, state decay, economic decline, and environmental scarcities that, by the end of the 1990s, threatened to tear the country apart (see Ali and Matthews 1998a).

After 1983 the ethnic-sectarian divisions intensified. The National Islamic Front (NIF), which dominated the regime that seized power in 1989, aimed to impose a fundamentalist Islamic state throughout the country. In pursuit of its goal, Khartoum armed "loyal" ethnic militias in the north and south, an action that encouraged some groups to prey upon their neighbours. Ethnic clashes spread to the central and northern areas, involving especially the Nuba of the Nubian Mountains and marginalized groups along the Ethiopian-Eritrea border. The NIF-dominated government also fractured the Sudan People's Liberation Army (SPLA) into warring factions by exploiting fears of Dinka domination in the south. Eritrea, Ethiopia, and Uganda supported the rebel forces, in retaliation for Khartoum's aid to their own hostile opposition groups. This external involvement threatened to transform a civil war into a regional conflict.

Despite this fragmentation the formation of the multi-ethnic National Democratic Alliance (NDA) in 1995 fostered a temporary reconciliation. A precarious coalition of opposition forces uniting the old sectarian parties with activists from the Sudan Alliance Forces—professional associations, trade unions, student and women's groups, and defectors from the army— and Colonel John Garang's SPLA, the NDA opened new fronts in eastern and western Sudan to complement the SPLA's campaigns in the south.

By the end of the decade political authority had decayed to the point that a slide into anarchy had become a terrifying possibility. One Sudanese expert, in 1989, referred to "the total administrative bankruptcy and the exhaustion of many of the institutions and organs of civil government" (Khalid 1990: 436). Nimeiri's regime had evolved into a weak and predatory state heavily engaged in corruption and nepotism—what one observer called a "textbook example" of a "soft state" (Umbadda 1989: 22). Even by 1989, the arming of private militias had spread uncontrolled violence throughout the country, and after that persistent economic decline limited public revenues and state capacity. As a result of war and shrinking revenues, social and physical infrastructure collapsed in many regions. Finally, the battlefield successes of the NDA and SPLA in 1997–99 created, in large stretches of the country, a power vacuum that the SPLA and Sudan Alliance Forces strived to fill (Ali and Matthews 1998a).

Economic decline compounds all of Sudan's problems. Detrimental factors are many: high inflation and counterproductive policies; corrupt and incompetent officials; civil war and political instability; prolonged and severe droughts; a paucity of private investment; declining terms of trade for exports; and a large foreign debt. These factors combined to produce a severe economic crisis (see Umbadda 1989; Gurdon 1991). Periodic stabilization programs underwritten by the IMF rendered a weak and divided state even more ineffective; the need to impose severe austerity measures at a time when people were already suffering fomented political turmoil on several occasions (Salih 1991: 61). Sudan's ineffective reforms prompted the IMF periodically to threaten the country's eviction from the organization.

Environmental scarcities, especially of arable land and forests, have interacted with the other factors to engender famine and intensified civil war. Natural conditions played a part in the genesis of the devastating famines of the 1970s and 1980s, and most recently in 1998. The period since 1969 has been unusually dry in the Sudan, generating periodic droughts; and the rural population more than tripled between independence in 1956 and 1989, with an accompanying explosion of livestock and demand for land and trees (Hulme and Trilsbach 1991: 7–8). These trends account, in part, for the disturbing evidence, derived from satellite photographs in the mid-1970s, that the desert margins had moved southwards by as much as 120 kilometres since independence; over 500,000 kilometres of the country were threatened by desertification (Hulme and Trisbach 1991: 8).

Yet the famines were largely the result of human activity, as a detailed analysis of famine in southwest Sudan concluded (Keen 1994). Famine among the Ngok Dinka of that region in 1986–89 resulted mainly from the predatory raids of the Baggara pastoralists to the north. These raids decimated the Dinka herds and displaced many inhabitants; the failure of the elected government of Sadiq el-Mahdi to come to their aid consigned the Dinka to destitution and hunger. Far from protecting these people, Khartoum actually armed the Baggara militia. It did this, according to David Keen, because the Umma government needed the support of the Baggara, but it lacked the resources to buy that support through development projects for this economically marginal people. (Desertification stemming from drought together with unsustainable agricultural practices in the government-allocated commercial farms had shrunk the Baggara's grazing land by the 1980s.) Instead, the government condoned the Baggara's attacks upon their equally marginal southern neighbours, attributing these to "traditional tribal enmities" (Keen 1994: 61). The raiders gained Dinka cattle, grain, and female slaves, but these divide-and-rule tactics also drove the Ngok Dinka into support of the SPLA in the increasingly bloody civil war. Environmental scarcities, economic decline, state incapacity, and ethnic tensions therefore provoked raiding, which in turn created famine, population displacement, and a widening of the civil war.

The CPE syndrome captures the major interacting symptoms of the conflict into which the Sudan descended after 1983. Humanitarian emergencies, like that in Sudan, are complex in that each of the political, economic, and ecological conditions is rooted in knotty and interacting historical factors.

The key question to reflect on is: how can this pernicious downward spiral be forestalled or, if underway, halted and reversed?

Democratization as Antidote

Democratization, at best, constitutes only one component of an effective preventive strategy. Neither forestalling deadly conflict nor "peace-building" in wartorn societies can succeed without a long-term and developmental approach (see Bush 1996). The root causes of humanitarian emergencies are political and economic; therefore, "The efforts to prevent humanitarian emergencies are part and parcel of the strategies of sound economic and political development" (Nafziger and Vayrynen 1999).

Democratization is therapeutic insofar as it widens opportunities to reform a society's dysfunctional institutions. "Institution" is a word open to many interpretations. I use the term here to refer to "a regularized pattern of interaction that is known, practiced, and accepted (if not necessarily approved) by actors who expect to continue interacting under the rules sanctioned and backed by that pattern" (O'Donnell 1996: 36). Political institutions are, thus, the formal and informal rules of the game that shape not only the behaviour of people when they contest and exercise power but also their, and the general public's, expectations regarding the actions of others. It is characteristic of neo-patrimonial political systems that the institutions that count are largely *informal* rather than *formal*. Formal institutions, whether elections, legislatures, parties, judiciaries, civil services, the separation of powers, local government, civil associations, or independent media, embody the formal or normative rules of gaining and exercising power. They are publicly honoured, and often privately circumvented. The informal institutions structure political behaviour and expectations, even though they are publicly unacknowledged or even condemned.

The essence of neo-patrimonialism is the private appropriation of the state's powers. The prime stratagems (informal rules) by which rulers gain, hold, and exercise political power are numerous. They include presidential supremacy over all organizations, the distribution of state-generated rents, sinecures, and benefits to political followers, the reliance upon personal and ethnic loyalties, and the ultimate resort to a personally loyal armed force. These institutions serve the short-term interests of the leaders and their followers; but some of them are dysfunctional in the sense that they create uncertainty, stifle an independent business class, waste scarce resources on unproductive activities, and foster ethnic or regional hostilities.

Whether democratization leads to institutional reform and rebuilding is widely debated. The problem is that institutions, particularly the unacknowledged informal ones, are notoriously resistant to change. They are rooted in the history and political culture of a society and the material interests of powerful social forces. Many experts are therefore skeptical, arguing that old neo-patrimonial traditions will quickly corrupt and even overwhelm fragile democratic institutions. Not only do the new democracies confront hostile socio-economic conditions and non-democratic historical legacies, but they must also cope with the social costs to key constituencies inherent in their structural adjustment programs. These circumstances, the skeptics argue, impel elected governments to centralize power and resort to populist rhetoric, clientelistic politics, and the cultivation of particularistic loyalties. Corruption, closely associated with pervasive clientelism, will also probably resurface (see, for example, O'Donnell 1994; Kohli 1993). The "governance" perspective is more hopeful, though it is focused specifically on promoting market-oriented reform. Democratization, that approach hopes, will empower domestic social forces that have a vested interest in defending a new order of limited and market-friendly government, accountable and honest officials, transparent decision-making, effective and predictable administration, and a rule of law that protects human rights, private property, and the sanctity of contracts (see, for example, Leftwich 1993; Van de Walle 1995).

Under certain conditions, democratization can be instrumental to institutional-building and reform. It can play a positive role *directly*, through the design of well-adapted constitutional and legal rules governing the contestation for, and exercise of, power. It can also play an important *indirect role* by opening up the political space for constituencies to mobilize behind their new formal institutions. Without the growth of associations, movements, and independent media to fight for institutional reform, the experiment will quickly fail, allowing the old ways to re-emerge. The danger is that political mobilization will occur along divisive, ethnic lines; constitutional reform and political practices will need to counteract this tendency.

To prevent deadly conflict in countries threatened by a vicious downward spiral of political, economic, and environmental decline, democratization must surmount three institutional challenges. Firstly, to build order and stability, democracy must restore political institutions capable of managing the conflicts and competition arising from ethnic/communal cleavages and the political tensions associated with growth. Secondly, to build prosperity and legitimacy, democracy must forge the institutional preconditions for functioning markets and poverty alleviation.[2] This challenge encompasses the first, because investors are unlikely to invest in fixed assets in the absence of stability and mutual confidence. Markets, however, also require the establishment of a compatible set of more narrowly economic and social institutions. Thirdly, to reduce environmental degradation and environmental scarcities, democracy must, at the least, empower local communities and ordinary citizens to become defenders of their local resources.

While these three challenges are generic, *there is no single set of appropriate institutional responses to these challenges*. Institutions have to be tailored to fit the traditions, socio-economic conditions, political problems, and segmental divisions of individual countries. The social pathologist can therefore aspire only to formulating general guidelines on institutional change.

Challenge: Developing Conflict-Management Institutions
Conventional wisdom in Africa's early postcolonial period held that multi-party democracy inevitably aggravated ethnic divisions and that one-party states were therefore advisable in plural societies. Democracy, few would deny, often degenerates into a zero-sum game, in which one ethnic group or coalition wins and others lose. The losers legitimately fear that their exclusion from power and public goods might be permanent. Hence, democratic contestation frequently heightens inter-ethnic mistrust, animosity, and polarization. One-party and military governments, however, have also not been adept at avoiding ethnic conflict (see Table 3.1); authoritarian governments, too, have tended to base themselves on a particular region or ethnic coalition at the expense of out-groups. Some of the continent's bloodiest civil wars have had little or nothing to do with democratization—as in Nigeria (1967–70), Somalia, Sudan (since 1983), Liberia, Sierra Leone, Chad, Ethiopia, and Zaire/Congo. Today one thus finds a more nuanced appreciation of the potential strengths, as well as weaknesses, of particular democratic arrangements.

Democracy can manage ethnic divisions, but only if its institutions foster compromise, inclusion, and co-operation across cleavages. This rather self-evident proposition seems to sum up the current consensus (Gunther and Mughan 1993: 274–75). Arend Lijphart did much to popularize the notion that "majoritarianism,"[3] not democratic contestation per se, was the real problem (Lijphart 1977: 28). Majoritarian or winner-take-all approaches were destructive because they raised ethnic tensions by excluding some groups from power and resources, sometimes indefinitely. Instead, institutions should encourage "consensual" governance, which builds mutual trust by including all groups in sharing power and public goods. This notion led Lijphart to advocate "consociational democracy," in which every political institution would promote co-operation and proportionality in the allocation of resources. While the European-derived model is probably too restrictive to apply holus bolus to African cases, the essential idea is germane. Similarly, Donald Horowitz (1991) advocates democratic institutions that align the self-interest of dominant political actors with policies of accommodating ethnic/religious groups other than their own. The aim is to create, before elections, "multi-ethnic coalitions of commitment" whose participants agree on the rules of the game. Although no single set of institutions can achieve this benign situation in all societies, Horowitz and others propose certain constitutional arrangements that appear better suited to the task than others.

1. Electoral systems. The debate among constitutional engineers has centred around whether proportional representation (PR) is more conducive to political harmony than the "first-past-the-post" plurality system. Few will deny that poorly designed electoral rules aggravate pre-existing ethnic conflicts, whereas appropriate ones enhance co-operation. Most experts contend that proportional representation is superior to plurality election within single-member constituencies because PR, unlike the plurality system, encourages coalition-building and consensual governance (Lijphart 1991; Reynolds 1995: 86; Gunther and Mughan 1993: 277). PR, at the least, ensures that even minor ethnic interests receive a voice in the legislature. The plurality system poses the danger that elections will produce an ethnically exclusive government—quite conceivably on the basis of a minority of the popular vote—which will use its mandate to discriminate in favour of its ethnic supporters. Groups excluded from power will probably refuse to accept such a situation, especially if they perceive that their exclusion may be permanent. Democratic rules will be unlikely to contain the resulting frustration and anger. But proportional representation also poses risks: it encourages the proliferation of political parties along personal or ethnic lines, rendering parliament a cacophony of particularistic voices.

African cases illustrate the drawbacks of both systems. In Kenya in 1992 and 1997, for example, the first-past-the-post system allowed the minority-tribes-based governing party (KANU) to prevail in both the presidential and parliamentary contests, because a splintered opposition split the majority opposition vote. This outcome further embittered the excluded Kikuyu, Luo, and Abaluhya and diminished the utility of democracy as a mechanism for reconciliation. Ethnic violence accelerated as each of the competitive elections approached. In Niger and Madagascar, though, proportional representation created a proliferation of parties and a succession of unstable governmental coalitions after the 1992 and subsequent elections.

Fortunately, hybrid electoral systems promise some of the benefits of each system with minimal costs (see Lijphart and Waisman 1996: 238–40). Two-round voting in multimember constituencies, with the second round a race between the top two parties, is a method of encouraging coalition-building in many districts. Another option is proportional representation that operates, not on a national list, but on the basis of territorial districts, with limited numbers of representatives and a high minimum threshold of votes to win a seat. This option should minimize the proliferation of parties that PR otherwise generates. Other complex but efficacious alternatives exist that mix the two polar systems. In the case of Mali, the National Conference that drafted the electoral code in 1991 wrought a compromise between, on the one hand, the many delegates who feared that PR would fragment parties and foster unstable coalitions, and, on the other, the representatives of minor parties who feared that a plurality system would exclude them from power. The code mandated proportional representation in nineteen urban commune councils and, at the national level, fifty-five multimember districts in which the party winning a majority in the first or second round took all the district seats (from one to six, depending on the population of the district). This system, while not preventing a frequent turnover in prime ministers (in a presidential system), nonetheless limits the fragmentation of parties, allowing several large parties to emerge.

2. Presidential vs. parliamentary systems. There is also a long-standing debate over which of these constitutional arrangements is superior in managing conflict. Some argue that parliamentary systems tend to exacerbate ethnic divisions by concentrating power in a single, regionally based party or coalition, while excluding others (Gunther and Mughan 1993: 276). Others contend, to the contrary, that presidential systems relying on direct elections are more antithetical to ethnic harmony (Linz 1990; Reynolds 1995: 94–95). The high stakes involved in contests in which the president bestrides the political system, the adversarial, winner-take-all nature of the election, and the long wait between contests (four or five years): all these factors can poison inter-ethnic relations in deeply divided societies. Because a prime minister will need to compromise and bargain with other parties, a parliamentary system is judged more conducive to reconciliation, especially with a PR electoral system.

This inconclusive debate indicates that either system can promote a winner-take-all, exclusionary mentality that deepens ethnic conflicts. Neither arrangement is, therefore, inherently superior to the other; circumstances and astute constitutional engineering determine which serves better to mitigate ethnic divisions (Horowitz 1992: 204–6). Parliamentary systems may foster reconciliation under certain conditions: no majority ethnic group exists; several parties emerge; and retaining power then requires the building of coalitions across ethnic divides. Presidential systems may also mitigate social divisions: if the electoral code stipulates that the successful candidate must win both a certain proportion of the vote in most regions and an overall plurality (Horowitz 1992: 206).

Sudan is an example of what can happen if an unsuitable institutional model is adopted. All three parliamentary regimes (1956–58, 1965–69, 1986–89) committed the same constitutional errors, and all three paid the same price—a coup d'état and inflamed ethnic/religious divisions. The two leading sectarian parties, the Umma and Democratic Union, could expect together to win a majority of seats based on the votes of their loyal Ansar and Khatmiyya followers. This condition encouraged their leaders to champion a majoritarian, winner-take-all parliamentary system. But this system inevitably alienated those in the south, west, and east who were generally excluded from power (Salih 1991). Parliamentary regimes therefore became just another face of northern, Muslim domination (Ali and Matthews 1998a).

Not that ingenious, well-balanced constitutional requirements will necessarily succeed. Reality is too complex for that degree of certainty. For instance, Nigeria's constitution in the Second Republic (1979–83) shrewdly endeavoured to build in mechanisms to promote co-operation and inclusiveness. These mechanisms included the separation of powers between the president and the assembly and the requirement that the president must win a plurality, plus 25 per cent of the vote in no fewer than two-thirds of the nineteen states. Although the Second Republic succumbed to a coup, this failure did not arise from an ethnic/regional conflict. Rather, the governing elite's mammoth corruption, culminating in the rigging of the 1983 elections, undermined the legitimacy of democracy, paving the way for a military takeover (Joseph 1987: ch.11). Similarly, Kenya's constitutional requirement that the president obtain a plurality plus at least 25 per cent of the vote in five of eight provinces appeared well designed to enhance inter-ethnic coalition-building. But this requirement was subverted by ethnic cleansing of provinces, divide-and-rule tactics in dealing with the opposition, and (according to many observers) election-rigging, all of which further inflamed ethnic hostilities.

In Botswana, Mauritius, Ghana, and Madagascar, constitutional arrangements have succeeded in muting cleavages. Key to this success is an inclusionary governing party or coalition—and an inclusionary opposition, too, in the cases of Mauritius, Ghana, and Madagascar. Since the governing party or coalition has a broad but shifting base and/or the opposition remains potent, no group is permanently excluded from power. In this case, democratic contestation has aided integration.

3. Unitary government vs. the devolution of powers. Studies of democracy in divided societies often advocate federalism as a way of reducing ethnic conflict. Lijphart's celebrated model of consociational democracy included federalism (a special case of "segmental autonomy") as one of its four features (Lijphart 1977: 41–42). Federalism, it is contended, can reduce ethnic conflict: by removing some divisive issues from the central government's jurisdiction; by fostering intra-ethnic disputes over resource allocation within ethnically homogeneous regions; and by lessening disparities among regions by redistributing revenues from the centre to the regions (Horowitz 1994). But federalism may also buttress parochial loyalties and the regional power of an assertive ethnic group, as appears to be true of the Zulu in South Africa's KwaZulu-Natal Province today. Federalism, in any case, has rarely long survived in Africa, succumbing to centralized control by insecure national governments or to attempted secession (Katanga, Biafra).

Secession, rather than federalism, may be the only answer in some countries. No amount of constitutional tinkering or decentralization will succeed unless communal leaders want the arrangements to work. Several commentators have argued in favour of secession in dysfunctional nation-states, especially if the development of European Union-type supranational associations accompanies separation (Herbst 1996/97: 136–39; Chirot 1995). Eritrea's peaceful separation from Ethiopia in 1994, following a referendum the previous year, reassured those who feared that secession in any African country would open a Pandora's box of violence and fragmentation. Such reassurance, however, was short-lived: the two countries went to war in 1998 over a disputed boundary.

Enhancing the prospect that democratization will moderate or channel ethnic tensions hinges on two conditions: astute constitutional design, and the likelihood that fearful elites and people in general will give democratic institutions a chance. The latter condition is more likely in some historical and structural circumstances than in others.

If an ethnic minority dominated the previous authoritarian regime, democracy's prospects will be bleak. Resentments and hatred will likely vitiate whatever institutional mechanisms are instituted (Welsh 1993: 67–68). In Africa political and economic domination by an ethnic minority has usually spawned violent explosions, as seen in the settler colonies of Algeria, Kenya, Rhodesia, and South Africa. Only South Africa has managed a conciliatory democratization in the postcolonial era. Postcolonial ethnic oligarchies have also provided a hostile terrain for democratic processes, as in Burundi and Rwanda (Tutsis), Zanzibar (Arabs), Liberia (Americo-Liberians), and Kenya (Kalenjin and allies under Moi).

More generally, a history of intense ethnic conflict and ethnic stereotyping will militate against reconciliation via democratization. The prospects for muting these communal divisions improve if the pro-democracy movement includes leaders of all ethnic origins, and if these leaders are able to negotiate institutional arrangements that foster power-sharing and compromise *before* the electoral transition takes place (de Nevers 1993: 40–46). Mali, with the exception of the Tuareg, satisfied these positive conditions, with workable compromises being expedited in 1991 through the mechanisms of a provisional government and a representative National Conference. Overarching loyalties engendered by Islam and the Bambara language fortified national integration in this case.

Certain structural conditions also impinge on the likelihood of democratization promoting ethnic harmony. If one communal group forms a majority, leaders of this group will be encouraged to strive for control rather than co-operation across cleavages, which was Sudan's unfortunate fate. Conversely, if ethnic groups are all small or similar in size and power, then political leaders may see little gain in making appeals to ethnic identity. Their interest will instead lie in forging coalitions; consequently, people will feel less threatened by ethnic domination under such conditions (Lijphart 1977: 55–65; de Nevers 1993: 39). Yet even these benign circumstances do not guarantee that democratization will not stoke communal tensions. Tanzania, as a one-party state for decades after independence, had an enviable reputation for social harmony in the context of many small ethnic groups and no dominant religion. But the combination of market-oriented reform and transition to multiparty democracy in the 1990s deepened ethnic/racial and religious (Christian/Muslim) tensions. Both processes, by creating winners and losers, raised fears that certain regional/religious coalitions would dominate government to the detriment of out-groups (Kaiser 1996). The issue is whether well-designed democratic institutions will, in time, channel and moderate these inevitable stresses.

If socio-economic levels in a plural society are not widely divergent along ethnic/regional/religious lines, the chances of reconciliation are enhanced. Conversely, marked inequalities along communal lines, as in Rwanda and Burundi, arouse suspicions and lower the prospect that democratization will enhance power-sharing and reconciliation.

The importance of leadership in all of this should not be discounted. Leaders are not merely the agents of historical and structural forces beyond their control. Leaders and movements, though constrained by social, economic, and political conditions, generally exercise some degree of choice on matters of war and peace. Astute strategy and tactics vastly enhance the prospects that democratization will support rather than undermine ethnic harmony. Leaders who avoid inflammatory speeches, restrain the tempers of ethnic followers, and work out compromises can overcome difficult circumstances (de Nevers 1993: 40). Nelson Mandela's key role in negotiating a peaceful end to apartheid in South Africa illustrates the significance of statesmanship. While outside observers were predicting a race war, Mandela, from his prison cell, shrewdly engaged his captors in talks that established the principles for a transition to majority rule. To advance the process Mandela was even willing to make commitments unsanctioned by the African National Congress. As he stated, "There are times when a leader must move out ahead of the flock, go off in a new direction, confident that he is leading his people the right way" (Mandela 1995: 627). Following the democratic transition, President Mandela used his personal authority to build a non-racial South Africa under very difficult conditions.

Challenge: Building the Institutional Foundations of Growth
A drastic decline in living standards and a concomitant rise in poverty form another dimension of the complex emergency syndrome. If democratization manages conflict via inclusionary institutions and an equitable regional/ ethnic distribution of resources, this enhanced stability will presumably facilitate economic recovery. Conversely, economic development will be conducive to the survival of democracy by providing the resources for ethnic reconciliation and heightened prosperity. A virtuous circle of democratization, ethnic harmony, and development will then counteract any slide towards state dissolution. Whether democratization can contribute to this synergy by promoting economic recovery is a key question.

Although there is no one-to-one relationship between democratization (or democracy) and economic growth, democratization may have an *indirect* effect on economic well-being by promoting the institutional reforms that are a necessary condition for market development. Sustained growth and prosperity are rare in Africa, for many reasons (Nafziger 1999): external terms of trade shocks, heavy external debts, natural and human-made disasters, poor initial conditions, predatory political institutions, and policy errors. Among these factors, the negative impact of weak and arbitrary neo-patrimonial governance now receives much attention. Governmental elites, in the absence of a legitimating formula, use the state to distribute economic resources to maintain their support and combat fissiparous tendencies. This process subordinates criteria of economic production to political considerations. Political-institutional reforms that forge a more capable, responsive, predictable, and production-oriented state boost the prospects for development.

The reform agenda is daunting, as it necessitates rebuilding the rule of law, constructing an effective, efficient, and non-partisan civil service, circumscribing the patronage system so that it does not destroy the productive economy, and enhancing accountability at all levels. The existing institutions are a product of the history, culture, and material conditions of particular societies; such ingrained behavioural expectations will therefore be highly resistant to change. How then will this task be achieved? The governance approach pins its hopes on democratization, because the alternative paths to institutional renewal appear so unpromising. Democratization, it is hoped, will empower domestic social forces that have a vested interest in defending a new order of limited and market-friendly government, accountable and honest officials, transparent decision-making, effective and predictable administration, and a rule of law that protects human rights, private property, and the sanctity of contracts.

In practice, though, as with ethnic tensions, democratization may worsen economic problems. Systemic corruption, for instance, can become a major drag on productivity and growth (Mauro 1997), and a return to democracy may encourage further corruption by providing both an opportunity and a motive for corrupt behaviour (see Harris-White and White 1996). The opportunity arises, ironically, from the economic liberalization that invariably accompanies democratic transitions in contemporary Africa. Adjustment programs increase inflows of external grants and loans while requiring the privatization of many public assets. By thus augmenting the resources in the hands of politicians, these programs provide new temptations to power-holders. A new motive arises from the high cost of mounting national election campaigns, because serious contenders must distribute patronage to potential supporters. These expenses push government leaders to welcome kickbacks on government contracts and to employ state resources (vehicles, personnel, media) for partisan purposes. As well, political uncertainty and the spectre of personal poverty motivate insecure politicians to build up their private fortunes by any means available. The weakness of procedural norms in fledgling democracies makes these pressures on officials all the more telling.

But this, again, is only half the story. Democratization also unleashes powerful reformist impulses. The constitution lays out the new formal rules of the game, together with agencies charged with overseeing and enforcing these rules, including independent auditors, courts, and commissions. The newly entrenched civil and political rights stimulate the organization and assertiveness of civil associations (Gyimah-Boadi 1996). Independent newspapers and opposition parties publicize the transgressions of political leaders and bureaucrats. Constituencies mobilize to defend new institutions. For example, law societies take the lead in championing the independence of the judiciary. Coalitions involving professional organizations, church bodies, students, human-rights associations, and non-governmental organizations form to press forward the goals of due legal process and constitutionally limited power. In Kenya, for instance, the National Convention Assembly united six hundred members in 1996–98 behind a demand that the Moi government permit public participation in constitutional reform.

Democratization does not guarantee the political-institutional reforms that might underpin a productive economy. Such reform involves a series of struggles over many years. But, as the experience of Ghana's Fourth Republic illustrates (chapter 5), emergent democracy probably does provide a more propitious context for needed socio-economic change than do the conceivable alternatives.

Challenge: Empowering Local Institutions of Environmental Defence
Environmental crisis is another key element of the multidimensional crisis we term a complex political emergency. Environmental degradation and growing scarcity of natural resources can form an interlocking circle with deepening rural poverty, predatory politics, ethnic tensions, and violent conflict between countries and/or communities. Protection of the local resource base, especially land, may therefore ease tensions that might other-

wise escalate into complex emergencies. Can democratization help address environmental degradation and scarcities?

The answer, at first glance, is apparently no. Third World democracies have generally failed to curb two critical local vectors of degradation: rapacious corporations and the desperate rural poverty that drives herders and cultivators to unsustainable husbandry. Yet democratization can mitigate environmental shortages in at least two indirect ways.

First, popularly elected governments have proved to be adept at quickly and effectively responding to famines, the most devastating manifestation of natural-resource scarcity in poor countries with large rural sectors. India has justly received praise for instituting a famine-relief system that has prevented famines since independence, despite periodic droughts. Although Indian democracy has its shortcomings, the electoral weight of the countryside has nonetheless motivated national governments to respond quickly to regional food shortages. In Africa, too, democracies have effectively distributed emergency food supplies in drought-stricken regions. Haile Selassie's autocratic government in Ethiopia was overthrown in 1974 owing partly to the public outrage evoked by its refusal even to acknowledge the drought and famine that had ravaged the countryside. In Zambia, by contrast, the government of Frederick Chiluba, following a democratic transition in late 1991, earned accolades for moving speedily to prevent a local drought from evolving into a famine. Similarly, Botswana, democratic since independence, has earned a fine reputation for drought relief. Politicians of the governing party have found that attention to this important program translates into popularity in their rural constituencies. According to J.D. Holm and R.G. Morgan (1985: 477), "Drought relief is coming to assume a role in Botswana politics comparable to education and welfare in industrialized countries." Hence, government leaders have resisted advice to reduce government expenditures by cuts in this area.

Second, democratization can empower local communities and nongovernmental organizations to promote and defend locally based strategies of resource conservation. The celebrated Brundtland report (World Commission on Environment and Development 1987) held that poverty was a prime cause of environmental deterioration, in that poor people had no option but to overwork or overgraze the land and overexploit the forests in order to survive. A contrary view was soon articulated: that poverty was not a prime *cause* of local-level environmental degeneration, but rather a *symptom* of a condition that produces this lamentable situation, namely, the disempowerment of rural communities (Vivian 1992; Watts 1991; Ghai 1994; Broad 1994). This disempowerment manifested itself as outside agents abrogated the traditional rights of people to use local resources and curtailed their ability to manage them. Insofar as, traditionally, local communities had set in place sustainable patterns of managing resources, this disempowerment often had negative environmental repercussions. Vast logging concessions, new mines, the establishment of plantations and ranches, the building of dams, irrigation schemes, roads, and railways: all these conditions have frequently devastated local livelihoods, cultures, and eco-systems. More socially and environmentally sustainable development, according to the empowerment perspective, requires the participation of the local communities in resource management.

The organization of the poor and indigenous groups is what empowers them to act effectively as managers and "environmental activists" (Broad 1994). Local community organization is crucial; this organization, however, needs the expertise, funds, and protection that environmental and human-rights NGOs and mass-based peasant or labour unions can provide. "A densely webbed civil society . . . creates a culture of popular resistance" (Broad 1994: 817). This culture makes it more likely that local groups will defend their natural resources against threats from governments, businesses, and landowners. Political liberalization, by instituting civil and political rights, expands the political space for such organizations and networks to form and resist environmentally destructive development. Local activists may confront commercial loggers or commercial fishing fleets, protest environmental pollution by mining and oil companies, resist enclosures of the commons by landowners and corporations, replant trees, and assert their right to manage community resources.[4]

The empowerment view of environmental sustainability gains support from abundant evidence of the capacity of local communities to manage their eco-systems in a sustainable manner (for example, Ghai and Vivian 1992; Friedmann and Rangan 1993). A striking recent confirmation derives from a study of a transitional forest-savannah region in northern Guinea (Fairhead and Leach 1996). The study contradicts the conventional "scientific" view that this region had formerly been forested, and that the people had degraded the forest into savannah. Instead, it finds the precise opposite to hold true: that the inhabitants and their ancestors had, despite population increase, fostered forest growth in the savannah wherever they had settled, cultivated, and raised animals. Rather, outsiders had threatened the environment. Government agencies and donor organizations, supposing the local communities to be incapable of conservation, had imposed master plans and regulations that declared time-tested farming practices illegal (Fairhead and Leach 1996: 292–93).

A quite different instance of environmental renewal at the grassroots comes from the Green Belt Movement (GBM) in Kenya (Ekins 1992: 151–52). Founded in 1977 as a project of Kenya's National Council of Women, it aimed to organize rural women around the project of reforestation. The GBM started tree nurseries, replanted public "green belts," and encouraged private farmers to plant trees on their landholdings. These activities not only combatted soil erosion, but also created jobs for rural women and enhanced their solidarity and power. In the first decade, between two thousand and three thousand women participated in the cultivation and planting of trees, with about two thousand new green belts and fifteen thousand replanted farms to show for their efforts (Ekins 1992: 151). Nonetheless, the authoritarian Moi regime soon saw the GBM and its leader Wangari Maathai as political threats. Its harassment of Maathai did not deter her: she played an important role in Kenya's democracy movement in the 1990s, thereby illustrating the close connection between environmental activism and political liberalization.

With qualifications, the empowerment view provides a practical way of confronting environmental decline. One flaw is the tendency to romanticize the relationship of poor and indigenous people to their environment. Local communities do not always prudently manage the local resources they depend on (Leach, Mearns, and Scoones 1997). Traditional ways of living in harmony with nature often do not survive the commercialization of natural resources that accompanies the extension of market relations. As well, the members of local communities rarely have a common interest: more often, they are neither undifferentiated nor democratic. An elite based on class, caste, or ethnicity often dominates local power structures and determines how local resources will be allocated. Local management, under these conditions, will certainly not reflect empowerment of the poor/local communities.[5]

Nonetheless, the poor have often acted as environmental activists—when their resource base is threatened by degradation, when they have a sense of permanence in an area, and when political conditions permit them to organize and engage in collective action (Broad 1994: 815–16). Democratization at the national level, while not guaranteeing decentralization and democratization at the local level, does widen the political space for national and international NGOs to organize to confront local oligarchies and press an agenda of resource conservation.

Thus, insofar as democratization attunes the central government to the food-security needs of rural people and furnishes a facilitative framework for environmental activism at the local level, it can indirectly respond to the destructive tendency of environmental degradation.

Prognosis: Uncertain

Whether human ingenuity can avert complex political emergencies is a question that has assumed growing importance with the proliferation of political upheavals. Nor have the upheavals been peculiar to Africa. One journalist, in a much-cited article, claimed that Sierra Leone in 1994 was a "microcosm" of what was occurring, "albeit in a more tempered and gradual manner," throughout much of the Third World: "The withering away of central governments, the rise of tribal and regional domains, the unchecked spread of disease, and the growing pervasiveness of war" (Kaplan 1994: 48).

Although this scenario was unduly pessimistic, it did reflect widespread anxieties as each headline brought further bad news.

The prevailing syndrome of four interlocking symptoms—ethnic polarization, weak and predatory governance, economic collapse, and environmental degradation—creates a vicious circle leading ultimately to civil war or state collapse. Democracy does not offer a quick fix to these problems. Indeed, democratization is a risky strategy because it unleashes tensions that may aggravate the underlying crises. But democratization can be an important component of a broad program to forestall deadly conflict. Its long-term promise is, under certain conditions, to replace the vicious circle with a virtuous circle of peaceful, prosperous, and ecologically sustainable development.

Political liberalization can advance this goal both directly and indirectly. Its direct effect is felt in the constitutional-legal institutions that manage conflicts in deeply divided societies, lay a foundation for economic prosperity, and recognize the traditional tenure rights of ecologically sensitive local communities. As these changes occur, the democratic state also enhances its capacity. Peace, governmental responsiveness, and growth generate the legitimacy, revenues, and legality on which a stronger state hinges. Indirectly, civil and political rights, independent media and courts, opposition movements, and grassroots associations generate the political space for constituencies to organize in support of valued institutions.

What then is the prognosis for closing this circle? For one thing, the earlier in a downward spiral that a democratic transition is attempted, the greater the chances of success. A breakdown into civil war will severely limit democratic prospects, owing to the heightened enmities, fears, and insecurities that such conflict breeds. It is also better if constitutions arise from negotiations, such as by means of a national conference; these negotiations generate compromises mitigating actual or potential cleavages. As well, the international community can play an important role. Although external interventions often exacerbate conflicts, they can also be positive. For instance, Mozambique's success in sustaining democracy and building peace in the 1990s can, in part, be explained by the continuing international oversight provided by the United Nations and donor countries. Moreover, democratic polities, to become consolidated, must deliver a better life to citizens. Such economic progress may require reform of the global economy, not just an increase in foreign aid. Finally, the growing willingness of African governments to intervene militarily in neighbouring countries further destabilizes countries by encouraging local insurgents; but there are ongoing negotiations to replace unilateral military interventions with regional peacekeeping forces.

Democracy movements confront enormous challenges. They search for suitable political, social, and economic arrangements in the face of multiple crises, recalcitrant domestic governments, and impatient and niggardly donors. But no longer should their quest be dismissed as wrongheaded on the grounds that only authoritarian regimes can create order. Although democratization often fails, it nonetheless provides a better opportunity for needed institutional reforms than the earlier, discredited autocracies.

FOUR

4 Democratization and Market Reforms

Until the 1980s, conventional wisdom held that authoritarian governments were better able to implement economic development than newly democratic ones. Authoritarian regimes, the belief went, were more insulated from the demands of special-interest groups than were elected governments, and they were not exposed to the populist temptations inherent in periodic electoral campaigns. Because of the autocrat's capacity to ignore or suppress dissent, the government could implement reform policies that imposed short-term costs on powerful strata, such as workers and civil servants. In Deepak Lal's blunt words, "A courageous, ruthless and perhaps undemocratic government is required to ride roughshod over . . . newly created special interest groups" (Lal 1983: 33).

Certainly, for influential groups the costs of stabilizing and liberalizing statist economies have been high. Devaluation raises the price of imports, including some of the urban population's basic consumer goods. Slashing governmental deficits usually means reducing public expenditures. Governments commonly achieve this cost-cutting by reducing public employment and salaries, by ending key subsidies—for example, on fuel—by rolling back educational and health services, or charging user fees, and by delaying the maintenance and building of public infrastructure, especially roads and schools. The elimination of price controls leads to higher prices for basic commodities, sometimes including food. Trade liberalization, including a reduction in tariffs, drives some local manufacturers into bankruptcy, thereby increasing unemployment and probably lowering industrial wages. A host of political cronies, key patrons who control their own clienteles, find their access to state-generated resources threatened. Economic stabilization and liberalization eliminate or diminish certain patronage resources: subsidized credit and foreign exchange, import licences, free or cheap utilities, bank fraud, public-sector jobs, sinecures, and opportunities for embezzlement. Although these costs of adjustment—except those to cronies—are supposed to be "transitional," they continue

75

for at least several years. Strategic groups suffer, and protest. No wonder, then, that observers were initially skeptical that elected politicians could impose adjustment policies and then expect the people to re-elect them.

Yet experience in the 1980s challenged the conventional wisdom regarding the developmental effectiveness of one-party states and juntas. Although certain authoritarian regimes consistently imposed market reforms—Chile, Mexico, and Ghana, for instance—many others in Latin America and Africa failed miserably as reformers. Many autocrats were not motivated to carry through fundamental political-economic change, because they and their supporters were reaping rewards and rents from the prevailing system of political capitalism. In contrast, in the 1980s or 1990s some democratic regimes—Argentina, Bolivia, and Mauritius, for example— excelled in neo-liberal adjustment, though others faltered. Clearly, no decisive relationship between regime type and economic development or effective market implementation obtained (see Geddes 1995: 60–63).

Hence, by the late 1980s, many observers, including researchers at the World Bank (1989), were questioning the conventional wisdom. Democratic governments, in the revised view, could have potential advantages in undertaking market reform. Democratic politics and the associated rule of law could be beneficial in motivating governments to implement workable reform programs, building popular support behind market-led development, and generating the improved governance demanded by investors.

These alleged advantages of democratization can be stated in a series of hypotheses. First, political liberalization may augment *governmental commitment* to market reform, in two ways.

⊛   **"New Broom" hypothesis.** Economic reform is doomed when a corrupt and illegitimate government, whose leading figures and supporters reap rewards from the prevailing statist arrangements, reluctantly accedes to adjustment in order to obtain much-needed loans from the international financial institutions. Such regimes will evade or negate the conditions attached to loans by the IMF, World Bank, and donors. But electoral transitions may elevate to power new political leaders who are not (yet) anchored in pre-existing clientelist networks and corruption. Hence the new broom provided by democratization may sweep away the economically unproductive clientele networks and government-enabled rents, unimpeded by formerly entrenched rentier groups.

⊛   **"Local Ownership" hypothesis.** If an elected government has freely adopted a reform program, has defended certain key changes in an electoral campaign, and governs with support of the legislature, it will feel that it "owns" reform. This sense of ownership can motivate a government to act consistently on economic policy. Moreover, in formulating its economic measures such a government can negotiate compromises with interest groups. This domestic consensus will facilitate their implementation.

Second, if market reforms are to be sustained despite the steep transitional costs of adjustment, a government must be able to *mobilize support* from putative beneficiaries. Corrupt and authoritarian governments are unlikely to succeed in this political task, because people will respond cynically to appeals for sacrifices for the common good. People will know that the regime profits from the prevailing order. Newly elected governments, in contrast, will benefit, at least during the early honeymoon period, from legitimacy, even in the eyes of sectors whose interests are hurt by adjustment. This legitimacy, reinforced by a pro-active policy of compensating those who suffer losses in the transitional period, may effectively mute opposition to the new order. In addition, electoral contests in theory will motivate pro-reform parties to mobilize the support of actual or potential beneficiaries of neo-liberal policies. These will include some sectors of the business community, farmers who produce cash crops, and certain segments of skilled employees and self-employed. Of course, the beneficiaries are assumed to wield considerable political influence, whether owing to numbers, organization, or resources. If this assumption is false, then the losers in policy reform may block costly reforms, using the democratic system.

A third political requirement for market reform is *restructuring of corrupt, arbitrary, and undisciplined state apparatuses*. Democracy, again in theory, will generate the necessary accountability of officials and transparency in decision-making, thus reassuring investors. Constitutional politics should also provide a conducive environment to reduce the clientelistic basis of the civil service and parastatals and augment their professionalism and probity. These measures will contribute to more effective economic reform.

But the reality in Sub-Saharan Africa diverges significantly from this threefold model. Democracy in the region, as we have seen (chapter 2), manifests fragility and limits. Indeed, general elections and multiparty competition do not banish—and may even aggravate—the clientelism, factionalism, ethnic/regional loyalties, and administrative weaknesses of the *ancien régime*. A monopolistic party or junta riven with factions is typically replaced with a fragmented party system formed around prominent personalities and regional or religious loyalties, rather than ideological differences. Political coalitions remain ambiguous and uncertain in a civil society that had for so long been suffocated by authoritarian rule. Public administrations in emergent democracies face many of the same constraints—fiscal austerity, a paucity of skilled personnel, low morale, indiscipline—that created their earlier debilitation.

In this weakened state, new governments confront high public expectations aroused by the election campaign. They must resolve the fiscal crisis, rebuild bureaucratic discipline, competence, and insulation, and maintain political support in order to satisfy these expectations through coherent economic reforms. This agenda is daunting.

If authoritarian-developmental regimes on the East Asian model were a practical alternative to emergent and weak democracies, they might be preferable as agents of order and reform. But Africa's historical, cultural, and material conditions are quite different from those that underpinned the developmental state in countries such as Korea or Taiwan (see Sandbrook 1991: 109–11). Hence, this East Asian model is now apparently out of reach.[1] Economic progress in Kenya, Malawi, Côte d'Ivoire, and Cameroon in the 1960s and 1970s rested on efficient, authoritarian-developmental regimes, but even those regimes decayed (partly because of external economic shocks) in the 1980s. The ensuing weak and predatory states represent—except for political breakdown and chaos—the worst-case scenario, given their propensity for both human-rights abuses and economically destructive political capitalism. Political democracies and market reforms offer some protection against both, as the cases of Mauritius and Botswana, two of the region's political and economic success stories, demonstrate. The hypotheses linking democratization to economic reform, therefore, merit further examination.

Governmental Commitment to Reform

To persist with reform despite opposition, the executive authority in a given country must be firmly convinced of the necessity of economic stabilization and liberalization (see esp. Wallis 1999). A politically astute leadership will mute opposition using such tactics as varying the pace and sequence of reforms and mitigating the costs to the most strategic groups. In contrast, a regime that is fractious or unpersuaded of the need for market-based reforms will probably adopt a stop-go approach to reform. This vacillation, usually induced by the conflicting demands of multilateral agencies and domestic support groups, may produce the worst outcome: an economy stalled between a weak *dirigiste* state and weak markets (Callaghy 1990).

Outsiders, who are not implicated in the spoils system, will probably be more willing to introduce reforms that disrupt neo-patrimonial practices (Bienen and Herbst 1996: 33). An executive's commitment to economic reform will be low if incumbent officials and their cronies are major losers of economic liberalization. Insiders benefiting from state-generated largesse will resist structural reform, or distort reforms in a manner they can exploit (see Hibou 1999). Democratic transitions may permit such outsiders to attain power. But experience suggests that these new brooms rarely sweep clean for long. Outsiders, whether authoritarian or democratic progeny, evolve into insiders playing the same old neo-patrimonial game.

Jerry J. Rawlings is an example of an outsider who came to power by means of the coup d'état. In June 1979 and again in December 1981, this young air force officer seized control of Ghana's government. Both times he acted as a new broom sweeping away the widespread corruption, clientelism, and cronyism bedeviling Ghana's political and economic life. In 1982 his radical-populist regime punished the corrupt, mobilized ordinary people in militant "defence committees," and urged hardy self-reliance, probity, and patriotism. When the economy continued to deteriorate in 1982 and 1983 (partly due to circumstances beyond Ghana's control), Rawlings and a few close supporters in the People's National Defence Council (PNDC) negotiated a structural adjustment agreement with the IMF. The move signified not a wholesale conversion to neo-liberal doctrine, but a calculation that the regime's survival in desperate economic circumstances required an accommodation with Western donors.[2] Economic stabilization and liberalization initially served Rawlings' populist objectives well enough, as the reforms undercut rent-seeking, rebuilt sagging state revenues, and promised a refurbished and more disciplined state apparatus. Because Rawlings and his coterie, as outsiders, held no stake in the prevailing clientelism and corruption that they professed to abhor, they moved decisively against these arrangements in the Economic Recovery Programs of the 1980s. Only when the external agencies pressed the regime to privatize and significantly reduce the size and role of the public sector did it resist. By 1992 the PNDC was no longer a new broom. Ironically, democratization accelerated the reversion to traditional clientelist methods of rule.

Although outsiders sometimes do violently seize power from autocrats and initiate fundamental reform, this phenomenon is rare. Some highly motivated rebels—for instance, Murtala Mohamed of Nigeria and Thomas Sankara of Burkina Faso—have been quickly assassinated by those threatened by their populist reforms. Other outsiders, such as President Laurent Kabila of the Democratic Republic of the Congo (Kinshasa), were merely regional warlords elevated to power by fortune, but incapable of transcending the obsessive security imperatives of warlord politics. Yoweri Museveni of Uganda is one of the few successful market reformers who seized power by force of arms. Still, a dozen years after his National Resistance Army assumed power in 1986, donors and the international financial institutions subjected even his much-praised administration to criticism for corruption and financial mismanagement (*Financial Times*, Dec. 9, 1998).

Whether democracy is more reliable an instrument for elevating committed reformers to power is dubious. Of the six countries featured in the discussion of democratization (chapter 2), four (Zambia, Niger, Mali, and Madagascar) experienced a change of regime in the early 1990s, but many of the new leaders soon fell into old neo-patrimonial patterns. In Zambia Frederick Chiluba's Movement for Multiparty Democracy (MMD) acted as a new broom when it swept Kenneth Kaunda's United National

Independence Party (UNIP) from power in the elections of October 1991. Chiluba was not implicated in spoils politics, because he had remained a union leader rather than enter UNIP politics. (Many of his cabinet ministers, however, were former UNIP stalwarts.) Chiluba employed his initial popularity to accelerate the reform package that UNIP had negotiated in 1990. Zambia by 1991 was in a severe economic crisis. While per capita income had declined to half its early 1970s level, Zambians were buffeted by soaring inflation, growing unemployment, a shortage of foreign exchange, and an eroding infrastructure (Simutanyi 1996: 828). In this desperate situation Chiluba quickly moved to institute several unpopular measures. He devalued the kwacha and liberalized foreign exchange. He decontrolled prices and removed subsidies, including those on the staple, maize meal. He tightened monetary policy and liberalized trade and agricultural marketing. In exchange for substantial inflows of loans and grants, the president allowed the international financial institutions to take the lead on issues of macroeconomic management. Yet the MMD government resisted donor pressure on matters that would directly undermine its ability to remain in power. Progress on reform of the civil service and privatization was minimal until the mid-1990s, and proceeded then only after extensive prodding by the donors (White 1997: 62). Also, in the face of strong objections from donors, in 1996 the government enacted controversial constitutional amendments disqualifying former president Kaunda as a presidential candidate. Indeed, the longer the MMD remained in power, the more it embraced the authoritarian and clientelist tendencies that had earlier animated UNIP. Persistent allegations of high-level corruption and drug-running, together with its high-handedness after 1995, sullied the government's reputation and reduced its legitimacy (Van de Walle 1997: 32).

Displacing leaders immersed in political capitalism may facilitate executive commitment to pushing through market reforms, but long-term implementation of controversial programs requires that governments and elected representatives "own" their own projects. Desperate for loans and grants, African governments have had little choice but to come to terms with IMF and World Bank demands. Still, this need to gain external approval has only encouraged certain regimes to play the game in order to secure credits, while the predatory state continues somewhat as before. The Zairean president Mobutu Sése-Séko, for instance, adeptly negotiated agreements with the IMF and World Bank, though apparently with little intention of adhering to their terms (Leslie 1987). If Western governments or multilateral agencies push governments too aggressively, they achieve not a political commitment to reform but a shallow and sullen acquiescence. This attitude, illustrated by these angry words of Mozambican President Joaquim Chissano, bodes ill for a long-haul reform process: "The U.S. said, 'Open yourself to OPIC, the World Bank, and the IMF.' What happened? . . . We are told now: 'Marxism! You are devils. Change this policy.' O.K. Marxism

is gone. 'Open the market economy.' O.K., [the ruling party] Frelimo is trying to create capitalism. . . . We went to Reagan and I said, 'I want money
for the private sector. . . .' Answer: $10 million, then $15 million more, then
another $15 million. . . . O.K. we have changed. . . . Now they say, 'If you
don't go to a multiparty system, don't expect help from us'" (quoted in
Bowen 1992: 272).

If donors impose reforms, governments will lack the motivation to
implement them effectively. As the World Bank itself observes, "Governments
and beneficiaries do not feel they have a stake when they have not contributed to the development of a program. Furthermore, 'homegrown' programs may be more effective in incorporating institutional capacity,
reflecting the needs of different domestic constituencies, and addressing
constraints" (World Bank 1995c: 6).

Yet the donors' practice diverges markedly from their rhetoric concerning the importance of local ownership. The IMF, World Bank, and bilateral
donors offer Sub-Saharan governments little latitude in devising their own
reform programs (Helleiner 1998). The IMF, in particular, wields enormous
influence; an agreement with this body is normally required before the
bilateral donors will negotiate their own agreements, and before the Paris
Club of official creditors will grant debt relief. The IMF, World Bank, and
donors negotiate an inordinate number of conditions that recipient governments must fulfil. One study of five adjustment-related agreements signed
by Zambia between 1990 and 1995 uncovered an average of twenty-five
conditions in each agreement (White 1997: 64). In that case, certain conditions required specific legislation, such as "parliamentary enactment of
business-related laws" and "enact amendments to land law" (White 1997:
64), which showed little respect for democratic processes, let alone local
ownership.

The top-down, secretive manner of negotiating adjustment loans and
grants also contradicts the principle of ownership through democratic
processes. Usually a few top technocrats from the country's central bank and
finance ministry act on behalf of the African government. Donors believe
that they must deal directly with governments on policy issues. They
assume that elected officials have a mandate to proceed with adjustment,
and that these officials will obtain ratification of any agreements, including
the conditions for loans. Donors also seem to believe that, since adjustment
requires unpopular sacrifices, a top-down decision-making process is preferable to a participatory one in which popular demands can derail "necessary"
reforms.[3] However, this approach removes key areas of economic and social
policy from the purview of representative institutions, so that elections and
legislative debates lose their meaning. Local ownership and governmental
commitment to reform only emerge from national debates over appropriate
policies. Local ownership means taking democracy seriously. At issue is

whether donors accept what ownership implies—that local programs will sometimes not accord with external priorities.

Crucial executive commitment, then, may build under certain conditions: if regime turnover installs outsiders as political leaders; and if this leadership develops a sense of owning a reform program. Then economic reform may persist despite setbacks and protests. But often democratization does not produce a beneficial condition, or the condition is short-lived.

Building Political Coalitions for Neo-Liberal Reform

A pro-reform government with a firm political base of beneficiary groups is best positioned to transform political capitalism by means of neo-liberal reforms. Are democratic regimes better able to provide such a political configuration than authoritarian ones? Democratization, in principle, would undermine the political power of the small coteries of state-dependent rent-seekers who have helped bring economic ruin. Political freedom would allow the allegedly more numerous and influential classes and interest groups who benefit from market exchange to organize and back pro-reform parties. Since numbers count in a multiparty electoral system, the vote should empower the formerly exploited peasant producers to support governments that will advance their economic interests. Political and economic liberalization also permits entrepreneurs, professionals, and others to develop their organizational and political power, helped by donor-assisted programs of institutional capacity-building. These changed power relations, together with schemes to compensate those groups paying the costs of adjustment, would permit reformers to override the inevitable opposition to economic liberalization.

Experience suggests that this theory of democratization and coalition-formation has its defects. The losers in structural adjustment include well-organized, vocal, and strategically located interest groups; their influence is further enhanced by the central role they played in the democracy movements of the early 1990s. Moreover, schemes to compensate those who suffer the costs of adjustment are unlikely to dispose of the resources needed to fulfil this goal in societies that suffer from mass poverty and have many losers. As well, the beneficiaries who should buttress a pro-reform regime (especially peasant producers) are weakened by divided interests and poor organization. To the extent that beneficiaries are unorganized and ambivalent, pro-reform parties are unlikely to take up the risky challenge of forging coalitions based on policy appeals. They are more likely to have recourse to the familiar patterns of clientelism, populism, and covert ethnic/regional/religious appeals. Indeed, electoral politics may stimulate clientelism and corruption, thus contradicting the market logic of resource allocation.

The first problem with the theory is that the influential groups that first championed democratic transitions are the main losers from structural adjustment. Liberal economic policies come at a high cost for many people: those who enjoyed privileged access when goods or foreign exchange were rationed; those who held public employment or benefited from subsidies; and those who profited from governmental intervention by means of price-setting in commodity and food markets. Yet many of these urban working-class and middle-class losers from economic reform were key supporters of democratization.

Popular struggles for democracy were impelled by economic decline and adjustment programs. Most of the authoritarian regimes that emerged in Sub-Saharan Africa in the 1960s and 1970s depended heavily for their survival on the politics of distribution. They favoured strategic urban strata and ethnic/regional allies in the allocation of public expenditures and the distribution of patronage via clientele networks. For many years financial repression, widespread state controls and regulations, and a large parastatal sector ensured the availability of significant resources for distribution. But by the early 1980s the economic mismanagement inherent in this mode of governance, combined with external and climatic shocks, undermined many economies.[4] Decrepit economies could no longer generate the surplus necessary to maintain an autocrat's political support. This reality left belea-guered governments with little alternative but to turn to the IMF and World Bank. However, structural adjustment is designed to *redistribute* resources; this principle is inherent in the changes in relative prices, the elimination of many controls and regulations, and the shifts in public expenditures. In Africa's agrarian economies, adjustment is intended in particular to shift resources away from certain urban groups (public employees, those employed in inefficient import-substituting industries, political insiders) and towards the producers of cash crops. This attempted shift, together with austerity programs, inevitably disrupted political alliances (see Grosh 1994).

Authoritarian governments, no longer as able to purchase political acquiescence, confronted the anger and frustration of well-organized and strategically located urban groups. Public employees, organized workers in general, students, and professionals were hurt first by economic decline and then by structural adjustment. Devaluation, inflation, and reductions in food subsidies shrank real wages. Planned privatization and downsizing of the civil service threatened existing public employees and those in educational institutions who aspired to that status. A reduction in subsidies to secondary schools and universities created higher fees and living expenses for students and a lower quality of education. Public services deteriorated. Consequently, economic grievances animated political protests as students, intellectuals, professionals, public employees, and workers blamed the economic crisis on the corruption and incompetence of autocrats. Subsequent transitions to democratic governance inspired public jubilation as democracy activists anticipated a return to better days.

Yet elected governments had little choice but to continue with the adjustment policies of their predecessors. Indeed, the IMF and World Bank demanded even more stringent implementation of stabilization, liberalization, and privatization programs. When such efforts did not soon produce economic benefits, some of the erstwhile elements of the democratic movements mutinied against the new governments. Although governments and donors erected social safety nets to cushion the effects of adjustment and reduce poverty, these efforts would have a limited impact. By the late 1990s public cynicism, strikes, and demonstrations had thrown the very survival of some democratic experiments into doubt.

This scenario, for example, played itself out in Madagascar, Mali, Niger, and Zambia, though not to any extent in Ghana or Tanzania. The first three countries adhered to a similar pattern. Although only a quarter or less of their populations reside in urban areas, secondary and university students, civil servants, and organized workers wielded a disproportionate political impact. Students, in particular, proved themselves to be organized, tenacious in the defence of their privileges, and capable of mobilizing unemployed and disaffected youth outside their own ranks. Students in all three cases initiated or spearheaded the urban rebellions that precipitated the transitions to democracy (see Fay 1995; Smith 1997; Gervais 1995a; and Allen 1995: 64–67, 96, 105). However, students and their urban supporters then expected their elected government to reinstate them in their earlier privileged position, an unreasonable expectation in light of the economic crisis and the adjustment response. Worse yet, economic reform did not generate a vibrant private sector to provide alternative careers for unemployed students and displaced public servants. The subsequent alienation of some of democracy's key urban supporters brought eruptions in street violence, the destruction of property, and peaceful demonstrations. Meanwhile, the illiterate and isolated rural majority played its largely passive role in national politics.

In Zambia, a far more urbanized country, a different pattern prevailed. Students played a less dominant role, and organized workers a more central one, in the oppositional coalition that prodded President Kaunda and the ruling UNIP to submit to a national election in 1991. Zambia suffered a severe economic decline after 1975 as the world price of copper (the economy's mainstay) plummeted. Borrowing offset the decline for several years. In the 1980s UNIP's periodic adoption of stabilization and liberalization packages further strained the living standards of its former supporters among copper miners, urban workers, public employees, professionals, and even business people.[5] The government's removal of a significant subsidy on maize meal twice acted as a flashpoint for urban riots in the 1980s, forcing the government to re-establish a subsidy. By 1990 people were blaming

UNIP's corruption and mismanagement for their economic hardships (Bratton 1994: 101–28). In 1991, after the united Movement for Multiparty Democracy harnessed this anger to defeat UNIP, the new government initially pursued adjustment with even greater zeal than its predecessor. After this honeymoon period some of the MMD's supporters became disillusioned with continuing austerity, high inflation, and declining services. A wave of strikes beset the new government. Not surprisingly, the government then procrastinated in the face of donors' demands that Zambia privatize state-owned enterprises and reduce the workforce in the publicly owned copper mines by half, as well as lay off seven thousand civil servants. By 1998, although some privatizations and redundancies ensued, the largest state-owned enterprises were still mostly intact.

In Ghana the politics of adjustment unfolded rather differently. Flt.-Lt. Rawlings seized power in December 1981 with the support of the lower ranks of the armed forces, the radical intelligentsia and students, and organized labour. This alliance was united in a vaguely defined populist revolution against a corrupt and exploitative elite of politicians and capitalists. Rawlings, however, changed course in 1983 by entering into a stabilization agreement with the IMF. By the mid-1980s his former urban supporters—minus the army—expressed their anger at this turn of events. The ruling PNDC met this opposition head on, detaining and harassing union leaders, closing the universities, and imprisoning middle-class opponents (Ho Won Jeong 1998: 219–20). Rawlings also obtained concessions in the adjustment agreements in 1986 to accommodate the interests of the protesters. In 1988 he launched PAMSCAD, a set of relief projects, to alleviate the distress of vocal groups, especially in the urban areas. By 1992, when Rawlings managed a transition to semi-democracy, his government could boast of some economic success. An 80 per cent rise in government salaries prior to the vote must also have allayed some of the urban disaffection. Finally, he succeeded in rallying a large rural constituency behind his banner of continuity. By then even the opposition parties were advocating modified adjustment policies.

Tanzania, in contrast to the other cases, has experienced neither a strong, urban-based democracy movement nor sustained urban opposition to structural adjustment. Public demonstrations against the single-party state, virtually non-existent between 1985 and 1988, peaked at only three or four instances in each of 1990 and 1991. The case for democratization was spearheaded by academics, prominent lawyers, and retired president Julius Nyerere, who demanded, in the pages of the independent press, the legalization of opposition parties. President Ali Mwinyi bowed to the continent-wide trend to multiparty systems in 1992, probably confident that a small and divided opposition would pose little threat. Certain features of the rule of the Chama Cha Mapinduzi (CCM) largely explain this weakness of an urban democracy movement. The governing party had managed to monopolize all popular organizations since the mid-1960s. Independent associations were co-opted into the party or saw their leadership dominated by party militants. The party's socialist, or *ujamaa*, ideology had restrained the privileges of the urban minority in this overwhelmingly agrarian society. When real incomes were halved between 1975 and 1983, urban employees accepted economic liberalization as an escape from the apparent dead end of existing socialist policies (Chege 1994: 276). The party's embrace of economic reform from the mid-1980s encouraged people; political liberalization appeared secondary.

Africa's emergent democratic governments can mobilize a strong coalition behind market reforms only with difficulty. On the one hand, their continued adherence to stabilization and adjustment policies risks alienating their erstwhile urban allies in the democracy movement. These vocal groups had initially protested against authoritarian regimes owing to their declining living standards occasioned by both economic decline and stabilization measures. Following the honeymoon period of the democratic transition, reforming governments have sometimes felt the sting of renewed urban protest. On the other hand, market reforms cannot rely on the economic interests of putative beneficiaries to forge a new governing coalition. For one thing, the economic interests of beneficiaries are not unambiguously market-oriented. One oft-noted political difficulty is that costs, in the form of lost jobs, higher prices, user fees, and bankruptcies, are felt immediately, whereas the benefits appear only in the longer term (Bienen and Herbst 1996: 32); and the longer term may be very long, indeed. Even if adjustment succeeds, economic growth in Sub-Saharan countries will proceed at only 4 or 5 per cent, according to the World Bank, while population grows at almost 3 per cent per annum. The living standards of beneficiaries would, therefore, rise at only very modest rates, at best.

Not only have few benefits yet emerged, but the interests of designated beneficiaries also diverge on key policy issues. Even the business class is rarely united in its support of economic liberalization. Although business should benefit from a free-market strategy, those entrepreneurs who owe their success to protection from foreign competition, subsidized inputs and credit, state-supported monopolies, and/or undervalued foreign exchange will usually resist the loss of these privileges. Even in Zambia, where business was a mainstay of the pro-reform MMD, firms were divided on key policy issues. All leaders of incorporated businesses agreed on the need to reduce inflation, liberalize the exchange rate, and privatize state corporations; but they parted company on the advisability of trade liberalization. Only the large, mainly transnational, firms supported a marked lowering of tariffs. The smaller firms engaged in manufacturing for the local market were adamantly opposed (Simutanyi 1996: 831). Indeed, rapid import liberalization in Zambia did lead to a wave of bankruptcies, layoffs, and declining output in the manufacturing sector (White 1997: 70). As well, many small operators in the informal sector did not regard themselves as adjustment's beneficiaries. The shrinking of formal-sector wage and salary employment drove many people into the informal sector, which came to account for a majority of the labour force in many cities (Bangura 1994: 9). As the informal sector expanded, competition mounted and returns fell.

Small agricultural producers also have divided interests. They benefit from higher cash-crop prices and the rehabilitation of rural services and infrastructure; they also suffer losses. Export-crop prices rise with economic adjustment, but so too do the prices of agricultural inputs, food, and user fees for services. Indeed, one economist has referred to "immiserated growth" as afflicting peasants in Madagascar. As many peasants are net purchasers of increasingly high-priced rice, liberalization of agriculture has led to both increased output *and* to deepening poverty (Barrett 1998). A contrary impression of a unified peasant interest in neo-liberal reform emerges from a study of Ghana's 1992 elections. This study argues that President Rawlings did, indeed, gain the smallholders' vote on the basis of their "rational" calculation of their economic interest in structural adjustment (Bawumia 1998). Certainly, Rawlings was more popular in most rural areas than in the towns and cities. However, certain facts suggest that voting patterns were not determined by a uniform peasant economic interest. For instance, people in the Ashanti region, though benefiting handsomely from adjustment (especially the rise in cocoa prices), nonetheless voted heavily for the opposition candidate. Also, ethnic voting prevailed throughout the country, as the study's author notes. As for the food-crop producers, they may not have gained from the reforms. They received a higher price, but they also had to pay more for fertilizer and services. Finally, patronage played an important role in securing rural votes for Rawlings' party.

Nor are the interests of peasants neatly separated from those of wage-earners. Peasants and urban workers are still not mutually exclusive classes in Africa; many workers who suffer from the effects of structural adjustment retain rights to small landholdings often worked by household members. This straddling of economic roles, coupled with the contradictory effects of price increases, vitiates any one-to-one relationship between class position and support for economic liberalization (cf. Bangura and Gibbon 1992).

A related problem is that the interest groups that might back a pro-reform government lack cohesive organization, as is obviously the case with widely dispersed peasants. Leaders in many countries have, therefore, appealed to smallholders on ethnic/communal lines or on the grounds of local issues, rather than on the basis of shared economic interests as producers of cash crops. The corporate elite, though divided on particular policy reforms, generally constitutes one of today's better organized interest groups. In the more highly industrialized societies, well-organized business associations have existed for many years. In Zimbabwe, for example, the Confederation of Zimbabwe Industries (CZI) played a key role in pressing the government to adopt the Economic Structural Adjustment Program in 1990. In 1987 the CZI abandoned its opposition to trade liberalization and joined the Commercial Farmers Union in advocating an opening up of the economy. The government eventually adopted this strategy, though against the opposition of the weak Zimbabwe Congress of Trade Unions (Skalnes 1995). Where capitalist production relations are less advanced, business associations have played a less influential role. In Ghana, Rawlings' populist perspective led him to regard business people as parasites and rent-seekers and to direct a panoply of punitive measures against them. Only in the 1990s did the Ghanaian government moderate its suspicion of business and open channels of communication with its associations. This new openness to the corporate elite stemmed, in part, from the pressure exerted on government by the international financial institutions and donors.

These external agencies have initiated a variety of programs to bolster the political influence of the private sector in African countries as a "natural" accompaniment to market-oriented reform.[6] They have lobbied African governments to institutionalize channels through which business associations can articulate their policy concerns to political decision-makers. The World Bank, the donors (especially USAID), and the donor-financed African Capacity Building Foundation have also directly assisted business associations in building their organizational strength, expertise in policy advocacy, and lobbying skills. For example, in the 1990s the USAID and the United States Information Agency arranged exchange visits between U.S. and African business associations, especially chambers of commerce, instituted training programs for the staff of business associations through the Center for International Private Enterprise, and sponsored Entrepreneurial International—a program to bring African entrepreneurs and chief executive officers to the United States for study tours. The two agencies also developed training and technical assistance programs to small entrepreneurs through the Human Resources Development Assistance Program and provided financial support for private-sector foundations and think-tanks in Africa to enhance capital's political influence (Kraus 1998: 45–47). Other donors, in particular the United Kingdom, have complemented and extended this ambitious set of initiatives. External agencies have also endeavoured to create regional networks of African business people to foster mutual support. For instance, the World Bank, USAID, and Club du Sahel helped create the West African Enterprise Network in 1993, with its headquarters in Accra.

Although the public aim of these programs is to develop a better business climate, thus encouraging more investment, they represent a potent external intrusion into the political dynamics of African countries. Whether these efforts to foster the autonomy and influence of a formerly state-dependent bourgeoisie will succeed remains to be seen. Capital, with its divisions and history of collaboration with political capitalism, remains an uncertain and far from hegemonic ally of liberalizing regimes.

The opposition of strategic urban interest groups and the weakness and ambivalence of the alleged beneficiaries of market reform, then, discourage direct appeals for political support on grounds of class interest. Under these conditions, democratization is unlikely to forge a policy-based coalition behind market reform. In poor peasant societies in which ideological differences are muted, political success in democratic contests will usually depend upon the tactics of populist appeals, patronage, and the manipulation of regional or sectional grievances. Yet adjustment requires the efficient allocation of scarce public resources and the predominance of a market-based economic logic. This dilemma presents a challenge to those who advocate both democratization and economic liberalism.

On the one hand, the free-market model demands a minimization of rent-seeking and populist distributional policies by governments. Neo-liberals argue that governments helped create the economic crisis in the first instance through heavy-handed interventions that promoted rent-seeking and pervasive clientelist politics. If adjusting governments succumb to populism and clientelism, neo-liberals contend, the economic reforms will unravel. Incompetence and corruption will reign in the public sector as appointments and promotions become fodder for political machines. Particularistic exemptions and deals will whittle away at the logic of stabilization and liberalization measures. As for public investments, if they follow a political logic of building support for incumbent politicians, they will contribute only minimally to production.

On the other hand, political competition and the instrumental expectations of constituents impel politicians to adopt populist stances and patron-client politics. As persistent recession and stringent adjustment alienate strategic supporters, elected leaders resort to machine politics to repair the political damage. Clientelism and a reliance on personal loyalties are familiar patterns in many poor, peasant societies. Such practices are deeply rooted in the history and culture of our six cases (see chapter 2). The neopatrimonial characteristics of preceding authoritarian regimes influence democratic transitions: the less institutionalized and more clientelist the authoritarian regime, the more likely the re-emergence of clientelism, personalism, and corruption in the new democracy (Bratton and Van de Walle 1997).

This oft-noted contradiction between economic and political logics is ineluctable in the democratic experiments of poor, peasant societies. Yet corruption and rent-seeking in the new democracies probably do not exceed that in the old authoritarian regimes. What changes is that such practices receive public exposure and criticism through resurgent private media outlets, opposition parties, and civil associations; and the contradiction is not as profound as often thought. Economic recovery depends fundamentally upon political stability and the political support that a reformist government commands. In heterogeneous peasant societies that have been further fragmented by years of recession and austerity, patron-client networks provide a basis—sometimes the only basis—for governance. In this sense, clientelism represents, not simply waste, but a necessary cost of adjustment. The real danger is that neo-patrimonial politics will become unrestrained and thoroughly corrupt, thus engendering the public cynicism, deinstitutionalization, and crony capitalism that will doom both democracy and market reform.

Democratization clearly does not ensure good governance and enhanced political capacity to enact economic reform. Adjustment will continue to alienate such volatile urban elements as workers, public-sector employees (including many top managers), and students; yet potential beneficiaries are ambivalent, weak, or unorganized. In many cases, the coalitional equation is even more complex. The government will need to placate the military, to keep it as a silent partner, presumably by protecting its perquisites while shrinking overall public expenditures. The government will also need to cultivate a regional/ethnic base through the distribution of patronage. Clientelism will continue as a means of building political support, though in partial contradiction to the goals of structural adjustment. Power in poor societies will remain a corrupting temptation to politically insecure officials in new democracies.

Administrative Capacity

"For governments to reduce their role in the economy and expand the play of market forces, the state itself must be strengthened" (Haggard and Kaufman 1992a: 25). This oft-noted paradox signals the pervasive importance of bureaucratic capacity in neo-liberal reform. The government will shed or curtail certain of its economic tasks: phase out its directive planning of economic activity and its direct participation in productive ventures; reduce its redistributive role by lowering or eliminating subsidies; and curtail the myriad of administrative regulations of economic behaviour. These changes are intended to bring the state's responsibilities more into balance with its limited administrative capacity (World Bank 1997). Yet at the same time the government must strengthen its effectiveness within its narrowed sphere if investors are to be enticed and markets are to operate efficiently. A government has four major tasks. First, it must be able to negotiate, implement, and monitor complex economic agreements with the IMF and aid donors. Second, it must furnish incentives to the private sector by means of complicated fiscal, monetary, investment, and trade policies. Third, it must resolve the infrastructural problems (in transport, power generation, water supply, health services, and telecommunications) that discourage private investment. Fourth, it must mediate the many conflicts within society, especially those between ethnic/regional interests, employers and workers, and factions of the military, that threaten social peace and stability. All these tasks increase the demand for scarce technical and administrative skills.

Yet administrative capacity sharply deteriorated after 1970 in most African countries (Schiavo-Campo 1996: 10). For one thing, neo-patrimonial governance had a corrosive impact upon the bureaucratic apparatus. Although the politicization of African bureaucracies is a complex story, its outlines are now widely known. Bureaucracy at independence was vulnerable as office-holders had not had yet imbibed a distinctive esprit de corps. The bureaucracy degenerated into patrimonial administration unless the political leadership shielded it from patron-client politics. Often, however, presidents treated the public administration as their personal property. They and their lieutenants arbitrarily filled the expanding ranks of the state apparatus with political appointees, selected the top administrators on the basis of personal loyalties, and assigned bureaucratic tasks. These public officials, in patrimonial fashion, then began to "treat their administrative work for the ruler as a personal service based on their duty of obedience and respect" (Bendix 1962: 345). The ruler may even have colluded with his officials by permitting them to act arbitrarily and corruptly. Consequently, the bureaucratic virtues of hierarchical authority, expertise, neutrality, predictability, and efficiency eroded (see Sandbrook 1985).

Even Tanzania, a country long noted for the probity of its leadership, suffered by the 1980s from what a Tanzanian academic graphically labels "bureaucratic feudalism" (Munishi 1989: 153–67). This term denotes a pervasive patron-client system, in which patrons secure positions in the civil service and parastatals for clients, who then owe loyalty to these patrons rather than to their hierarchical superiors. These transorganizational factions advance the interests of their members, often to the detriment of the public they supposedly serve. Hence, "Without accountability, both foreign aid and internal surpluses will be deflected to the nodes of power in the political system at the expense of popular socioeconomic development" (Munishi 1989: 166). Civil services elsewhere had earlier exhibited such characteristics.

A second trend, fiscal austerity, also vitiated administrative effectiveness. As the economic crisis shrunk public revenues and fuelled inflation, and as external development agencies pressed African governments to reduce budget deficits, the salaries, perquisites, and facilities of civil servants steadily declined. Public servants in many countries went unpaid for weeks or even months in the 1980s and 1990s. In Sudan, basic starting salaries fell by four-fifths between 1970 and 1983, while in Ghana and Uganda real starting salaries had plummeted below subsistence level by 1983 (World Bank 1988b: 115). In Guinea the average salary in the civil service was the equivalent of only U.S.$18 per month in 1985 (Graybeal and Picard 1991: 289). Although most governments have more recently endeavoured to improve the lot of civil servants, middle-level officials in most Sub-Saharan countries still can barely feed—let alone adequately house, clothe, and edu-cate—their families on their paltry salaries. These conditions led to an exo-dus of skilled personnel out of public employment and into the private sector or employment abroad. For the rest, morale, probity, and efficiency decayed. Civil servants since the mid-1980s have often lacked the basic tools to do their jobs: transport in the rural areas, petrol, computers, typewriters, even typewriter ribbons. As salaries and debt repayment consumed an increasing proportion of recurrent expenditures, allocations to operations and maintenance items typically fell. Lacking facilities and motivation, many civil servants filled in their time by chatting, reading newspapers, or absenting themselves from work. Many also turned to bribes, embezzlement of public funds, and/or moonlighting to supplement their meagre salaries and benefits. Commonly, officials were unavailable during working hours because they were attending to their private business affairs, often informal-sector activities.

The governance approach proposes that democratization will generate a conducive context for the reform of a public sector crippled by these administrative weaknesses (Dia 1993; Van de Walle 1995: 161). Civil-service reform can hardly succeed in neo-patrimonial systems without a substantial improvement in governance. Where neo-patrimonial authoritarian regimes prevail, rulers will be opposed to bureaucratic reforms that threaten their control of patronage and self-enrichment. "An underpaid, unskilled civil service is actually desirable [in neo-patrimonial systems]—public employees dependent on the regime's discretionary largesse are forced to become corrupt, cannot quit their jobs, and reluctantly become the regime's accom-plices" (Schiavo-Campo 1996: 13). Simply downsizing such a civil service, coupled with technical reforms—providing more training to managers, instituting meritocratic procedures for hiring and promotion, and paying more adequate salaries—may not improve technocratic and administrative capacity much. These changes may simply produce "a small and well-paid but no less inefficient or corrupt civil service" (Schiavo-Campo 1996: 12). More fundamental or structural changes are needed. Democratization may generate such changes; it potentially forges a more open, accountable, and legitimate state, rebuilds legality, and strengthens the civil associations and interest groups that advocate institutional reform.

Accordingly, Mamoudou Dia (1993), who once headed the World Bank's Capacity Building and Implementation Division, has proposed that before any civil-service reform is attempted in a country, its "institutional environment" be evaluated. This approach ranks a country as high, low, or average in a patrimonial profile. A high ranking indicates a lack of checks and balances on the executive, the absence of the rule of law, the use of the state apparatus to reward the politically loyal, a corrupt tax administration, and state-dependent rent-seeking on the part of entrepreneurs. It also means the exploitation of the budget to meet the political needs of the powerful rather than the funding of projects that benefit the broader public. If a country ranks average or high on this patrimonial scale, administrative reform will require a "comprehensive institutional approach" to succeed. This comprehensive approach involves "institutional adjustment"—the forging of a more open, accountable, and legitimate state, the rebuilding of legality, and the strengthening of civic associations and interest groups. Without these deep institutional changes, Dia contends, the more minor reforms of incentives, procedures, and management will fail. Such a comprehensive institutional approach can only realistically be implemented when a new regime takes power without a vested interest in the neo-patrimonial state and political capitalism.

Dia's schema thus boldly links administrative reform to more fundamental institutional changes in state-society relations. At the centre of this reform process are certain hoped-for benefits of democracy: accountability, transparency, and the rule of law. Needless to say, such a comprehensive approach is both complex and lengthy. Yet, in the short run, democratization may *expand* debilitating clientelist pressures. Electoral transitions from an authoritarian regime will usually impel a broadening of patronage beyond the narrow elite of political notables to include some ordinary voters. In Senegal clientelism at the national and local levels persists despite a democratic transition dating from 1974–75 (Diop and Diouf 1992). In Nigeria democratic interludes have been periods of heightened "prebendalism" or clientelist politics (Joseph 1987). In democratic India, corruption and the politics of patronage have induced bureaucratic lethargy (Wade 1985). In the short run, then, democratic contests may actually heighten the attraction of using the public sector as "jobs for the boys."

The root-and-branch governance approach also ignores the dilemma of state-building in Africa. Clientelism serves an important function. The recent tragedies of Chad, Liberia, Sierra Leone, Rwanda, Somalia, Sudan, and Angola remind us that political disintegration is the gravest threat in Sub-Saharan Africa. Patronage is a glue binding together weakly integrated, multi-ethnic peasant societies with very brief histories as united entities. Reformers, in their zeal to eliminate bureaucratic waste and rent-seeking activity, will need to avoid undercutting the material basis of consent. Some degree of pork-barrel politics is unavoidable. A study of state disintegration in Sierra Leone (Reno 1998a), for instance, traces the country's descent into warlord politics to the disruption of clientele networks occasioned by economic decline and structural adjustment. In a context of diminished state revenues, donors further restricted the central government's stock of patronage resources in the late 1980s by requiring fiscal stringency and channelling aid through non-governmental agencies. When central patrons had little to distribute, regional leaders lost their incentive to co-operate with the central government, turning instead to "freelancing" as warlords, establishing their direct control of valuable local resources such as diamonds. The slide into civil war and chaos, accelerated by support for the rebels from Liberia's warring factions, had begun.

State reform and economic liberalism, then, need to balance the political logic of system maintenance against the economic logic of efficiency and accumulation.

Adjustment and Reform

Structural adjustment aims to displace the social regime of accumulation that I call political capitalism. Adjustment is not only a matter of "getting the (macroeconomic) policies right." It is, more profoundly, a matter of transforming the institutional nexus within which economic behaviour is embedded. Market reforms, therefore, offer societies the possibility of escaping the short-term rationality of economies dominated by neo-patrimonial states.

Democratization generally does little to advance this agenda in the short run, though experience varies. Mauritius, for instance, mounted a highly successful stabilization and adjustment program in 1979–86, and the pluralist political system apparently figured centrally in this success (Gulhati and Nallari 1990: 58–59). But Mauritius is an unusual country: its population was so small (one million) that its political elite could develop trust through face-to-face interaction; and the economy was already much more thoroughly transformed by market forces (through the domination of agriculture by sugar estates) than in the Sub-Saharan economies. Democracy was therefore more firmly established, and neo-liberal reform faced a less daunting institutional challenge, than on the continent. In Africa there is "little association between economic reform and the degree of political liberalism, one way or the other," as John Williamson and Steven Haggard (1994: 569) conclude from studying Australasian, European, Asian, and Latin American cases. Occasionally the tensions between political and economic liberalization have even unleashed disaster. Gambia in 1994 was one of Africa's longest-established democracies, having maintained a stable, pluralist regime and respect for human rights and the rule of law for nearly thirty years. But that year saw Senegal, in concert with the other countries of the franc zone, accept a 50 per cent devaluation of the CFA (Communauté Financière Africaine) franc as part of a belated adjustment program. By crippling Gambia's re-export trade, this program instigated a rapid decline of the country's living standards and widespread alienation from President Dawda Kairaba Jawara's elected government. This situation set the stage for a coup in July (Da Costa 1995). Whether democratization facilitates more effective market reform is thus contingent upon a variety of factors.

Effective reform requires a committed political leadership, supported by a strong coalition of potential beneficiaries and a competent and disciplined bureaucratic apparatus. Democratization will often not foster these winning conditions. Competitive elections may enhance the government's commitment to market reform by bringing outsiders, those not implicated in political capitalism, to power. However, new brooms do not sweep clean for long, and competitive elections have not provided the only path to power for such outsiders. Coups have also served, as the case of Rawlings illustrates. If parties compete for support partly on policy grounds, debate policies in the legislature, and respond to critiques in the privately owned media, democracy may also augment the sense of local ownership of reform, and hence build commitment. But such a beneficial sense of ownership is diminished by two common factors: "issueless" politics in which competing parties differ very little on policy; and the secret and top-down process by which foreigners negotiate conditional agreements on policy and institutional reforms.

Democracy is also unlikely to build a strong pro-reform coalition: the costs of adjustment to vocal urban groups are high; economic recovery is slow; group interests are ambiguous because of mixed costs and benefits, and because of the practice of families and individuals straddling occupations; and clientelism and regional/ethnic loyalties remain salient. Rarely, therefore, will a pro-reform party boldly seek to mobilize a constituency on policy lines. Contending parties in this ambiguous situation will most likely retreat to the formula of patronage, populist appeals, and identity politics. Not only will such a political formula contradict the rationality of market reforms (if carried too far), but it will also not build a coalition with any great loyalty to market reforms and sacrifice.

In the long haul democracy may generate the societal reforms that will facilitate bureaucratic capacity-building. In the short term a government intent on retaining power may continue to view the administrative apparatuses of the state and parastatals as the "employer of last resort" for wavering supporters. Again, political logic is not necessarily conducive to building the strong bureaucracy required by market transformation. Yet democratization still offers a better long-term opportunity for needed changes than does neo-patrimonial authoritarianism. At least democracy opens political space for constituencies outside the public sector to mobilize to defend or advance institutional reforms, as we will see in the case of Ghana's Fourth Republic.

Democratization and State Rehabilitation

How can Africa's societies reorient and rebuild state apparatuses in which predatory, neo-patrimonial governance rules?* This question emerges as crucial if one accepts that dysfunctional institutions—and not simply poor initial conditions, hostile international factors, external shocks, and policy errors—have impeded economic recovery. Although analysts weigh these various causes differently, few dissent from the recent consensus that political-institutional reform is a necessary condition for recovery in Africa (see, for example, Grosh 1994; Helleiner 1994; Killick 1995a; Mengisteab 1995; Sahn 1994: 381–84; Schatz 1996; World Bank 1997: 3).

Neo-patrimonial rule inhibits economic development by subordinating economic objectives to the short-run exigencies of political survival (see chapter 1).[1] Certain neo-patrimonial practices foster an unpropitious economic environment.

- The use of governmental powers to reward political insiders encourages rent-seeking behaviour and concomitantly discourages productive, entrepreneurial activities. Rents are derived from a variety of sources: for example, the award of public contracts at inflated prices to insider contractors; the manipulation of regulatory powers; and the levying of preferential rates for public services, such as utilities.
- The distribution of state jobs by political patrons to followers, particularly in combination with the government's tacit acceptance of bureaucratic corruption, has negative consequences. It fosters incompetence, indiscipline, and unpredictability in the civil service and state-owned enterprises. These deficiencies in turn undermine

---

* This is a revised version of an article co-written with Jay Oelbaum and published in *Journal of Modern African Studies* 4 (1997). Jay Oelbaum should not be held responsible for any errors inadvertently introduced here.

public services, discourage productive investment, and demoralize
competent, honest public servants. These public servants will then
join the political game, depart for the private sector, or emigrate.
Moreover, clientelism encourages rulers to appropriate more and
more resources to service their political machines. A likely consequence of this is the proliferation of inefficient, debt-plagued state
corporations.

- The ruler's acquiescence, if not active involvement, in the misappropriation of public funds by his political cronies lowers the rate of
public investment, especially in infrastructure, education, and health
care. This underinvestment in human and physical capital then
restricts the growth potential of national economies that operate
within highly competitive global markets.

- Neo-patrimonial rule often threatens private property through the
weakness or non-existence of the rule of law—a consequence of
some combination of political instability, undisciplined troops and
police forces, arbitrary officials, and political determination of judicial decisions. Again, the unfortunate economic result is to discourage long-term, fixed investments and encourage political
investments, speculation, and capital flight.

To counter these obstacles, reformers must set in motion a major
program of institutional change. They will have to limit the arbitrary and
predatory nature of government by improving its accountability, transparency, and responsiveness to popular demands. They will need to reassure
investors through wide-ranging administrative and legal reforms designed
to rebuild expertise, predictability, and protection for private property and
contracts. Since neo-patrimonial institutions are rooted in the history, political culture, and material interests of powerful social forces, changing the
rules of the game will meet with considerable opposition. Reformers may,
therefore, discover that there are "no shortcuts to progress," that capitalism
requires nothing less than a bourgeois revolution (Hyden 1983: ch.8).

Or perhaps not. Perhaps institutional reform need not await the rise of
a bourgeoisie with the capacity to mould a disciplined state and a bourgeois
culture. Decisive strategies have occasionally wrought significant social and
political change.[2] First, "revolutions from above" have sometimes been
engineered by populist/reformist leaders who seize power in a coup d'état
(Trimberger 1978). But to be successful in reorienting national institutions,
the reformers must meet stringent conditions: a unified leadership; a coherent nationalist/statist ideology; a foreign threat; and an absence of personal
or professional links between the traditionally dominant classes and the new
leadership. These conditions have rarely existed in postcolonial Africa.
Consequently, populist military interventions have proved notoriously
ephemeral. In West Africa, such leaders have either succumbed to compro-

mises with ingrained institutional practices (Rawlings in Ghana) or been assassinated (Murtala Mohamed in Nigeria, and Thomas Sankara in Burkina Faso).

External support of institutional reform may prove effective. Although structural adjustment programs have not yet delivered economic breakthroughs, they do address certain domestic institutional constraints on economic development. Optimally, reformers within government will use support from external agencies and middle-class constituencies to build technocratic enclaves within a state apparatus hitherto dominated by clientelistic criteria. But external support for institutional reform is inevitably limited in its impact: nationalists will reject institutions foisted on them by foreigners, and donors will succumb to fatigue brought about by the long-term commitments inherent in governance reforms.

If populist leaderships, local technocrats, and foreign supporters will not suffice, can democratization spur institutional change? Opinions diverge on this question. On the one hand, a positive or governance perspective holds that democratization can be instrumental to institutional reforms where predatory and authoritarian states prevail (chapter 4). Democratization may empower domestic social forces that harbour a vested interest in promoting a new order of limited, accountable, and market-friendly government. Much of what the IMF and World Bank advocate—economic liberalization, financial-sector reform, the creation of stock markets, privatization, legal reform, the support of economic think-tanks—is designed to foster a bourgeoisie with the confidence, resources, and political clout to anchor a functioning market economy. Democracy may generate a sustained pressure for institutional reform if sizeable segments of the middle class and rural poor also desire a break with the past.

Still, skeptics maintain that old neo-patrimonial traditions will quickly corrupt and even overwhelm fragile democratic institutions, thus undercutting market-oriented reforms (Callaghy 1995; O'Donnell 1994; Kohli 1993; Grosh 1994: 38). Not only do the new democracies confront hostile socioeconomic conditions and non-democratic historical legacies, but they must also cope with the social costs to key constituencies inherent in their market reform programs. These circumstances, the skeptics argue, impel elected governments to centralize power and resort to populist rhetoric, clientelistic politics, and the cultivation of particularistic loyalties. Corruption, closely associated with pervasive clientelism, will also soon resurface. These practices will, among other things, imperil macroeconomic stability, divert public revenues, and reintroduce instability and uncertainty. Beneath the trappings of liberal democracy, the ingrained informal institutions of neo-patrimonial governance will re-emerge to jeopardize fragile economic reforms.

Ghana provides an excellent case for reflecting upon these competing views of institutional change. Inasmuch as institutional change is *context-specific*—the outcome of struggles over normative rules—we need to focus upon a particular country, and Ghana represents a best-case analysis of

African democratization. In certain other respects, this country has traced a typical political and economic trajectory since independence in 1957. It emerged under Kwame Nkrumah in 1959 as one of the first (de facto) one-party states. Nkrumah's regime introduced the informal institutions of neo-patrimonialism at the national level. Although Nkrumah was overthrown in 1966, the institutions were to prevail until J.J. Rawlings' second populist coup of December 1981. Brief experiments in redemocratization in 1969–72 (the Second Republic) and 1979–81 (the Third Republic) modified but did not eradicate neo-patrimonial patterns. Partly as a consequence of this persistent institutional pattern, the economy entered into decline from the mid-1960s, and this downward slide accelerated in the 1970s. The Ghanaian economy was on the point of collapse by the early 1980s. To attract loans and grants from the IMF, World Bank, and bilateral donors, Flt.-Lt. Rawlings and his Provisional National Defence Council (PNDC) had little choice but to adopt stabilization and adjustment. The PNDC received accolades from its foreign supporters for adroitly and consistently implementing top-down, stroke-of-the-pen stabilization and liberalization measures in 1983–92. But the more complex reforms associated with the second, or institutional, phase of adjustment were another matter. Donors joined with an indigenous democracy movement to urge political reform, in the hope of buttressing the regime's legitimacy and effectiveness, and a partial democratic transition occurred in 1991–92. The first five years of the Fourth Republic (1993–98) provide a suitable case study for assessing the connection between democratization and institutional reform.

Although this period of institutional struggles is too brief for drawing definitive conclusions, the Ghanaian experience provides some basis for the positive view that democratization can facilitate institutional change. The situation, however, is highly contradictory. On the one hand, democratization since 1992 has stimulated the resurgence of neo-patrimonial institutions under the guise of liberal democracy—to the extent that by the mid-1990s the Rawlings regime resembled the Nkrumah regime that Rawlings had once decried. Pervasive clientelism in 1992 predictably undercut macroeconomic stability as the government opened up the sluice gates of patronage to win the election. Budget deficits and mounting inflation forced the government to accept, at least nominally, the IMF's stringent terms for a new stabilization program. On the other hand, beneath the surface, and in tandem with the strengthening of middle-class civil associations, important institutional changes running counter to the logic of neo-patrimonial traditions were underway. These included the fortifying of liberal-democratic political and intermediary institutions, the legal system, and, to a minor degree, the bureaucratic apparatus. Perhaps, some speculated, Ghana could transcend the low savings and investment rates that had impeded recovery during its first decade of adjustment.

This contradictory outcome—continuity of neo-patrimonial practices in combination with some liberal institution-building—mirrors Ghana's contradictory historical legacies. Neo-patrimonial traditions are well-entrenched in Ghana's political culture; yet liberalism too has extensive historical roots.

The Politics of Economic Decline and Renewal

Counterproductive policies and practices bear a heavy, though far from exclusive, responsibility for the economic problems that Ghana experienced between 1960 and 1982 (Killick 1978; Rimmer 1992; Leith and Lofchie 1993; Toye 1991; Green 1987). Successive governments failed to furnish adequate incentives to rural producers and instead emphasized state-led industrialization. This strategy, from its inception, had a political logic. Nkrumah's Convention People's Party (CPP) was handicapped because the opposition liberal elite, together with the traditional authorities, controlled a large share of the country's wealth, especially in cocoa-growing regions. Nkrumah endeavoured to overcome this liability by expanding the public sector—and hence the CPP's access to patronage—at the expense of the private sector (Price 1984). By the time Nkrumah was overthrown in 1966, Ghana had fifty-three public enterprises, twelve joint state-private enterprises, twenty-three public boards, and extensive price, credit, and exchange controls. Virtually none of the import-substituting industries could be justified on the basis of domestic resource cost calculations, and most operated at far below their capacities.

The reasons for the failure of state-led development included the use of inappropriate technology, poor project planning, and, above all, neo-patrimonial relations. Ministers frequently interfered in the day-to-day affairs of state enterprises. CPP stalwarts expected favours: appointments of unqualified clients to staff positions; the bypassing of regulations; purchases of nationalized businesses at inflated prices; and the directing of loans from publicly owned banks to "insiders" (Brownbridge and Gockel 1996; Killick 1978; Rimmer 1992). Import controls accelerated the inflationary tendencies in the economy by closing off the import safety valve, as well as fuelling corruption. Currency controls generated a rent-seeking constituency that profited from the overvaluation of the local currency (the cedi) and from governmental allocation of foreign exchange; this constituency would later prove resistant to reform (Herbst 1993; Toye 1991; Rimmer 1992). In 1961 the regime responded to a crisis in the balance of payments by assigning the Ghana Trading Corporation, an inefficient parastatal, monopoly rights to import a wide variety of basic commodities. Even legitimate traders often had to stoop to bribery to secure scarce licences to import or distribute goods and to obtain foreign exchange (Owusu 1970; Killick 1978; LeVine 1975; Herbst 1993; Rimmer 1992).

In the post-Nkrumah era, economic decline accelerated. Ghana's share of the world cocoa market fell from 35 per cent in the mid-1960s to less than 10 per cent by 1982 (IMF 1996). Recurrent budget deficits, which peaked at over 13 per cent of GDP in 1976, underpinned an entrenched inflation that averaged 58 per cent in the decade 1972–82. This situation contributed to a dramatic fall in the cedi's value: by 1982 the black-market rate of exchange for the cedi was twenty-two times the official rate. Inflation also led to the erosion of real wages and substantial wage compression in the public sector. By 1982 a messenger's real basic salary was 40 per cent of its 1975 level, while a principal secretary's had plummeted to an astonishing 11 per cent (Lindauer, Meesok, and Suebsaeng 1988). This situation resulted in administrative decline. The average public-sector worker spent only fifteen to twenty hours a week on the job by the early 1980s (Green 1987). Furthermore, import restrictions, coupled with the fall of export earnings, caused massive import shortfalls, eroding infrastructure and undermining production. Domestic investment fell an average of 5.9 per cent per annum between 1970 and 1983. Finally, price and other controls furnished incentives for the growth of untaxed and unrecorded parallel-market activity, which, based on one estimate, accounted for 32 per cent of GDP by 1982 (May 1985).

By that year the economic collapse had exacted a devastating human price. One-half of the urban and two-thirds of the rural population subsisted below the poverty line; estimated per capita daily caloric intake was only 68 per cent of requirements; and previously eradicated diseases such as yaws and yellow fever had resurfaced (Green 1987). Daily survival became even more of a challenge in 1983 as the economy faced two external shocks: a prolonged drought with attendant crop-damaging fires, and the return of a million Ghanaians expelled from Nigeria.

Ghana's newly installed PNDC, desperate to survive in the face of this crisis, undertook an orthodox stabilization and adjustment program in April 1983.[3] This was a surprising development given the radical-populist orientation of Flt.-Lt. Rawlings and his comrades. It was even more remarkable that a government of the PNDC's complexion in a country with patrimonial traditions consistently implemented stringent neo-liberal measures. The reasons for the PNDC's success included its ruthlessness in dealing with opposition, the depth of the economic crisis, which clearly demanded a new direction, the generous inflows of donor finance, and the weakness of potentially oppositional associations.[4] Organized labour, which strongly opposed austerity measures and privatization, was severely weakened by the economic crisis. Industrial decline had undermined union strength by reducing employment and the unionized workforce. Splits in the Trade

Unions Congress further diluted labour's political influence (Graham 1989; Nugent 1995; Herbst 1993).

Other influential groups did not oppose the new economic direction. Urban consumers, who elsewhere had resisted the removal of subsidies and price controls, were not deeply affected by such measures because they had already been paying inflated parallel-market prices for "free" public services and "controlled" consumer goods. Civil servants had already adopted survival strategies, including moonlighting and/or corruption. Business people generally greeted structural adjustment with relief. Not only did neo-liberal reforms signal a retreat from the rhetoric and practice of anticapitalist class struggle, formalized by the dissolution of the People's and Workers' Defence Committees in December 1984, but they also relaxed the import constraint. Ghana's remaining professionals and entrepreneurs had been cowed by the capricious Defence Committees, the shocking murders of three Supreme Court Justices in 1982, and the extrajudicial bodies established by the PNDC to root out and punish corrupt practices. Business people nonetheless were to remain suspicious of Rawlings' real intentions for many years (Tangri 1992).

Although the PNDC's autocratic style allowed it to swiftly adopt policy reforms, especially those involving deregulation and price changes, this style was not conducive to deeper institutional reforms. Yet such reforms, the World Bank and others realized by the early 1990s, were essential for restoring investors' confidence and stimulating greater savings and investment. A less top-down, more consultative approach was needed to secure the co-operation of the groups concerned. Hence, the World Bank advocated broader participation in political life in its 1990 *Country Strategy Paper*, believing that this tactic would enhance such co-operation for long-haul reform. Political liberalization itself, however, became something of a top-down operation.

Although Ghana's political liberalization resulted from external and internal pressures that had been intensifying since 1988, the PNDC maintained control over the institutional arrangements and timing of the transition (Nugent 1995; Ninsin 1993a). Formal debate over national political arrangements commenced in August 1990 with a series of government-orchestrated seminars held at regional capitals. Since individuals opposed to the PNDC were excluded from these meetings, most of the participants supported a no-party option. Nevertheless, popular support for a return to multiparty politics was transparent, and Rawlings found this sentiment more palatable when two government opinion surveys in 1990–91 indicated that he would win a contested election. Thus in January 1991 Rawlings presented a transition timetable, and in May he confirmed that the country would return to a multiparty system.

After a referendum in April 1992 approved a constitution, the ban on party activity was lifted. Opposition parties rushed to establish themselves in the seven months before the election, organizing against a government that had enjoyed an eleven-year incumbency. Nevertheless, a significant political transition commenced. In January 1993 a Fourth Republic was born.

Neo-Patrimonialism Resurgent: Rawlings as the New Nkrumah

Rawlings' first elected government (1993–96) resembled a pseudo-democracy or what Guillermo O'Donnell (1994) refers to as a "delegative democracy," a form of rule that differs from Nkrumah's authoritarian regime principally in the willingness of the Rawlings government to hold periodic, more or less free, multiparty elections and to respect, more or less, the civil and political rights of citizens. Individuals enjoyed freedom of movement. They could form associations, including political parties, subject to certain legal requirements (albeit quite onerous). Amidst acrimony and threat, an independent press exercised its freedom of expression. Yet under the democratic façade the old neo-patrimonial rules of the game came to the fore. Centralization of power in the hands of the president, personal loyalties, pervasive clientelism, growing corruption, and unofficial presidential control of his own, personally loyal armed force: all these informal institutions undercut the formal democratic institutions that were designed to monitor, check, and discipline the government between elections. Patrimonial traditions, persistent political insecurity, and the strain of imposing unpopular austerity measures accounted for the president's efforts to escape day-to-day accountability. Competitive elections and civil liberties were the price he had to pay to build legitimacy in the eyes of potentially violent opponents and potentially ungenerous foreign donors.

Strongly contested national elections in 1996 moved Ghana closer to the model of an accountable and representative democracy. The danger remained, however, that resurgent neo-patrimonial practices would impede capitalist development, as in the earlier postcolonial era, unless mitigated by ongoing institutional reforms.

Elections

In two sets of presidential and parliamentary elections held after 1992, foreign observer teams judged the voting, on the whole, to have been "free and fair." But the question of fairness is tricky (Geisler 1993). Observer teams often focus on election day alone. In particular, they assess whether the correct procedures for validating voters and tallying votes are observed, and whether voters are subject to intimidation. But the electoral outcome may have been shaped by irregularities and unfair practices that long preceded voting day. Governments employ such tactics as using invalid electoral rolls, denying opponents access to the publicly owned media, restricting opposition campaign meetings, using militias to intimidate the supporters of opposition parties, and buttressing their support by the distribution of patronage. Judged by these broad standards, Ghana's second elections, in December 1996, were fairer than the first set, in November-December 1992. We can therefore speak of a partial institutionalization of the electoral rules of the game: a real, though fragile, achievement.

Although a Commonwealth Observer Team pronounced the 1992 presidential election free and fair, this judgement remains controversial. Academic observers disagreed vehemently over the legitimacy of the results (Jeffries and Thomas 1993; Oquaye 1995). The opposition parties denounced the presidential contest as fraudulent and boycotted the subsequent parliamentary elections. The New Patriotic Party (NPP), the main opposition party, issued a report that included hundreds of detailed allegations of irregularities in one hundred of the country's two hundred constituencies (New Patriotic Party 1993). Many of these charges related to the conduct of the voting, especially the allegations of systematic, planned rigging of the results by a partisan Interim National Electoral Commission. But other charges related to practices that preceded voting day. One concerned the electoral roll. According to the International Foundation for Electoral Systems, the roll contained many irregularities: multiple entries of the same voter; inconsistent name order (even Rawlings was unable to locate his name when he came to vote in the 1992 referendum); failures to record corrections; ghost entries; and failure to list about 5 per cent of the eligible voters. An estimated 1 million of the 8.4 million entries were erroneous (Cooper, Hayward, and Lee 1992).

In addition, Rawlings and his newly minted National Democratic Congress (NDC) fully exploited the advantages of incumbency in the 1992 campaign. The government handed civil servants an 80 per cent pay raise just before the election, an action that pushed the budget into deficit. Rawlings had targeted the rural areas as a major base of governmental support since 1988. He campaigned extensively in the countryside in 1992 and dispensed patronage to local communities in the form of electricity extensions, water supply, feeder roads, and school improvements (Green 1995). This rural strategy (which nicely complemented the higher producer prices for cocoa under structural adjustment) paid off, as many rural constituencies outside Ashanti (the NPP's heartland) favoured Rawlings in the election. NDC candidates also relied on government vehicles and public radio and television to conduct their campaigns. Government officials confounded the opposition parties by delays in granting permits to hold rallies (Rothchild 1993; Haynes 1993).

Many of these same campaign practices also characterized the 1996 election, though the electoral roll and election-day procedures involved fewer irregularities. The government launched Phase 2 of its Self-Help Electrification Project in 1995 with the goal of bringing electricity to one thousand towns and villages. Donor funds also underwrote various government-directed rural infrastructure projects in 1996. Rawlings again won over 50 per cent of the vote in the presidential election, including a majority in all regions except Ashanti. In contested parliamentary elections, the NDC came out with 132 seats to the 65 won by the Great Alliance of the NPP and People's Convention Party. This time the opposition accepted its defeat. Indeed, it congratulated Rawlings on his victory, in marked contrast to the rancour associated with the 1992 elections. Concessions won by the opposition in the preparations for these elections account for this conciliatory attitude. A committee representative of the opposition as well as the government oversaw the Electoral Commission's registration of voters, its preparation of the voters' list, and the arrangements for voting day. The government also agreed to use transparent ballot boxes to allay suspicions of prior stuffing of ballot boxes by government agents.

Nonetheless, the ruling NDC enjoyed various strategic advantages in the 1996 campaign. With an enormous financial advantage over the opposition—widely attributed to kickbacks on government contracts—it could mount an unmatchable media blitz. (The advent of independent radio stations, though, provided the opposition with access to a larger audience than hitherto.) The governing party and its wings could also afford to distribute election gifts such as T-shirts, wrist watches, wall clocks, bicycles, umbrellas, and sewing machines to potential rural supporters.[5] In Akim Oda, in the Eastern Region, an NDC pickup truck was seen distributing new colour television sets to villages the day before the election. As well, the governing party continued to cultivate its rural constituency with large expenditures on rural infrastructure. Ghana's capital budget amounted to 6 per cent of GDP in 1995 and about 4 per cent in 1996, and half of this went into road construction (*Financial Times*, July 9, 1996). Gift-giving and infrastructural development, when combined with the boost to cocoa production,[6] gold mining, and forestry, sectors integral to the aims of structural adjustment, proved a winning formula for Rawlings. The urban areas languished, however, with rising prices and limited employment opportunities stirring discontent.

Besides material considerations, urban residents, unlike rural dwellers, had grown increasingly aware of government corruption as Accra's independent scandal sheets daily splashed sordid stories on their front pages. But peasants had limited access to the disclosures of governmental corruption furnished by Accra's and Kumasi's independent media. Normally deferential to authority and largely ignorant of affairs in Accra, they tended to support the government even if, as in the case of smallholding subsistence farmers, they reaped few benefits from the long years of structural adjustment.

Beyond gaining strategic advantages, some participants flouted the rules. Reports alleged that NDC agents had purchased Voter Registration Cards from NPP supporters in order to vote in their stead (*Ghanaian Chronicle* [Accra], Oct. 10, 1996). The electoral register, though much improved, still generated suspicion. Members of Ghana's Network of Domestic Election Observers questioned how 9.2 million valid voters could be registered in a country of 17 million people, with about half the population under the age of sixteen (Gyimah-Boadi 1997: 83). Assaults on suspected supporters of opposition parties and party agents occurred from time to time (*Ghanaian Chronicle*, Jan. 25–28, 1996, April 18–21, 1996). Some incendiary speeches by NDC leaders threatened to use any means to crush the opposition, which was characterized as "thieves and rogues who are desperate for the spoils of the nation's wealth to enrich themselves" (*Ghanaian Chronicle*, April 18–21, 1996). Even Rawlings reportedly warned a Sekondi rally that, if the NDC lost the election, "Perhaps we can only get it [power] through another June 4th [coup]," and "If June 4, 1979 repeats itself 10 times, I will do what I did then 10 times over" (*Ghanaian Chronicle*, Nov. 15–18, 1996; reported also in *Free Press* and *The Independent*).

Even though the incumbents enjoyed many campaign advantages and incivility and electoral abuses occasionally erupted, the concessions made to the opposition on the ground rules lent legitimacy to the electoral process. The opposition was willing to abide by the rules and bide its time. Therefore, a fragile institutionalization of electoral norms was evident by 1996–97. Still, the informal institutions of neo-patrimonialism also strengthened their hold, in tension with electoral norms and other formal institutions of a democratic society.

Presidential Rule under Rawlings

Highly centralized personal rule sanctified by periodic elections characterized the Fourth Republic. In some ways, little changed from the days of the PNDC. Rawlings continued to dominate the scene from his seat in the Castle-Osu, chafing against restraints on his power imposed by the constitution and civil society. He retained personal control of a significant coercive apparatus. In other ways, however, much had altered from his early days. Rawlings, who carried out two coups ostensibly to stamp out the informal institutions of neo-patrimonial rule—especially clientelism and rent-seeking—ended by surreptitiously embracing these same stratagems. He and his lieutenants constructed a political machine that rivalled Nkrumah's CPP. Pervasive clientelism and personalism inevitably stoked the fires of corruption.

In the Fourth Republic Rawlings continued to govern largely as he saw fit. Presidential supremacy derived partly from the 1992 constitution, which apportions extensive powers to the executive. The constitution creates a hybrid presidential-parliamentary system in which the president is ultimately responsible for the determination of policy. Subject to the approval of Parliament, he appoints and chairs a cabinet with members drawn from Parliament and elsewhere. The cabinet assists the president in designing legislation, which the responsible minister then submits to Parliament for hearings, amendments, and approval. Budgets must also receive parliamentary approval.

The president has wide powers of appointment and confirmation of status, which enabled Rawlings to project his influence down to the district level. Rawlings retained considerable leverage over chiefs, who remained respected opinion leaders in most of the country. Until the 1992 constitution, their legal status depended upon their recognition by the government, a requirement that discouraged their overt criticism of government. Rawlings had also elevated pliant chiefs to paramount status, thus increasing their powers and their revenues—for instance, royalties from mineral exploitation (Haynes 1995: 106). Not surprisingly, many chiefs supported the government's agenda, even to the extent of propagating "the ideals or aims of the revolution" at durbars—open-air village meetings (Owusu 1996: 341).

Although the constitution withdrew the president's authority to recognize chiefs, Rawlings manoeuvred to maintain influence over the chiefs' allegiance. Before the 1992 and 1996 elections, chiefs were wooed with gifts, sometimes very significant ones such as tractors. Some chiefs reported being quietly cautioned about potential sanctions in the form of withheld economic support, if they failed to support the government. The governing party also kept a close watch on chiefs. One internal/confidential NDC analysis of the 1996 elections identified chiefs who, while secretly backing opposition candidates in their traditional areas, simultaneously represented themselves to the party hierarchy as NDC supporters.

The 1992 constitution also empowers the president to appoint the district chief executives (DCEs), who play a prominent role in the 110 district assemblies by virtue of their seat on the executive committees. The DCE may be removed from office by a vote of no confidence supported by at least two-thirds of all members of the district assembly. Challenges are rare, though, because the president also appoints 30 per cent of the assembly members in each district. This central influence is significant, as the 1992 constitution allocates not less than 5 per cent of national revenues to the district assemblies. This allocation prompted widespread fears that DCEs in NDC-controlled district assemblies would penalize communities that favoured the opposition by directing development funds to other areas (see, for example, *West Africa*, March 14–20, 1994: 438–39; *Ghanaian Chronicle*, Feb. 15–18, 1996).

Besides using his broad constitutional powers to build acquiescence, Rawlings sought to neutralize formal institutions that asserted their right to hold the government accountable between elections. The legislature was hobbled by the near-monopoly of seats enjoyed by the governing coalition before the 1996 election. Nonetheless, it was far from supine even in 1993–96; two independent members posed embarrassing questions to ministers, and the committee system provided opposition leaders with a forum from which they could criticize legislation and budgets. Opposition parties and the independent press voiced persistent critiques of governmental policy and behaviour, but a lack of resources and periodic intimidation inhibited their impact. The Supreme Court and other judicial bodies delivered some courageous judgments that circumscribed presidential discretion and reasserted the formal rules of fair play.

In the realm of civil society, the Ghana Bar Association, the Christian Council of Ghana, the Ghana Bishops Conference, human-rights organizations, and to a lesser extent the Trade Unions Congress and the National Union of Ghanaian Students monitored government actions, publicized abuses, and criticized policies, as they did during the latter days of the PNDC. Yet organized centres of potential opposition to the regime attracted the attention of NDC stalwarts, who sought to control or split the organizations. The fate of the Ghana Association of Private Voluntary Organizations for Development (GAPVOD) is revealing. Registered in 1980, GAPVOD aspired to become the umbrella body for indigenous and foreign non-governmental organizations. But in the highly charged political atmosphere of 1990–92 the organization ran into trouble. The immediate issue was the management of a $600,000 grant from the United Nations Development Programme. But the belief that NDC agents were seeking control of GAPVOD in order to control the NGO sector alienated many member organizations, and this promising experiment virtually collapsed in factional conflict in 1992 (Gary 1996).

President Rawlings also apparently retained extensive personal control over a coercive apparatus. Although a president in a constitutional system should have only an arms-length association with the armed forces and militias, many Ghanaians believed that Rawlings retained a tight personal control over the armed forces.[7] Junior officers and lower ranks twice carried out coups (June 4, 1979, Dec. 31, 1981) in order to elevate Flt.-Lt. Rawlings to power. In 1983–84 Rawlings placed loyalists in charge of the army, navy, and air force after retiring many senior officers. The armed forces and intelligence agencies constituted an important power base of the PNDC, especially after 1983 when IMF-supported adjustment alienated other supporters such as the urban workers and university radicals. Rawlings' revolution was, in part, a movement against the established military hierarchy. This aspect of the revolution was manifest in the authority exercised within a highly politicized military by the Armed Forces Defence Committees, which, as with the Committees for the Defence of the Revolution (CDRs), reported through their own hierarchy to the PNDC. Reworked as a "voluntary" association, an Armed Forces Association for the Defence of the Revolution continued to operate under a Forces Sergeant-Major after the return to constitutional rule in January 1993. During its first administration, the NDC government had therefore not abandoned the model of a politically engaged armed forces in favour of an apolitical, professional, and hierarchical military establishment. The military remained shielded from the scrutiny prescribed

by the constitution. Despite being legally required to audit the accounts of
the military, the auditor general was prevented from doing so.

Apart from the military, Rawlings apparently commanded other armed
groups in the period under scrutiny. During PNDC rule, the paramilitary Civil
Defence Organization (CDO) operated alongside the CDRs as an intimidating
presence, especially in the countryside. With the advent of the Fourth
Republic, the CDOs were absorbed into special units of the armed forces and
police service. But newspaper reports and informed observers insisted that
the Castle retained direct control over these units and occasionally mobilized them for action against demonstrators.[8] Adding to the mix, a presidential guard unit reported directly to Rawlings.

If Rawlings' presidential rule showed continuity with the preceding
authoritarian structures, a major discontinuity came in the resurgence of
neo-patrimonial mechanisms as a means of building support and accumulat-
ing wealth. The National Democratic Congress was founded in 1992 as the
successor to a military regime that, during its decade in power, had not
converted itself into a mass movement. The PNDC had rested heavily on its
base in the military and intelligence agencies, its cadres in the form of the
CDRs, and its paramilitary CDOs. With the advent of a multiparty system,
the NDC had to develop a popular constituency with haste. Opposition parties laid claim to the two main political traditions of the country: the liberal
mantle of Danquah-Busia and the radical-populist mantle of Nkrumah.
Although the fledgling NDC allied itself with one faction of the Nkrumahist
family (the National People's Convention), it still required a popular base.
The party built one primarily through the construction of a political
machine that drew heavily upon state resources.

The NDC, in contrast to the opposition parties, was well-financed and
well-organized on a countrywide basis. It boasted an impressive headquarters in Accra, with full-time officials and a full array of regional and district
branches. In 1994 the top officials were all former PNDC activists. The
general secretary, appropriately enough, was the former head of the
Committees for the Defence of the Revolution. One of his deputies was the
full-time secretary of the 31st December Women's Movement (31DWM).
Some of the officials also held government appointments to public boards
and offices.

Informally, the NDC constructed clientelistic networks that penetrated
to the grassroots. The former CDR hierarchy, the 31st December Women's
Movement, and the Council of Independent Business Associations (CIBA)
played key roles in building these networks. An array of smaller organizations also played their part: the Ghana Private Road Transport Workers
Union (GPRTU), the market women's associations, and the many associations affiliated with 31DWM and CIBA. In exchange for their partisan
support, these associations received sources of revenue from the govern-

ment, usually in the form of the right to collect rates and taxes from their members and others and to allocate assets, such as market stalls.

During the PNDC reign, the Committees for the Defence of the Revolution constituted the cadres of the populist "revolution." They were organized at five levels, from Accra, through the districts, and down to the zone, ward, and units (the last located in a village or small town). Paid salaries and benefits by the government, the CDRs (as the militants were called) were not really revolutionary. Local studies reveal that the CDR cadres often usurped chiefly, security, and police functions. Often they involved themselves in ongoing local disputes over land and chieftaincy (Jonah 1993; Asibuo 1994). They were an intimidating presence.

Under constitutional rule, the CDRs lost much of their arbitrary power and, indeed, found themselves converted into supposedly non-governmental organizations (Associations for the Defence of the Revolution—ACDRs). No longer could they be treated as civil servants. Hence, the NDC found new employment niches for them, especially in the government-funded but ostensibly independent National Commission for Civic Education (NCCE), directed by a former PNDC ally.[9] The opposition parties, not surprisingly, wondered how objectively such cadres would deliver civic education. After 1993 the ACDRs continued to serve as NDC activists throughout the country. They acted as youth wingers at campaign rallies. They continued to partici-pate in local government institutions, from the unit (village) committees and town councils to the district assemblies (see, for example, Lemarchand 1994). These positions gave the NDC activists a continuing influence over the allocation of resources at the local level, in particular development funds.

The 31st December Women's Movement, headed by First Lady Nana Konadu Agyeman Rawlings since 1984, was the second pillar of the NDC's political machine. Founded in 1982 as one of the "revolutionary organs" of the December 1981 "revolution," in the late 1980s the 31DWM declared itself a non-governmental organization in order to qualify for grants and assistance from donor agencies and international NGOs. Despite this legal change, the 31DWM informally operated as a women's wing of the NDC, receiving financial support from the public treasury that financed a large headquarters in Accra and covered the travelling expenses of the First Lady (Gary 1996: 161). Many of its organizers received salaries from state min-istries, though they worked full-time for the Movement. For instance, in 1994 Cecilia Johnson was general secretary of the 31DWM, national women's organizer of the NDC, deputy minister of local government, and a member of the council of the state-organized National Council for Women and Development (NCWD). NDC insignia and signs were conspicuously dis-played at the organization's headquarters. Undoubtedly, the resources and projects distributed by the First Lady were perceived as part of the largesse of the NDC.

The National Council for Women and Development was an ostensibly independent organization that worked closely with 31DWM. Established by the government in 1975 to co-ordinate women's groups and advance women's economic and social interests, NCWD fell under the sway of the NDC in 1992–93. The government gradually replaced the independent executive secretary and council members with 31DWM and the NDC activists. The NCWD channelled donor and government funds into some 31DWM projects, with the credit redounding to the benefit of 31DWM and NDC. Nonetheless, even Ghanaian critics allowed that NCWD executed useful functions: it developed a resource centre on women's issues; it attracted donor funding to worthwhile rural projects; it used its regional and district offices to help organize local activities by Accra-based women's groups; and it provided a monthly forum in which women's groups worked out problems.

The 31st December Women's Movement was Ghana's only mass women's movement, claiming over a million members, both directly and indirectly through its twenty-eight affiliated women's groups. Most of the rural members remained inactive, at least until a visit by Nana Konadu Rawlings and other dignitaries galvanized them into action. The affiliated groups were diverse in membership and function. They included, for instance, the Hairdressers and Beauticians Association, the EP Church Women's Union, the Police Wives Associations, the Nurses Association, and numerous so-called "ladies clubs" organized in government departments or parastatals. This network constituted a formidable force whose mobilization during election campaigns created significant support for the NDC. Material inducements, such as the right to collect rates from members, ensured organizational loyalty to the 31DWM, which itself had an organizational presence throughout the country. It boasted offices with paid staff in Accra, the regional capitals, and all districts, and it claimed to have active organizers and volunteers in most zones and even units (villages).

The 31DWM undertook a variety of projects designed to assist mainly rural women. The Movement was associated with the construction of storage silos, gari-processing, and palm-oil processing mills, the growing and spinning of cotton, the promotion of craft industries such as pottery, weaving, and tie-and-dye clothing, the organization of revolving-credit schemes for members, and the building of day-care centres. It financed these projects through donor support, contributions from local businesses, profits derived from 31DWM enterprises, and transfers from collaborating government ministries, such as the Ministry of Health. Critics claimed that the 31DWM used its control over productive facilities such as gari-processing factories and microcredit organizations to exclude women who were not government supporters.

The innocuously named Council of Indigenous Business Associations (CIBA) constituted a third leg of Rawlings' clientelist network. CIBA ostensibly represented the interests of twenty associations of small entrepreneurs before governmental agencies, and it promoted microenterprises through the construction of industrial estates, the provision of low-interest credit, and the regularization of tax collection from members. In practice, CIBA was a creature of government that posed as an NGO (its constituent associations were actually registered as NGOs). Some ten of its member associations had no choice in their affiliation, in that the legislation listed them as members of CIBA with no provision for withdrawal. The PNDC promulgated the law creating the Council as one of its last acts in early 1993. Its president and founder was a deputy minister, and its chair was Nana Konadu Rawlings. The government in 1993 donated 150 million cedis to the fledgling organization as a "capacity-building grant," with more to follow if the organization performed well (Nana Konadu Rawlings, as reported in *The Pioneer* [Kumasi], Feb. 9, 1994). The inflow of funds to the CIBA from both the government (ostensibly to promote small business) and the 31DWM led to a well-publicized scandal in the run-up to the 1996 election. Leaders of both the NDC and the Movement demanded that the CIBA account for the "billions" of cedis it had received (*Ghanaian Chronicle*, May 6–8, 1996).

CIBA apparently acted as a major conduit of NDC patronage. Tax-farming was one means by which CIBA provided a material payoff to associated organizations and their leaders and employees. Many of the constituent associations were granted the questionable right to collect taxes from their members on behalf of the Internal Revenue Service and/or the municipal assembly, in exchange for a commission. CIBA itself collected rates in Kumasi on behalf of the (irate) Kumasi Municipal Assembly, receiving a 10 per cent commission for its efforts. Tax-farming created jobs for NDC supporters, as well as providing substantial revenues for compliant associations. In addition, the allocation of scarce credit, subsidized equipment, and work sites to small entrepreneurs handed ample political leverage to CIBA officials. CIBA also imported 330 containers of election gifts—umbrellas, hairpins, plastic chairs, hairdressing equipment—in August 1996, with foreign exchange provided by the Bank of Ghana (*Ghanaian Chronicle*, Aug. 26, 1996).

The Ghana Private Road Transport Union (GPRTU) was a more minor cog in the patronage machine. Drivers and their assistants composed the membership of this staunchly pro-NDC organization. By assuming responsibility for collecting daily tolls from drivers at lorry parks, as well as managing these parks, the GPRTU provided "jobs for the boys." In addition the union benefited from extensive government "loans," which were not repaid.[10] According to critics, these loans subsidized the vehicles, tires, and lubricants purchased by GPRTU members.

All of this clientelism entailed largely dyadic relationships—one patron provides one or two clients with patronage, and each client may in turn act as a patron to further clients. Since the networks penetrated to the grass-roots, the NDC won many tens of thousands of adherents. The beneficiaries included those who received benefits directly from government, especially in the form of contracts to party loyalists.

Another side of the president's machine involved "aggregative" clientelism, whereby political leaders allocated public investments to the benefit of selected regions or communities in order to maximize their electoral or general support. Generous salary increases to civil servants, as well as extensive infrastructural investments in potentially supportive rural constituencies, figured heavily in 1992, and, in the case of infrastructural investments, again in 1995–96. The hometown of a long-time minister (and former PNDC secretary) in the Central Region graphically illustrated the rewards of political loyalty. In 1994 the town boasted an unusual array of newly constructed amenities: a well-maintained main road, a recent electricity connection, a bore hole, a day-care centre, latrines, and a workshop for the junior secondary school. The NDC had little to fear there in the 1996 elections.

Corruption kept pace with the extension of clientelism, as Rawlings himself acknowledged in a speech in 1993 to mark the first anniversary of his election as president. He warned of the corrupting effect of political power: "The victory we won was not a victory we have come to eat" (*Ghanaian Democrat* [Accra], Nov. 15–21, 1993). He pointed out that opportunism had led to the demise of earlier ruling parties, including Nkrumah's CPP (in 1966), Busia's Progress Party (in 1972), and Hilla Limann's People's National Party (in 1981). By 1995–96 the signs of corruption were legion. Rawlings administered a severe beating to his vice-president in December 1995, allegedly because the vice-president had publicly accused his cabinet colleagues of corrupt activities (*Ghanaian Chronicle*, Jan. 2–7, 1995). In October 1996 the government-appointed commissioners of the National Commission of Human Rights and Administrative Justice issued a courageous report, reprimanding two cabinet ministers and the presidential advisor on cocoa affairs for various nefarious activities. The independent press was filled with reports of irregularities in the award of government contracts, particularly for road-building and drainage works. To win a contract, contractors allegedly needed to be NDC supporters and to pay a kickback. These allegations gained further credibility when an NDC member asked in Parliament "whether the government was trying to develop a new class of businessmen where Political Party card qualifies one for assistance" (*Ghanaian Chronicle*, Feb. 26–March 3, 1996). In 1997–98 public servants expected to receive "dashes" (bribes) for their performance of even routine duties.

Democratization and Macroeconomic Performance

Certain skeptics maintain that electoral contests have stimulated this resurgent neo-patrimonialism and have thereby contributed to undermining Ghana's hard-won economic gains. Following redemocratization in 1992 the economy failed to meet many targets set by the government and donors. Ghana had to seek a Structural Adjustment Facility loan from the IMF in 1995, but then breached the conditions required to renew that loan in 1996. Democratization, however, is not solely responsible for Ghana's recent economic problems. As early as 1990 fiscal control slackened, in part owing to unbudgeted outlays for a summit meeting of the Non-Aligned Movement and peacekeeping operations in Liberia (Overseas Development Institute 1996). Deficiencies in adjustment policies, poor harvests in 1993 and 1994, and withheld disbursements of loans also played their part.[11]

The elections nonetheless promoted fiscal laxity. Total government expenditures in the 1992 election year grew by almost 45 per cent, partly because of politically inspired rural infrastructure projects and an increase of 80 per cent in public-sector wages. The broad budget deficit reached 4.8 per cent of GDP, reversing the fiscal surpluses attained in the previous six years. This fiscal shock had wide ramifications: the money supply increased by more than 50 per cent; the current account deficit deepened; the depreciation of the cedi accelerated; and inflation surged from 10 per cent in 1992 to 25 per cent in 1993 and 60 per cent in 1995 (IMF 1996). A combination of large nominal interest-rate hikes and high government borrowing then caused a major contraction of credit to the private sector. Primary budget surpluses were restored in 1994, albeit only by the budget's treating divestiture receipts as normal revenue. The highest-profile divestiture entailed the sale of 30 per cent of the government's shares in Ashanti Goldfields Corporation, which reportedly netted U.S.$316 million. Using such funds to cover budgetary deficits helped to conceal the unsustainability of Ghana's fiscal position.

Yet some of the political expenditures were defensible on economic grounds. Although electoral considerations influenced the timing of the 1992 public-sector wage boost, it was claimed that this wage-bill "explosion" was partly due to an earlier failure to implement the selective salary increases for civil servants proposed by World Bank officials, only to be rejected by the IMF (Armstrong 1996: 43). Wages continued to be too low to rebuild the morale of public employees, who still registered high rates of absenteeism and expected side payments to perform regular duties. Road construction was also driven by political imperatives. With 98 per cent of freight moved by road and more than half of trunk roads remaining unpaved (Economist Intelligence Unit 1996), however, it is hard to argue that such expenditures are frivolous. The Ministry of Roads and Highways' six-year roads program, which it launched in 1995 at a projected cost of 2.1 billion cedis, should be assessed in this light.

Less defensible on economic grounds were government loans to state-owned enterprises and private organizations such as the GPRTU. Many Ghanaians suspected that a share of the large loans extended to the Ghana National Petroleum Company (GNPC), headed by one of the president's closest associates, found its way into NDC coffers. The World Bank (1995b) reported that the 1992 fiscal shock in Ghana was in part caused by the decision to write off fourteen billion cedis in taxes owed by the GNPC, whose central bank borrowing in 1994 led to a 46 per cent rise in the money supply and higher inflation.

Other incidents that seem to confirm the economic costs of democratization are more ambiguous than they first appear. For example, fiscal problems in 1995 derived partly from the government's withdrawal of a value-added tax (VAT) following mass demonstrations in Accra, led by an alliance of opposition politicians who harnessed popular grievances to their own political agendas. Still, the controversy and subsequent withdrawal of the VAT were not simply a case of democratically unleashed populism undermining sound fiscal practice. There were serious problems with the implementation of the VAT: it was introduced at a difficult time—the peak of the lean season for local foodstuffs—and the educational campaign led by the VAT secretariat was inadequate. By design or inadvertence, vendors applied the 17.5 per cent charge several times to the same goods and service (ISSER 1996: 17). The public backlash against VAT was therefore quite understandable.

Although the dismal performance of Ghana's manufacturing sector is sometimes attributed to the macroeconomic instability engendered by democratization, deficiencies in the design and implementation of adjustment policies, apparent long before the fiscal shock of 1992, largely account for the difficulties. Manufacturing growth was substantial after 1983, as imported inputs again became available to struggling factories with excess capacity. However, too rapid liberalization of imports and exposure to world competition led to a deceleration of output growth after 1987 (Lall and Stewart 1996). Even the guarded World Bank acknowledged that problems in Ghana's manufacturing arose from the poor design and sequencing of trade liberalization and the failure of financial reform to redirect credit towards besieged manufacturing firms (Armstrong 1996: 49–50).

It is, therefore, an oversimplification to blame Ghana's fall from economic grace in the mid-1990s wholly on democratization.

Countermovement: Liberal Institutional Reform

Democratization fostered the institutionalization of formal electoral rules, but the process also reinvigorated the informal institutions of neo-patrimonial governance. The Fourth Republic of Jerry Rawlings resembled Nkrumah's First Republic (see, for example, Bretton 1966). Clientelism, personalism, and corruption returned with a vengeance, contributing to macroeconomic instability.

But this tendency was only one side of the story. The other was the gradual strengthening of some important institutions of a liberal-democratic order. This contradictory tendency should not be dismissed as a mere epiphenomenon; the future of Ghana's capitalist development may hinge on continued progress in this direction. Ghanaian politics in the 1990s was shaped by a tension between neo-patrimonialism and liberalism, though the former was undeniably the stronger current. This liberal countermovement shows up in institutional reform in three core arenas: the parties, the courts, and the public service.

A Stable Party System?
If democratization improves governance by promoting the accountability, transparency, and responsiveness of decision-makers, then an institutionalized party system will be key to this change. Most conducive to stable democratic governance, according to conventional wisdom, is a two-party system. When only two or three parties compete for power, they will all court, and thereby integrate, diverse constituencies, and the losing side will possess the resources and incentive to monitor the government and galvanize opposition to poor policies or abuses of power.

Ghana is better-placed than most African countries to develop a two- or three-party system. Until the coalition disintegrated in early 1996, President Rawlings' NDC and its allies (the National Convention Party and the tiny Egle Party) controlled all but two legislative seats. When the NDC emerged in 1992 it was as a personal vehicle for Rawlings, a lineal descendant of the PNDC, which Rawlings had headed for a decade. It displayed little uniformity of viewpoint. Its leadership included former Marxists, Nkrumahists, and Danquah-Busia supporters (Essuman-Johnson 1993). Besides the three allied parties, four other parties contested the presidential elections of November 1992 and then boycotted the December parliamentary elections. One was the substantial New Patriotic Party, the inheritor of the conservative Danquah-Busia tradition. The other three, like Rawlings' erstwhile ally, the NCP, were parties in the Nkrumahist tradition. Despite this multiplicity of parties and the personalistic basis of the president's party, some historical probing reveals an incipient two-party tradition in Ghana.

A 1947 split in the nationalist movement set the mould for Ghanaian politics.[12] On the one side was Dr. J.B. Danquah's elite-led, liberal, and

moderate United Gold Coast Convention (UGCC), which drew disproportionate support from the relatively well-off Ashantis and Brongs. On the
other side was Nkrumah's breakaway Convention People's Party, with its
militant, populist appeals, its petty-bourgeois base in early school leavers,
and (in time) its disproportionate strength among the Ewes and people of
the Northern Region. Competitive national elections pitted parties in these
two traditions against each other on four occasions: 1954, 1956, 1969, and
1979. The winning tradition avoided fragmentation. However, the 1992
multiparty elections appear to contradict this incipient two-party model,
since the victorious NDC, in serving as a personal vehicle for Rawlings,
represented neither tendency.

In early 1994, most of the Nkrumahists merged into a People's
Convention Party (PCP), and two years later Rawlings' Nkrumahist ally, the
NCP, terminated that alliance. But the governing NDC had already declared
itself the true embodiment of the Nkrumahist philosophy. The old opposition between the Danquah-Busia tradition and the Nkrumahists had thus
surfaced anew, though now two major contenders, the NDC and the PCP,
and one minor one fought over the Nkrumahist mantle (*West Africa*, Sept.
25–Oct. 8, 1995). In the run-up to the 1996 elections, an opportunistic
Great Alliance of the NPP and PCP emerged to challenge Rawlings. But the
governing party responded effectively by means of machine politics and an
advertising campaign that, among other things, cast Rawlings and his wife
as the embodiment of Nkrumah and his wife. The NDC won, thanks largely
to shrewd advertising and campaigning, blatant patronage, and the disunity
of the Great Alliance, whose members bickered incessantly.

Adherence to the Danquah-Busia or Nkrumahist tradition has much
more to do with style than substance, but the division is no less important
for that reason. The Danquah-Busia parties profess a commitment to a
market economy and liberal values; they have usually enjoyed wide backing
from business people, professionals, civil servants, and the educated elite in
general; and they have always had a strong base in Ashanti. The Nkrumahist
parties all revere the memory and achievements of the *Osagyefo* (Redeemer),
though they no longer adhere to his doctrine of socialist-oriented, or at
least heavily state-led, development. All leading politicians agree on the
need for a market-oriented economic strategy, differing only in the mix,
pace, and sequence of market reforms. Yet the Nkrumahist parties, including the NDC, continue to echo the old CPP's populist denunciations of the
exploitative elite who take advantage of the suffering masses.[13] The division
is reminiscent, in certain respects, of the gap between the Republicans and
Democrats in the United States.

The institutional capacity of all parties was limited in the 1990s. A
major constraint on all of them, except the NDC, was a weak financial base.
Running a political party in Ghana is an expensive enterprise. Registered
parties are legally required to maintain offices in all ten regions and at least

two-thirds of the 110 districts. Although most offices were run by volunteers in the 1990s, parties still had to rent space and pay salaries of office staff. Additional expenses included the maintenance of the head office and especially the organization of campaigns, rallies, regional seminars, and party conventions. Nkrumahist leaders suggested that one reason for their financial plight was the paucity of wealthy donors who supported their parties, which, after all, were populist in tone. Finances were not as significant a problem for the NPP, because it did have the support, albeit unobtrusively, of some wealthy people. Still, its leaders felt constrained by the Political Parties Law, which restricted the maximum annual donation to one million cedis and prevented firms from making political contributions. Undoubtedly, those who depended upon the government for contracts were loath to be seen as opposition supporters. On several occasions Rawlings publicly urged his supporters to boycott the products of firms whose proprietors allegedly backed opposition parties. Potential donors, therefore, remained aloof from damaging commitments.

Financial weakness translated into meagre or non-existent formal party organization. None of the opposition parties in 1995 maintained offices in all the regions or most of the districts. At the grassroots, these parties were represented, if at all, by volunteers in makeshift offices or private homes. Only the governing NDC had offices in all ten regions and in over 90 per cent of the constituencies, though some of the constituency offices actually served two or more adjacent areas and relied upon volunteers. Even the governing NDC, however, exhibited organizational problems, in this case springing from the party's origins as a vehicle built around its leader. The party's personalistic basis bred opportunism and factional struggles, and few of its committees played any role in policy formulation. Most prominent NDC officials were cabinet ministers or members of Parliament and/or held one or more state appointments. The line between party and state had thus blurred.

Despite financial stringency, the NPP maintained a capacity for formulating policy and criticizing governmental actions. It established eighteen sectoral committees in 1993; their task was to monitor the activities of the relevant ministry or ministries and formulate the party's position on the issues of the day. These committees, which were formally subcommittees of the National Executive Committee, presented briefs to various committees of Parliament—for example, critiques of the government's budgets and proposals for electoral and other reforms. Its sectoral committee on legal and constitutional affairs mounted several successful Supreme Court challenges to the government based on constitutional requirements.

An institutionalized party system is one in which both government and opposition not only sustain an organizational and programmatic presence, but also accept each other's legitimate role and the rules of electoral competition. In Ghana one positive sign of this acceptance exists. Soon after the controversial 1992 elections, marred by vitriol, the opposition restrained its outraged militants and pursued only peaceful actions within the constitution. Forming an Inter-Party Coordinating Committee, the opposition announced that it accepted "the present institutional arrangements" and urged its supporters to "give the NDC-led government a chance to prove that it is genuinely interested in the institutions and restoration of democracy" (*West Africa*, Feb. 8–14, 1993). This action defused the tensions accompanying the elections and the subsequent scattered riots. The formation of an interparty advisory committee in April 1994, chaired by the head of the Electoral Commission, was another encouraging sign. A compromise involving identification cards, registration procedures, and the training of registration assistants and party observers set the stage for a peaceful second election in 1996. That both opposition and government made conciliatory gestures at the conclusion of this second election seems to have further entrenched the normative rules of party competition.

The Fourth Republic, then, featured an incipient two-party tradition, with organizations that built a sustainable presence, and a fragile elite consensus on rules of contestation. Following the 1996 elections, a large and talented bloc of NPP parliamentarians daily criticized the actions and policies of a shrewd NDC government. Governments became more accountable than hitherto.

A Rule of Law?

Ghanaians have only sporadically enjoyed the rule of law (see Amissah 1981). Most of the time, they have suffered the whims of strongmen, who have undermined judicial independence, detained opponents, countenanced (or practised) rent-seeking and corruption, and, in 1982–83, empowered public tribunals to confiscate private property and jail businessmen for "economic crimes." These practices had several detrimental consequences. Among them, the insecurity of property rights and contracts and the indiscipline of officials discouraged productive investments in favour of speculation, political investments, and capital flight (Aryeetey 1994). Many hoped that the Fourth Republic would restore constitutionalism and the rule of law and, in the process, reassure investors and entrepreneurs.

An encouraging development in the early years of the Fourth Republic was the evident self-confidence of the country's top judicial authority, not least since the 1992 constitution assigned jurisdiction to the Supreme Court over all matters pertaining to the constitution. Having boycotted the 1992 parliamentary elections, the opposition could not use Parliament as a forum in which to curb the government. It therefore looked to the independent judiciary to enforce rules of fair play. In the early years the NPP won four major constitutional challenges. The Supreme Court directed the government to accord the opposition equal access to the state-owned media, cease using public funds to celebrate the 31st December coup, change its practices in the election of district chief executives, and stop requiring police permits for political demonstrations.

Although the government sought to tame this assertive court, supportive constituencies emerged to defend the hard-won gains. In particular, the Ghana Bar Association and the independent press resisted what they perceived as politically inspired threats to judicial independence. Inevitably, such struggles involved intricate manoeuvres. Consider, for example, one rather convoluted contempt case. When the government appointed I.K. Abban chief justice in February 1995, the Ghana Bar Association challenged the appointment largely because it was not consulted. During the parliamentary hearings on the appointment, the *Free Press* published an article questioning Abban's suitability for the post and alleging breaches of acceptable judicial conduct in a case concerning the celebration of the December 31st Revolution as a public holiday. The attorney general laid charges against the relevant newspaper staff, and the Supreme Court found the publisher, editor, and writer of the article guilty of contempt of court. Hefty fines were imposed, and the journalist concerned was sentenced to one month's imprisonment with hard labour. Two judges who delivered dissenting verdicts in this contempt case were later retired, for technically legitimate but involuntary reasons, and two of the four appointments subsequently made to the Supreme Court aroused suspicions of pro-government bias in the minds of opposition leaders and lawyers. Neither of these appointees had served on the Court of Appeals (the usual stepping-stone to the Supreme Court), and one who lacked judicial experience was widely reputed to have close ties to the NDC.

Still, the Supreme Court has occasionally ruled against the government on important constitutional matters. In 1996, for example, the Court ruled in favour of the NPP in a case concerning freedom of association. PNDC law 312 of 1993, which established the CIBA, included a list of indigenous business associations that could not withdraw from the Council. The Court declared this provision inconsistent with constitutional provisions on freedom of association, and therefore null and void.

But the Supreme Court has more often ruled in the government's favour. One decision of mid-1996 permitted non-officials to institute proceedings for criminal libel, strengthening the hand of the president's wife, who did not hold any official position, in dealing with the press. That same year the Court also found that the Frequency Board, an agency of the executive, could legally enforce a regulation requiring the licensing of radio stations. That regulation had been used to prevent a prominent opposition politician from operating a radio station in 1995, even though chapter 12, section 162(3), of the 1992 constitution specifies, "There shall be no law requiring any person to obtain a license as a prerequisite to the establishment or operation of a newspaper, journal, or other media for mass communication." In March 1997 the Supreme Court rendered an equally questionable decision by accepting the constitutionality of an Nkrumah-era law that made it a criminal offence to "publish a false report which is likely to injure the reputation of the state." Ghana's legal experts regarded this seditious libel law as inconsistent with the constitution. Critics viewed the decision as a dangerous development in the government's battle to contain threats to its authority—whether through scurrilous excesses or legitimate watchdog reporting—by the country's independent media.[14]

Consider next the Commission on Human Rights and Administrative Justice, instituted by the 1992 constitution, which was given a mandate similar to that of an ombudsman. It possessed broader powers, too, because it was authorized to sue in court to enforce its findings. Despite initial concerns in the opposition, the Commission became an effective agency committed to redressing human-rights violations and the misappropriation of state resources and powers. The Commission enjoyed wide support among the urban elite and received a great deal of media attention. This strengthened its hand vis-à-vis the government, as the commissioner and his deputy both attested.

Although most of the cases heard by the Commission concerned allegations of wrongful dismissals, its most publicized activity involved probes of government officials. In October 1996 the Commission submitted an interim report on an eleven-month inquiry into allegations of abuse of office by a minister of the interior, a trade and industry minister, a presidential adviser for cocoa affairs, and the most influential presidential adviser (P.V. Obeng). Of these individuals, only the last was exonerated. The others were found guilty of financial impropriety or negligence causing losses of revenue to the state.

The government's reaction to this embarrassing report revealed much about Ghana's informal rules of the game. While it did not publicly respond to the report, the government did comply with the initial recommendations. The two ministers resigned, and money was returned to state coffers. But the NDC's subsequent decision to allow one of the former ministers to contest (and win) a seat in the 1996 parliamentary elections implicitly condoned abuses of office by NDC stalwarts. For its part, the Commission continued to monitor abuses of power, thereby reinforcing the formal rules of accountability and probity. In 1997 its investigation of the financial affairs and opulent lifestyle of the minister of roads and highways produced several embarrassing, and widely reported, revelations. The struggle seemed likely to continue, since the government was periodically endeavouring to limit the scope of the Commission's authority and impede its ability to investigate and prosecute violations of human rights and official misconduct.

A Reformed State Bureaucracy?

Ghana's public sector sharply deteriorated in the 1970s and 1980s. Its short-comings in the early years of the Economic Recovery Programs (ERPs) in the 1980s were legion:

> Shortages of skilled professional and technical personnel were endemic, while considerable overstaffing was evident in the junior levels. Non-labour inputs, such as paper, office machinery, pharmaceutical supplies, and tools, had become extremely scarce. Productivity was . . . extremely low in all of the basic functions of government, a condition exacerbated by absen-teeism, moonlighting, poor morale, lack of supervision, and an absence of pride in work and rewards for good performance. Contributing to this state of affairs was the inadequate level of remuneration, political instabil-ity, and the evasion of checks and balances designed to limit expansion in staff, enforce discipline, and control corruption. (Gregory 1996: 196)

Although civil service reform was a component of the ERPs, little had appar-ently changed on the eve of the Fourth Republic. One observer concluded that many of the earlier shortcomings had persisted to produce a "limited institutional capacity" in the civil service (Leechor 1994: 167). To promote productive investment and efficiency, Ghana clearly needed more respon-sive, expert, disciplined, and motivated civil servants, state corporations, and regulatory agencies.

Neo-patrimonial rulers are likely to be uninterested or even strongly opposed to bureaucratic reforms that threaten their control of patronage and self-advancement. But those who advocate the governance approach (Dia 1993; van de Walle 1995: 161) or institutional approach (World Bank 1997: ch.5) hope that democratization will forge a more open, accountable, legitimate, and effective state apparatus. According to this view, technical reforms in pay and incentive systems, procedures for recruitment and promotion, and public management will not succeed without these deeper institutional changes.

In Ghana, the advent of multiparty politics stimulated a resurgence of neo-patrimonial rules, as well as a countermovement of rational-legal reformism. That the tendency towards the neo-patrimonial predominates was crudely indicated by the growth of the civil service. Although struc-tural adjustment aimed to reduce expenditures and increase the salaries of those remaining by trimming redundant staff, the Fourth Republic reversed this trend. Whereas the number of core civil servants fell from 131,000 in 1987 to about 105,000 in early 1992 (Ayee 1995; Armstrong 1996), by January 1997 it had again grown to 183,717, an increase of roughly 70 per cent since 1992.[15]

The governance emphasis on building the capacity of key economic agencies also produced disappointing results. Although the Bank of Ghana and the Ministry of Finance relied on their own specialized analysts for the formation of fiscal and monetary policy, both organizations had difficulty in recruiting directors for their research departments.[16] The reason, according to the donor-backed National Capacity Building Assessment Group in Accra, was not so much the low pay as the limited freedom to initiate appropriate projects to support policy development. If so, one of the potential benefits of political liberalization—increased freedom for civil servants to question and redesign policy—had not materialized by 1997.

No major pockets of technocracy had developed in the civil service by early 1998. World Bank documents (Armstrong 1996; World Bank 1995b) continued to lament not only the lack of predictable and transparent regulatory procedures governing private-sector transactions, but also the persistence of rent-seeking by officials. One senior World Bank official, long resident in Accra, noted a major disjunction between the government's rhetoric on public-sector reform and the reality of limited and partial reform.

Nonetheless, certain agencies crucial to recovery of the private sector showed modest improvements. For instance, the cumbersome registration process for exporters was streamlined; the registrar-general and Ghana Investment Promotion Centre now had only five days within which to register a business or inform the applicant of why registration had been denied. Also, revenue collection and the efficiency of customs improved. Goods were cleared through customs more expeditiously than earlier in the decade, a point confirmed by businessmen and representatives of their associations.[17] That the Internal Revenue and the Customs Services were better endowed than other public agencies, and operated with more autonomy from day-to-day political interference, may have accounted for their superior efficiency. These semi-autonomous units offered relatively attractive terms of employment.

Another encouraging development concerned the Divestiture Implementation Committee (DIC), authorized under PNDC law 326 with implementing and overseeing all government policies respecting the privatization of public assets. Entrepreneurs and the press had criticized the divestiture process as both opaque and politicized. But in March 1995 DIC finally published its rules and procedures governing divestiture, and thereafter it more consistently released information to the mass media. In September 1996 the government published a full list of enterprises divested between January 1995 and July 1996, including the names of the new owners, the sale prices, and the outstanding balances (Gyimah-Boadi 1997).

Nonetheless, doubts remained about the transparency of the process. In 1996 a policy of outsourcing divestitures to private firms became operational. When Ghana Telecom was sold to a Malaysian telecommunications company in partnership with a local consortium in early 1997, controversy erupted. This privately managed sale was condemned because the purchase price for a 30 per cent share was only $38 million, despite a Coopers and

Lybrand valuation of the firm at $316 million. Critics charged corruption, and the ensuing furore illustrated that key stakeholders were demanding greater transparency than hitherto in the privatization of public assets.

Considerable progress was made in reform of the financial sector. After restructuring in 1991, the state-owned banks—with the exceptions of the Ghana Cooperative Bank and perhaps the Bank for Housing and Construction—generated respectable rates of return. In 1995–96 the government belatedly sold part of its holdings in banks, such as the Social Security Bank and the Ghana Commercial Bank. Several new commercial and merchant banks entered the country's financial markets after 1992, and most of them had major equity participation from local investors.

These changes raised new regulatory challenges for the government. On the one hand, banks were now confronting less political pressure to stock their portfolios with unviable and unsecured loans to political clients, as was formerly the case. On the other hand, insider-lending and heavy foreign borrowings emerged to threaten the security of the financial sector.[18] In 1995 the local subsidiary of Meridian BIAO was closed after incurring a large foreign-exchange exposure to its parent bank, a debt that the Bank of Ghana did not address in time. Also, when the Securities Discount Investments Company was placed in liquidation in 1996, it transpired that this company had never been licensed under the 1993 Non-Bank Financial Institution Law and that it had violated its legal exposure limits, extended credit to its director, and failed to obtain adequate security for about half of its outstanding loans (Brownbridge and Gockel 1996). This experience did not reflect well on the regulatory powers of the Bank of Ghana, which excused itself on the grounds that its supervisory capacities as regards non-bank financial securities were not operational when the infringements occurred.

Another insider banking scandal, revealed in 1997, raised further doubts about the regulatory capacity of Ghana's central bank. The case involved the Ghana Commercial Bank (GCB) and the managing director of a Ghanaian supermarket chain who owned 4 per cent of GCB. The director, with the apparent collaboration of senior bank staff, took advantage of a generous overdraft facility to cash over seventy-five billion cedis from the coffers of GCB and two other banks (both of which were subsequently removed from the central bank's clearing system). Opposition MPs created an uproar, demanding to know why the Bank of Ghana did not detect the scandal and calling for its governor to appear before Parliament to answer for his conduct (*Ghanaian Chronicle*, March 14–20, 1997).

Institutional reforms in the public sector were, thus, limited, obstructed by clientelism and scarce managerial skills. A professional, non-partisan, and disciplined public sector to support economic growth cannot be built overnight.

Historical Legacies and Institutional Change

Institutional reforms in the Fourth Republic to the end of the 1990s were contradictory, discontinuous, and fraught with contention. Democratization had accelerated the reintroduction of neo-patrimonial institutions, as the pessimistic thesis predicted. Although clientelism, particularism, and corruption had reappeared in the final years of the PNDC (Nugent 1995: 192–93), competitive elections magnified their salience. This reinvigoration of economically dysfunctional institutions threatened again to undermine capitalist accumulation. Yet realists expect the early years of democratization to be tumultuous as weak parties vie to mobilize constituencies. Two transitions are necessary—to a market economy and a democratic polity—and each produces losers as well as winners. The promise of democracy, therefore, belongs to the longer term.

But the Ghanaian experience had not yet disproved those who expected democratization to spur institutional reform and enhanced governance. Not only had the Fourth Republic already outlasted earlier democratic interludes, but it had also spawned, albeit in the midst of conflict and compromise, a fragile institutionalization of some key rational-legal organizations and procedures. A complex electoral system worked quite well during its second test in 1996. An incipient two-party system further consolidated itself. Struggles to impose legal limits on state officials persisted with some victories and some defeats. Although initial efforts to augment the efficiency and accountability of public servants foundered, modest successes were achieved. Underpinning this whole experience was the resurgence of civil society, especially as manifest in the intermediary institutions of the press, the professional, employer, and labour organizations, and other NGOs—a story for another book (but see Gyimah-Boadi 1994).

How do we explain this contradictory experience? Robert Putnam (1993) and others argue that today's institutional performance is shaped by traditions established over many years, if not centuries. In Ghana contemporary clashes over institutions reflect the co-existence of contradictory historical legacies. A well-established patrimonial tradition contends with a weaker, more elite-based, but no less indigenous, liberal tradition. This unusual historical pattern imparts an open-endedness to institutional struggles that does not exist to the same degree in neighbouring countries.

Ghana's patrimonial legacy requires little comment—its existence is widely acknowledged. Many have argued that this traditional political pattern of southern Ghana, especially that of the Akan peoples, who constitute about 45 per cent of the country's population, has persisted into the colonial and postcolonial periods to shape relationships between the governors and the governed: the so-called "Big-Man, Small-Boy Syndrome" (Price 1974). In the pre-colonial era, according to Maxwell Owusu (1970), chiefs ruled partly on the basis of "traditional legitimacy," but largely based on the extent to which they could provide for the material well-being of their subjects through ritual observances and personal gift-giving. This system fostered a highly instrumental approach to politics on the part of both leaders and followers.

As Owusu (1970: 251) describes it: "What tied the follower to the political leader was . . . economic necessity, a reciprocal tie that at times assumed the form of a patron-client relationship. . . . The relationship held so long as the patron honored his material and economic obligation, and the client his duty to vote at elections and perform various other services for the patron, including ritually praising him in public."[19]

In the context of such a political culture, certain practices flourish: personal loyalties, clientelism, and the use of state resources by patrons to build factional support; deference towards those who conspicuously command power and wealth; and even corruption (Chazan 1983: 98–102). The neo-patrimonial governance evident since independence can only be understood by reference to this tradition; and the corollary of such a system is a high premium placed on political power—a tendency for politics to become a struggle with few restraining rules, leading to recurrent oligarchies, instability, and violence.

Yet a second, contradictory, tradition also emerged over the past century or so, whereby influential groups championed civil and political rights, including the notion of popular sovereignty, against both authoritarian colonial governments and more recent military regimes. Several factors account for the development of a hardy liberal ethos among the urban middle classes in particular. Firstly, colonial rule was established early along the Gold Coast (1850), but avoided the presence of a white settler community that would have given colonialism an oppressive cast. Notions of legal rights and due process, parliamentary democracy, and national self-determination circulated in the Gold Coast from early times, which is not to say that they were honoured in practice by colonial governments. However, those governments were willing to tolerate "liberty of speech, of movement, of organization, and . . . a considerable degree of abuse from Press and public platforms" (Kimble 1963: 557). Secondly, by the late nineteenth century the early establishment of schools in the coastal towns had led to the emergence of an educated elite. Many among this elite were lawyers whose wealthy merchant or royal families had sent them abroad for study. Thirdly, the development of a prosperous cocoa economy in African hands fostered an individualistic ethic with a natural affinity for liberal doctrine (Fage 1959: 69–70). Wealthy farmers have long hired labour and invested in transport, timber companies, urban property, and the higher education of their children.

Finally, Akan political traditions were not antithetical to liberal notions of individual achievement and constitutional limits on political power

(Austin 1964: 18–21). Although chiefs were drawn from one or more royal lineages, no right of automatic succession existed. Usually the Queen Mother, assisted by the elders, selected a new chief; and personal qualities such as wisdom, generosity, and courage, as well as achievement, often influenced the choice among those who were eligible. Today, achievement continues to shape the choice of chiefs, many of whom are well-educated people who work in towns and cities. In addition, chiefs who abused their authority could be ousted or "destooled" if certain strict procedures were followed. As explained by David Kimble: "One of the recognized grounds for destoolment was habitual disregard of [the advice given by the elders' council]; and the Chief's duty of consultation with the representatives of his people, coupled with the possibility of removing him in the last resort, meant that even if the system did not approach democracy, at least it avoided the dangers of autocracy" (Kimble 1963: 127). In this context an urban elite, especially lawyers and journalists, championed civil and political rights and equality of opportunity for Africans. As early as 1875, Colonial Office despatches were referring to "educated natives" as a "thorn in the side" of the Gold Coast government (Kimble 1963: 91). Many African-owned newspapers in Accra, Cape Coast, Sekondi, and Kumasi sharply criticized colonial policies and practices and demanded greater African representation in government.

Protest movements also emerged at an early stage. The Aborigines Rights Protection Society successfully defended African rights to land in 1897–98, just about the time when colonial rule was being installed in East Africa. The Society continued to press political demands until it was replaced by the National Congress of British West Africa in 1921. Not surprisingly, Africans were always better represented in the Gold Coast than in other British colonies. Even the first Legislative Council in 1850 included a prosperous African merchant among its five unofficial members. Throughout the early twentieth century, demands that the British authorities remove all impediments to African progress in the public service and professions kept up the pressure on the colonial power to practise its preachings. The post-war period of political ferment, from 1946 to 1952, therefore drew upon nearly a hundred years of struggle.

Several discordant institutional tendencies today reflect these contradictory legacies. The neo-patrimonial tradition is doubtless more deeply rooted in the history and culture of Ghana, not to mention better adapted to its poverty, limited class formation, and peasant origins, than the liberal-democratic tendency. Yet the latter, after a century of nurture in the Ghanaian, middle-class soil, can hardly any longer be regarded as an alien intrusion. It provides roots for liberal institutional reform to a degree that is rare in Africa. The World Bank and the donors, in buttressing the organizational power of business associations in the 1990s, built on this tradition.

Where traditions conflict, broader scope may exist for political movements to shape institutional reform by selectively drawing upon historical memories. As well, the disastrous examples of chaos in Liberia, Sierra Leone, and elsewhere focus the mind of Ghana's political class on compromises that might avoid the abyss.[20] These circumstances, together with donor pressure, may yet facilitate the gradual institutional change that can support a market economy.

Closing the Circle

How might a virtuous circle of democratization, growing prosperity, and state rehabilitation be nurtured in Sub-Saharan Africa? The pragmatic neo-liberal answer offers an interventionist strategy extending beyond a simple faith in untrammelled markets. Market-oriented policy reforms, export orientation, and privatization, it says, will need to be supplemented by institutional change, improved (democratic) governance, and human-capital development. Since these reforms will meet with resistance, they must be accompanied by measures to alleviate the misery of the destitute and the vocal groups who pay the cost of neo-liberal experiments. Donors should support these programs with conditional aid and debt relief to consistent reformers, pragmatic neo-liberals contend, because Africa's narrow tax base cannot bear the burden alone.

But persistent poverty threatens to sabotage this vision of democratic development. Poverty is a trap that breeds both more poverty and tyranny. Closer African integration into global markets will most likely not generate the growth required to escape this poverty trap. Yet the foreign sponsors of structural adjustment, focused as they are on the domestic roots of Africa's malaise, have not accepted that the global economy they revere fails to serve Africa's interests. As the *Human Development Report 1997* graphically observes: "The greatest benefits of globalization have been garnered by the fortunate few. A rising tide of wealth is supposed to lift all boats, but some are more seaworthy than others. The yachts and ocean liners are rising in response to new opportunities, but many rafts and rowboats are taking on water—and some are sinking" (UNDP 1997: 9). African countries are the rafts and rowboats, and some have already sunk. Does it make sense therefore to advise Africa's governments to adapt further to the exigencies of competition within this global economy?

Democratic development, in Africa as elsewhere in the world, would be greatly bolstered by the reforming of economic globalization—towards what I call "social-democratic" globalization (Robinson 1995). Although democratic development requires massive reforms of domestic institutions and policies in Africa, it depends also on certain facilitative changes at the global level. Chief among the latter are debt cancellation, social restrictions on global markets, and mechanisms for redistribution of income on a North-South basis. Such changes are not as impracticable as they may at first appear to be, and that is because they serve the interests of most people in the North as well as the South.

The Pragmatic Neo-Liberal Strategy

First and foremost, according to neo-liberal advocates, African governments must adapt their economies to global market forces. "Globalization is proceeding inexorably and sub-Saharan Africa must decide how to live in a more complex and more competitive world," asserts the associate director of the IMF's Africa Department. "Africa has little to lose from globalization . . . and much to gain, provided it is accompanied by policy changes in several areas" (Hernández-Catá 1999: 11). These changes will facilitate the deeper integration of African economies into global markets:

> First, transaction costs . . . need to be reduced. In particular, transportation is expensive because of monopolistic, cartelized, and/or subsidized sea, air, and rail links. Globalization coupled with a reduction in transaction costs could shift comparative advantage toward manufacturing and raise output while helping to diversify the region's economy. Second, fiscal policy will have to shift toward the provision of infrastructure and education to prevent local capital from being moved to other countries where the quality of physical and human capital is higher. Third, a further reduction in barriers to foreign trade . . . would improve resource allocation and increase competition. . . . Finally, more African countries will have to deal with episodes of large and potentially reversible inflows of foreign capital. . . . This will require strong fiscal policies and prudent debt management, tough bank supervision, and flexible monetary policies. (Hernández-Catá 1999: 11)

Second, reforming governments must address poverty issues in their impoverished societies. Vocal and well-organized urban groups will grow politically hostile if they are left to suffer the costs of adjustment measures. As well, the poor must feel that they have some stake in market reform and the democratic system, if they are to co-operate with central authorities and vote in elections. Most corrosive is the popular belief that elected politicians concern themselves only with self-aggrandizement, primarily through corrupt activities.

In theory, adjustment policies enhance equity in Africa by benefiting the poor, who are largely rural, at the expense of the allegedly privileged urban dwellers (Azam 1994; Killick 1995b; Sahn, Dorosh, and Younger

1997). Currency devaluation and increases in the locally paid prices of export crops have raised the incomes of rural producers, including the many smallholders, though declines in world prices since 1995 have nullified this positive effect. Market liberalization often also raises the price of food, but this hurts the rural poor, who are largely self-provisioning, less than it does the urban poor. Adjustment should also help rural dwellers by redirecting public resources to the rural areas. In principle revenues will depend more on urban-based taxes, such as gasoline and value-added taxes, and less on taxation of primary exports, whereas expenditures should favour the primary education, primary health care, and rural infrastructure of benefit to the rural majority.

In Ghana adjustment does seem to have supported the redirection of resources to the rural areas.[1] Ghanaian smallholders gained ground after the late 1980s by benefiting from a higher share of the world price for cocoa, a shifting of more of the tax burden to urban consumers, a decentralization to the districts backed by central transfers for development projects, and major investments in rural infrastructure, including rural electrification, feeder roads, and schools. The motivation of this rural policy bias has probably been as much political as economic: it enabled President Rawlings to build political support in the populous countryside.

Elsewhere, adjustment's distributional impact remains controversial. Various policies had divergent effects on income distribution, and relevant data on those effects are unavailable or unreliable. Hence, deductive reasoning based on economic models, anecdotes, and hunches replaces clear evidence. Critics have long maintained that adjustment packages are defectively designed: they rarely create the sustained growth required by poverty alleviation; they increase the burden of the poor in general, especially women; and they offer compensatory schemes that are too meagre and urban-biased to be of much use (for example, Stewart 1991). The World Bank's acknowledgement of some of these problems led to its 1990 adoption of poverty reduction as a separate goal of structural adjustment.

The neo-liberal view, after 1990, was that "social dimensions of adjustment" (SDA) programs should target not only the "new poor" and other vulnerable groups hurt by adjustment, but also the "chronic poor"—including people whose low productivity had condemned them to poverty long before the advent of adjustment (see African Development Bank, UNDP, and World Bank 1990). SDA programs would not simply compensate losers; rather, they would reduce poverty in the targeted groups by raising their productivity. This approach would entail investments in human capital and household assets, changes in relative prices to favour the poor, the promotion of wage employment, and the organization of targeted groups within "empowering" community organizations.

Practice has fallen short of these lofty aims. Although IMF and World Bank adjustment lending has long included provisions to address poverty and the social costs of adjustment, the anti-poverty programs do not dispose of the resources needed to combat the widespread deprivation. Nevertheless, such projects are better than nothing. Meanwhile, plans to incorporate poverty reduction into the design of adjustment programs have yielded mixed results.

Consider the effectiveness of social safety nets, which are of two types (Marc et al. 1995). Social Action Programs (SAPs) are "regular investment projects," implemented in most cases by existing governmental departments. Social Funds (SFs) involve the formation of a more-or-less independent agency to administer funds contributed by donors and the host government. These agencies respond to the proposals of NGOs and local governments for pertinent projects, supervise their implementation, and monitor their effectiveness. Both arrangements—SAPs and SFs—support similar projects. The most effective in assisting large numbers of people are labour-intensive public-works projects. They have not only created thousands of temporary jobs, but have also usefully rehabilitated streets, drainage systems, sanitation facilities, water supplies, schools, health facilities, and markets (Marc et al. 1995: 63–65). Other types of projects include assistance to laid-off public employees and to the unemployed graduates of secondary schools and universities, and credit and training schemes aimed at managers of microenterprises, in particular women. SAPs have also dedicated funds to restoring basic social services for the poor, such as basic health and educational facilities, and to supplying essential medicines and nutritional programs.

Students of these initiatives lament their limited impact (Marc et al. 1995: 22; Graham 1994; Hutchful 1994). In places where most of the population is poor, scattered projects will not improve the lot of very many. Because the bulk of the poor generally live in rural areas, the urban bias of projects further reduces their impact. This bias does, however, address the political realities of adjustment, namely that the most vocal and best-organized opponents of adjustment reside in the cities. If neo-liberal reform is to proceed, these opponents must be compensated. Finally, certain governments divert funds designed to alleviate hardship into patronage channels. The anti-poverty thrust of social programs is, thus, further diluted. Such diversions are not inevitable, though. Independent and politically insulated agencies, in Zambia and elsewhere, have successfully administered Social Funds, especially through labour-intensive public works (World Bank 1995d; Graham 1994).

The World Bank and other agencies advocate three other anti-poverty strategies in addition to establishing safety nets: shifting public expenditures from military budgets and less essential services to primary education and primary health care, directing credit to microenterprises, and improving the marketing of agricultural products (see, for example, World Bank 1990). The data in Table 6.1 suggest that, in aggregate terms, defence spending has fallen—from 3.4 per cent of GDP in 1980 to 2.5 per cent in 1995—but these figures are misleading. For one thing, they mask enormous variations in defence expenditures. South Africa, by far the largest military spender in the region, has reduced its expenditures by half in real terms since 1989 (SIPRI 1998: 196). This reduction accounts for much of the overall decrease. Also, military outlays in countries undergoing civil wars, especially the Democratic Republic of the Congo (Kinshasa), Congo (Brazzaville), Sierra Leone, Angola, and Sudan, are either unreported or unreliable, and exclude expenditures by rebel forces (SIPRI 1998: 195). As for the Bank's emphasis on primary health care and education, this approach, if implemented, would promote both productivity and equity. In practice, overall health expenditures have declined while those on education have grown (see Table 6.1). Again, South Africa's increase in educational expenditures would seem to account for much of the additional spending on education. As African governments have struggled to service exorbitant external debts (see Table 2.1) and maintain a reliable military apparatus, health and educational spending has often suffered. Other recommended measures to augment equity and the productivity of the poor—such as targeted credit to microenterprises and small farmers, the provision of marketing services, and research on appropriate technology—prove difficult to implement for political/institutional reasons. Few countries boast the requisite depoliticized and effective administrative apparatus.

Table 6.1 Government Expenditure in Sub-Saharan Africa			
	Defence Expenditure as % of GDP	Public Expenditure on Health as % of GDP	Public Expenditure on Education as % of GDP
1980	3.4	5.8	4.1
1985	3.0	5.7	5.2
1990	2.8	2.4	4.2
1995	2.5	1.6	6.3
Source: World Bank.			

If market adjustment and democracy are to endure, people must eat. Yet the shortcomings of these neo-liberal poverty-reduction measures suggest that many Africans are eating poorly. Social safety nets, though minor in their societal impact, do help reconcile vocal urban critics to continuing adjustment. Experience suggests that separate agencies that enjoy autonomy from the executive and the civil service are most effective in responsibly administering Social Funds. But, even in the case of this modest success, will donors fund these programs on a long-term basis?

Even if they do, a knotty challenge remains: building a state with the will and capacity to maintain order, implement economic reforms, and foster poverty reduction. Regardless of the degree of democratization, little can be done without an effective state. The World Bank now endorses, in principle, the rebuilding of state capacities to prepare governments for a more active role in market economies. The Bank and donors seem galvanized by the spectre of state collapse. As one Bank report observes, states that fail to reform face greater risks than "just" postponed growth and social development—namely, deadly conflict and even state disintegration: "The enormous cost of state collapse has naturally turned attention to prevention as a preferable and potentially less costly course of action. . . . Once the spiral into collapse has occurred, there are no quick fixes" (World Bank 1997: 15).

The Bank's two-part strategy in *World Development Report 1997* represents a belated endorsement of a position long advocated by centre-left political economists (see, for example, Mkandawire 1996). First, the state's current economic role should be limited to what it can effectively handle—which in Africa's case would extend only to maintaining order, instituting "correct" macroeconomic policy, and supplying some infrastructure, especially roads. But "capacity is not destiny" (World Bank 1997: 3). The second part of the strategy is, thus, to undertake the long-term process of "reinvigorating public institutions." When a state's political and administrative capacities improve, it can expand its economic role, perhaps even to the point of promoting an industrial policy.

The problem in state capacity-building is generally a paucity of administrative capacity. Declining revenues, clientelism, and limited bureaucratic esprit de corps have produced civil servants who are poorly paid, inadequately trained and supplied, prone to corruption, and hence inefficient workers. Augmenting the accountability of state officials at all levels, while making public transactions more transparent, is one piece of the solution. Here democratization connects with state revitalization.

Pragmatic neo-liberals recognize the need for a more democratic—participatory and open—mode of economic and social policy-making. Donors and African governmental technocrats have engaged in centralized and top-down negotiations on budgets and adjustment programs (see chapter 4). But intellectuals, civil associations—especially professional and employers' associations, trade unions, and human rights groups—and the independent press have long demanded more open and responsive governance in emergent democracies. A more participatory mode of decision-making will heighten the risks of "macroeconomic populism" (Dornbusch and Edwards 1990) by motivating elected officials to respond to the demands of voters for relief. Against this possibility, proponents weigh the potential advantages: increased support for popularly approved adjustment measures and strengthened democratic institutions.

If a more participatory style is to evolve, intermediary institutions will need to develop their capacities. Political parties, parliaments, interest groups, and the press all operate under onerous constraints (see chapter 2). Parties tend to fragment and lack ideological or policy coherence. Few parties boast sufficient financial and technical resources to sustain a capacity for policy analysis. Parliaments lack many experienced deputies or access to the financial and economic information and expertise with which to develop critiques of technically complex budgets and legislation. Legislators make do with rudimentary or non-existent parliamentary libraries. They lack expert parliamentary staff and the funds to hire consultants. Governments often refuse legislators' requests for information on adjustment agreements on the grounds that such information is "classified." Interest groups lack a capacity for policy analysis and advocacy owing to decades of authoritarian controls and the corrosive deal-making of clientelist politics. Lacking professional expertise and financial resources, the press cannot engage in incisive analysis of the complex issues surrounding recovery. Hence, international agencies, donors, and private foundations try to remedy these deficiencies through capacity-building initiatives: they buttress parliamentary libraries, train policy analysts, establish independent think-tanks, assist in the organizational strengthening of parties and interest groups, and fortify the analytical capacities of the press, as well as assist in electoral reform, decentralization, and judicial reform.

Whether this pragmatic neo-liberal strategy will succeed in promoting democratic development will, according to proponents (for example, Diamond 1997: 37–38), depend partly upon the willingness of the United States and other donors to transfer resources to Africa. Sub-Saharan countries are too poor and weakly organized, they suggest, to raise the resources needed to underpin rapid growth, sustain safety nets and basic services, renovate state apparatuses, and invigorate democratic institutions. Resource transfers should take two forms: generous and well-targeted aid, and debt relief.

Neither of these avenues seems equal to the task at hand. True, Africa has received ample aid, although experts question its effectiveness. Official development assistance in 1997 represented 12.4 per cent of Sub-Saharan Africa's GNP, whereas it represented only 1.1 per cent for all low- and middle-income countries combined (*The Economist*, March 13, 1999). Many countries were heavily dependent on aid—for instance, aid accounted for 37 per cent of GDP in Mozambique and 13 per cent in Uganda and Tanzania. Sub-Saharan governments have had to rely on official sources of credit because private banks have been unwilling to lend to countries with threatening debt overhangs, bleak economic prospects, and unstable governments.

Aid, however, has declined, as have development grants from non-governmental organizations. Total aid to all recipients, which peaked at U.S.$59.6 billion in 1994, stood at U.S.$49.7 billion in 1998 (OECD 1999). The United States registered the sharpest reduction in 1996–97—28 per cent—which reduced its contribution to only 0.09 per cent of its GNP. Japan, the largest donor, announced a cut of 10 per cent in 1998, though some of the funds were later restored. Only the Scandinavian countries and the Netherlands continued to devote 0.7 per cent of their GNP to aid trans-fers. Aid to Sub-Saharan Africa remained constant at about U.S.$17.3 billion between 1990 and 1995, but then declined sharply, by almost U.S.$4 billion over two years (World Bank 1999a, Table 12-1). Not only are Western governments unlikely to restore earlier aid levels, but an increasing share of existing aid is devoted to handling growing emergency relief efforts in Central America, Eastern Europe, and Asia, as well as Africa. Hence, the earlier promises that consistent policy reform in Africa would be rewarded with substantial official inflows are not being honoured.

Debt relief, virtually a necessary condition for recovery in Africa, has so far remained limited. By the 1990s many Sub-Saharan countries were insol-vent, in the sense that they were unable to service their debts. Therefore, external debts were periodically rolled over, thereby compounding the long-term problem by expanding the capital owed. Some thirty-three Sub-Saharan countries were classified as Highly Indebted Poor Countries in 1998; these countries struggled to service their debts by curtailing expenditures in infrastructure, health, education, and other key services. High debt burdens also deterred private investors.

In 1996 the donors agreed on a debt-relief scheme, but this delivered limited benefits to few beneficiaries. Highly indebted countries required six years of consistent market reform to qualify, and then received enough relief to reduce external debts to twice their export earnings. Only Uganda and Bolivia had benefited somewhat from the scheme by 1998. Massive demon-strations organized by a coalition of civil associations (Jubilee 2000) at the G7 summit of industrial countries in Birmingham in 1998 and the G8 finance ministers meeting in 1999 pressed for more substantial debt relief as a key to recovery in the poorest countries.[2] This protest apparently suc-ceeded: in June 1999 the G8 agreed to a debt relief package said to be worth U.S.$50 billion. The number of eligible countries expanded from twenty-nine to thirty-six, most in Africa; and the qualifying time for debt relief was reduced to three years (*The Guardian Weekly*, June 20, 1999).

Jubilee 2000 supporters argued that the new deal was only a slight improvement. About half of the advertised U.S.$50 billion cost of the initiative involved writing off irretrievable debts. Moreover, donors had already dedicated aid to cover some overburdened recipients' debt repayments; critics suspected that these aid payments would cease, bringing little net benefit to poor countries. And those who received aid under the agreement would still be expected to devote a fifth of government revenue to debt service. Even this meagre debt relief effort suffered a setback in 2000. The 1999 initiative stalled, owing to Japanese indifference, the refusal of the U.S. Congress to accept President Clinton's request for full funding of the U.S. share of the HIPC Trust Fund, and the European Union's unwillingness to release its main contribution until the United States complied.

That debt relief and aid to support democratic development are limited is only part of the weakness of the neo-liberal strategy. Pragmatic neo-liberalism, to be sure, is a welcome advance over orthodox liberalism, insofar as it envisages a limited welfare role for the state, complementary programs in state-building, and attention to some degree of democratic deepening. The model's flaw lies at its core: its insistence that Africa's redemption lies in adjusting its policies, institutions, and modes of governance to permit its deeper integration into the prevailing pattern of neo-liberal globalization.[3] In this emerging global economy, many are called but few are chosen. Very few African economies will feature among the elect.[4] But if an outward orientation fails to raise living standards, safety nets will remain too minimal to cope with the mass destitution. Consequently, pragmatic neo-liberalism is unlikely to overcome the vicious circle of poverty, state fragmentation, and reversions to tyranny.

Neo-liberal globalization does not favour Africa's progress. This region shares with other areas certain generic shortcomings of globalization that its critics, and even some of its supporters,[5] identify:

- global financial instability, linked to liberalization of capital markets, giving rise to periodic financial crises in vulnerable economies;
- growing inequalities, as certain countries, regions, ethnic groups, and classes win while others lose in global competition, together with growing insecurity of employment and income, both or either of which can lead to social disintegration, conflict, and crime;
- environmentally unsustainable economic practices that ineffectual governments desperate for investment cannot or will not control, and which produce scarcities (especially of water and land), pollution, disease, and further poverty; and
- an augmentation of the power of capital, and in particular of financial markets, which constricts fiscal, monetary, and social policy options at the national level and thereby dilutes democracy by removing key issues from the public arena.

In addition to these generic problems, Africa suffers specific disadvantages. Export-led development, a key element of neo-liberal strategy, is unlikely to benefit most African countries under prevailing conditions. Sub-Saharan Africa's share of world trade has steadily declined over forty years—from 3.1 per cent of world merchandise exports in 1955 to just 1.2 per cent in 1990 (Yeats et al. 1996: 38). By 1997 the entire continent accounted for a lesser share of the world's exports than tiny Belgium (2.3 per cent against 3 per cent). Africa's weak position will probably continue because the region's comparative advantage, owing to relatively abundant natural resources and scarce human capital, lies in primary production, especially agricultural and mineral production, and in related unskilled activities (Helleiner 1997: 69). But the market prospects for Africa's traditional primary exports are bleak. According to the World Bank's projections, real non-oil commodity prices are declining by an average 2 per cent per year in 1995–2005. Tropical beverages, which contribute more than a third of total exports in ten African countries, will experience a fall in prices of 5 or 6 per cent per annum. Further, this export profile is deleterious because, as a noted development economist points out, "Unskilled labour-intensive activities can be a technological 'dead-end,' unconducive to the productivity enhancement and indigenous learning upon which development is now generally believed to depend" (Helleiner 1997: 69).

To make matters worse, recent changes in global trade rules have created further impediments. Rules established by the Uruguay Round of GATT (General Agreement on Tariffs and Trade) and the more recently established World Trade Organization (WTO) reduce preferences that the region enjoyed under the European Union's Lomé Convention and the Generalized System of Preferences, and bar significant protection of infant industries. Also, the North, and the European Union in particular, have been allowed to retain high tariffs on textiles and agricultural imports that compete with local production. How then will an export orientation spur the growth needed to support democratic development in Africa? Considering the limited growth of non-traditional exports during fifteen years of adjustment (Helleiner 1997: 67–68), one cannot be sanguine that Africa will reap gains from international trade, even in the longer term.

Sub-Saharan Africa, in addition, has not experienced significant inflows of foreign investment, even though many of its governments have undertaken policy and institutional reforms to foster favourable investment climates.[6] Foreign direct investment, which fell to an abysmal 1 per cent of the developing countries' share in the 1980s ("Recent Trends in FDI for the Developing World" 1992: 51), stagnated in the early 1990s. At its high point in 1997, foreign direct investment had risen sixfold (to U.S.$5.2 billion) from its 1990 level, while gross portfolio investment had grown from an outflow of U.S.$31 million in 1990 to a more respectable U.S.$1.2 billion inflow in 1997 (World Bank 1999b). But in the following year panicked investors withdrew their funds from all emerging markets in the wake of the East Asian and Russian financial collapses. New investments, moreover, have flowed largely to South Africa and Nigeria, and mainly into the mining and petroleum sector. Despite periodic panics, foreign investors perceive superior opportunities in East Asia, Central Europe and Latin America. (East Asia and Latin America typically account for two-thirds or more of foreign direct investment to developing countries.) Investors still regard Africa as a risky place for investment. The thinness of capital markets in Sub-Saharan countries, together with capital-account liberalization, suggests that investments in Africa will be as volatile and disruptive as in other parts of the world.

Under these circumstances, it is implausible to claim that Africa has "little to lose, and much to gain" from globalization. Neo-liberal globalization is unlikely to generate sustained growth in Africa. As even billionaire Ted Turner recognizes, "Even as communications, transportation and technology are driving global economic expansion headway on, poverty is not keeping pace. It is as if globalization is in fast forward, and the world's ability to react to it is in slow motion" (quoted in UNDP 1999).

Even some who present a case in favour of neo-liberal globalization arrive at equivocal conclusions. Nicholas Van de Walle (1999), for instance, argues convincingly that Africa's current marginalization within the global economy and dependence on the international financial institutions are detrimental to democratic survival on that continent. What is needed, Van de Walle says, is sustained growth to legitimate democratic structures. Countries can achieve this growth, furthermore, through integration into global markets via the consistent implementation of neo-liberal reforms. But his case loses momentum when he moves beyond citing economists who claim a correlation between sustained growth and global integration, to engage African realities. More tentatively, he observes: "High growth may be possible in the longer term, once the necessary bases have been put in place, but it is probably illusory to expect higher growth in the near future for most of the countries of the region, even with macroeconomic stabilization" (Van de Walle 1999: 107). Moreover, "While competing in international markets may in time promote growth and political stability, there is no clear road map that shows how to get from the current state to a reasonable ability to compete" (p.113). Van de Walle's analysis exhibits a common tendency: to portray the alternatives as, on the one hand, marginalization or, on the other, integration via consistent market reforms into the global market. He may believe that it is simply unrealistic to discuss any other options. Although time may prove his calculation to be correct, his stark alternatives unduly restrict a debate on desirable futures.

Democratic development in Africa will be unlikely in the absence of a new global order.

A Social-Democratic Globalization?

The proponents of globalization often present the alternatives in falsely dichotomous terms: the deepening of a generally beneficent and technologically driven free-market globalization, or a retreat into (or retention of) defensive protectionism. Yet many of the critics of globalization do not advocate protectionism. They accept that markets, including global markets, enhance efficiency and create wealth. They insist, however, that markets, if unrestrained, also produce volatility, inequalities, concentrated economic power, and environmental degradation. Hence, they advocate imposing social restrictions on market forces to ensure that the economy serves the common good.

The problem, from this alternative viewpoint, is therefore not globalization; it is *neo-liberal* globalization. And the solution is not protectionism; it is *social-democratic* globalization. Pragmatic neo-liberals accept the inexorability and, usually, the desirability of global free markets. They seek merely to mitigate their worst effects, but without challenging the interests of the rich and corporate capital. Social democrats champion the building of integrated, *but socially embedded*, markets for goods, capital, technology, and skills. They believe that the structures and inequalities of capitalism require democratic reform, including a redistribution of income and power from rich to poor.

This notion of subjecting markets to social boundaries is not really a radical idea. As economist Dani Rodrik (1997: 35) observes, in a book sponsored by the Institute for International Economics, "Every society has restrictions, legal and moral, on what kind of markets are allowed."[7] Restrictions on free contracts are regarded as legitimate, he points out, in the case of unequal bargaining power among the parties concerned (p.36). Social democrats argue that the same logic should apply to global, as to national, markets. Few would deny the vastly unequal bargaining power that obtains in global markets. Global trading rules, for example, are negotiated among the major industrial powers with scarcely any reference to the concerns and interests of the weak and vulnerable countries of Sub-Saharan Africa.

A social-democratic pattern of globalization requires two types of enforceable international agreements.[8] One set will regulate international competition among firms and states so as "to yield socially and environmentally desirable outcomes" (Robinson 1995: 374). As critics of neo-liberal globalization (see, for example, Martin and Schumann 1997; Greider 1997) suggest, such agreements would include, at a minimum:

- a *social charter* banning child and forced labour and ethnic or gender discrimination in employment and guaranteeing basic union and bargaining rights; and

- an *environmental charter* setting minimum environmental standards for participants in free trade.

Both accords might be enforced through the WTO, in the same way as unfair trade practices are today.[9] A country found contravening either charter by a WTO tribunal would have punitive duties imposed on its exports. An obvious objection is that industrial countries would use the agreements as a weapon to negate the comparative advantage of developing countries in a cheap and docile labour force and a disposable environment. But such an objection must be balanced against the charters' benefit to people in Third World countries: basic protection against exploitation and a poisoned environment and against an unfettered race to the bottom to attract investment by the transnational corporations. Moreover, the transfer of clean technologies to the South and redistributive measures would compensate developing countries for the inevitable losses of investment stemming from such accords.

So the application of social-democratic principles to the global economy also requires new redistributive mechanisms. These accords would redistribute "a substantial part of the economic gains from globalization to those who are most in need and most vulnerable to the massive restructuring that globalization brings in its wake" (Robinson 1995: 374). The idea would be to tax undesirable transnational activities—speculative movements of capital and environmental pollution ("green" taxes), for example—in order to transfer resources to depressed regions (such as Africa). Such transfers, if well targeted, could encourage the growth that would allow societies to escape the poverty trap and support democratic development.

One useful tool could, for instance, be a tax on international currency transactions, in particular a "Tobin tax." Nobel economist James Tobin first proposed such a tax in 1978 to "throw sand in the gears" of speculative capital markets (Tobin 1978). Hundreds of billions of dollars wash about the globe each day as speculators seek to exploit minor inter-country interest-rate differentials and shifts in exchange rates. Daily transactions in foreign exchange markets totalled U.S.$1.2 trillion in the mid-1990s, according to the IMF.[10] When capital surges in and out of countries, these shifts magnify volatility. Periodic financial meltdowns result, as in Mexico, East Asia, and Russia in the middle and late 1990s. Liberalized capital markets, through these demonstrations of their power, dictate conservative monetary and fiscal policies to intimidated national governments. To alleviate these problems, Tobin originally conceived of a currency exchange tax being set at 0.5—1 per cent of each exchange. Later, proponents revised this tax downwards to 0.25 per cent or even lower—a rate low enough not to deter long-term investments or trade in real goods and services, but high enough to dampen the nine-tenths of currency trading that concerns short-term speculation. This tax would discourage a negative, destabilizing practice, *and* generate substantial revenues. Assuming that a tax of 0.5 per cent would reduce the volume of currency transactions by 35 per cent, it would yield about U.S.$1.5 trillion per year (Robinson 1995: 378). A United Nations agency might disburse these revenues to member countries, perhaps on the basis of population, subject to certain conditions. To receive transfers, governments might be required to (a) be demonstrably democratic, and (b) respect the rights protected in the social and environmental charters (Robinson 1995: 378). Developing countries' relatively large populations and debts would encourage them to accept this package. Some question the feasibility of the Tobin tax. For instance, could it be collected? Would it drive foreign-exchange markets into offshore havens? But many experts believe it is workable (see, for example, Martin and Schumann 1997: 84).

Is the notion of applying social-democratic principles to the global economy merely a pipe dream? Is it not a council of despair to propose that democratic development in Africa may depend upon supportive reforms in the global economy? After all, the 1970s witnessed a major campaign to achieve a New International Economic Order more favourable to the interests of the developing world. That effort foundered as the heavy indebtedness of Latin American and African countries during the "lost decade" of the 1980s revealed their weak and dependent position within the global order. Do new factors make a new order any more politically feasible today?

Very little has altered at the governmental level. Major Western governments, especially those of the United States, Britain, and Germany, have embraced and nurtured neo-liberal globalization. It did not matter in the 1990s that governments in Britain, Germany, and most other European countries identified themselves as social-democratic, that a Democrat occupied the White House, and that a traditionally nationalist and welfare-oriented Liberal Party governed in Canada. Owing to the formidable power of vested interests, these key governments were still wedded to a pragmatic neo-liberal strategy (dubbed the Third Way by President Bill Clinton and Prime Minister Tony Blair).[11] Transnational corporations are still pushing hard for measures, such as a Multilateral Agreement on Investment and a General Agreement on Trade and Services, that will further ease international movements of capital, goods, and services by restricting the scope for national regulation. Corporate power stems from a variety of well-known developments. A hegemonic ideology portraying globalization as an inexorable force of nature paralyzes many who regard the global economy as defective. The greater the ease with which investors can shift their assets across boundaries, the greater is their leverage over national and local governments, communities, and employees. Transnational mobility enables corporations to pit one national government, community, and workforce against the others in a competition for the available investment and jobs. Also, neo-liberal globalization has fostered economic concentration on a global scale. Concentrated economic power shapes political power in diverse ways: for instance, expensive advertising campaigns to influence public opinion; a conservative editorial line in the mass media moulded by concentrated media ownership; the funding of seemingly independent think-tanks on economic policy; charitable donations by foundations to universities and other organizations; elaborate lobbying programs; and the financing of increasingly expensive election campaigns. The decline of organized labour magnifies the power of capital. The relative immobility of labour, together with the shrinking proportion of the labour forces in industrial employment and high unemployment and underemployment, vitiates its political role. But, above all, footloose finance capital now has the capacity to devastate any economy whose government loses its confidence.[12] Hence, the governments of Europe, the United States, and Japan are unlikely to negotiate a social-democratic pattern of globalization—unless their hands are forced by a popular movement or a catastrophe, such as another Great Depression or ecological disaster.[13]

How likely is a movement to mobilize popular support behind the project of a new global order of regulated capitalism and redistribution? The nineteenth- and early twentieth-century struggles to tame the destructive features of free-market capitalism occurred under very different circumstances. In Britain and in the other European industrializers, the struggles took place within nation-states and featured growing socialist or left-wing parties linked to vibrant labour movements. Today, however, "social democracy in one country" is increasingly difficult to maintain or build, especially in the smaller and more vulnerable economies. National governments have diminished powers vis-à-vis transnational capital, while labour movements are defensive and waning in influence and socialist parties have lost their vision. To be effective, popular movements must operate on a transnational as well as national and local basis. They will need to unite the new social movements of the past thirty years—the environmental and development-oriented NGOs, human-rights associations, peace activists, consumer protection groups, anti-poverty alliances, church and ecumenical coalitions, students' associations, women's groups, research institutes—with the older movements, especially labour. Global grassroots activists advance this agenda.[14] "We the people of the world," boldly declared the NGO Forum at the Earth Summit in Rio de Janeiro in 1992, "will mobilize the forces of transnational civil society behind a widely shared agenda that bonds our many social movements in pursuit of just, sustainable, and participatory human societies."

These global grassroots activists have initiated some innovative protests and campaigns. Although we must be careful not to romanticize these disproportionately Western-based activists, transnational social movements do exhibit certain strengths. One set of strengths is their energy and idealism, and thus their ability to stir the public's conscience. They also excel at networking via electronic mail, Internet sites, and the fax machine. They have exchanged information and co-ordinated their actions on a regional or global basis in several campaigns.[15] The "50 Years Is Enough" campaign, for example, successfully challenged the effectiveness of World Bank and IMF programs on the occasion of the fiftieth anniversary of these organizations. Development-oriented and environmental NGOs employed various strategies—demonstrations, advertisements, op-ed pieces in newspapers, and special issues of journals and newsletters—to advocate cuts in the funding of these two bodies. James Wolfensohn, who assumed the World Bank's presidency in 1995, responded to the challenge by instituting a new sensitivity to the ecological and social effects of Bank lending and a new openness on Bank activities. He also sought to forge links with the NGO community, as well as the private sector.

The Multilateral Agreement on Investment (MAI) was also successfully opposed in 1997–98. Negotiations on this treaty began quietly within the Organization of Economic Co-operation and Development (OECD) in 1995. The MAI aimed to facilitate the movement of capital across borders by harmonizing investment rules, restricting the legal powers of national governments to regulate or impose conditions on foreign investment, and providing foreign investors with legal remedies against governments if they felt their rights had been violated. Citizens' groups charged that the transnational corporations would use the MAI to erode national laws protecting the environment, workers, and culture. Strident campaigns within the twenty-nine OECD countries, facilitated by the rapid exchange of information and strategies among networked national committees, aroused public opposition to the proposed treaty. This opposition, together with divisions among the OECD members, aborted the negotiations in 1998, at least temporarily.

Although this transnational movement can claim a certain measure of success, it faces major hurdles in forging a less defective global order. The potent myth that "there is no alternative" to neo-liberal globalization constitutes one of the barriers. Hegemony rests on the prevalent imagery of globalization as an inexorable process, a force of nature driven by technological change. If this notion is accurate, then all individuals, communities, and countries must adapt to increasingly ruthless global competition. But the image is misleading. Global capitalism is not a force of nature; technological innovations in information-processing, communications, and transport buttress globalization, but they do not dictate a particular form of global economy. The neo-liberal order is a "constructed system" (Block 1999: 10). What has been constructed through international agreements and the practices of transnational actors can be reconstructed.

Another major hurdle to a transnational movement is the North-South divide. Will not workers in the developed world perceive a threat from the Third World, as transnational corporations transfer production facilities to low-wage developing countries where unions lack clout? But reserves of cheap, unskilled labour, the economists tell us, are no longer as attractive as they were in the past, owing in part to the introduction of robotics. In various ways, people in both the North and South share an interest in governing global market forces. Financial deregulation has fostered turbulence, tight monetary policies, and pressures on social programs in the North as well as the South. Global warming and climatic change, deforestation and desertification, a poisoned environment, and the depletion of the world's major fisheries are problems that harm people everywhere. Even the rich cannot fully insulate themselves from the effects of environmental degradation. Growing insecurity hurts the majority in the North as well as the South. Critics of globalization in Britain speak of a "40-30-30" society today, one in which 40 per cent of the population derive major benefits, 30 per cent work harder, longer, and in more insecure employment to maintain a stagnant living standard, and 30 per cent are marginalized in unemployment, welfare, petty crime, and part-time, unskilled work. Inequalities, moreover, are reaching grotesque proportions, both within and between countries. The *Human Development Report 1999* observes that the combined wealth of the world's three wealthiest families is greater than the annual income of six hundred million people in the least developed countries. Inequalities grew between 1993 and 1997: the world's two hundred richest people doubled their wealth (to more than U.S.$1 trillion), whereas the number of people living on less than one U.S. dollar a day remained unchanged at 1.3 billion (UNDP 1999). People in the North and South have ample grounds for anger. But whether this anger feeds a transnational social-democratic solidarity or a xenophobic-protectionist, even neo-fascist, reaction remains to be seen.

Another challenge is to build agreement in the North for some redistribution to the South—from the proceeds of a Tobin tax, for example. Jorge Castaneda (1993), writing from the perspective of a Latin American social democrat, outlines a "Grand Bargain" between North and South in which a new international deal rests on a series of trade-offs. People in the North need the co-operation of the South in dealing with many urgent issues: global warming, deforestation, and species extinction, illegal South-North migration, the international drug trade, and the migration of industries to the South, where labour and environmental regulations are more lax. Perhaps governments in the North, Castaneda speculates, will eventually agree to some redistributive measures in exchange for social and environmental charters plus accords on immigration, drug trafficking, and global capital movements. But some economic or environmental calamity may have to intervene before such trade-offs occur. It might take a major systemic crisis to loosen the constraints on state action imposed by global economic forces and hence to create an opening for social movements to pressure national governments into renegotiating international economic regimes.

Although social democrats may disagree on the tactics and prospects for democratic development, on one thing they do agree: closing the circle, in Africa and elsewhere, entails global as well as domestic reform agendas.

Notes

1 Patterns and Perspectives

1. There are now forty-eight Sub-Saharan countries. Eritrea separated from Ethiopia to become an independent country in 1994.
2. Gambia fell prey to a coup in 1994.
3. For similar arguments see Cammack 1997 and Abrahamsen 1997.
4. On Nigeria, see Ibrahim 1997; on Ghana, see chapter 5 below. For a general discussion, see Bratton and Van de Walle 1997: 31–33.
5. See also Huntington and Nelson 1976: ch.2.
6. But see, for an excellent analysis, Biersteker 1995.
7. A "rent" is an unearned or windfall gain, that is, the return that an individual or firm receives from a transaction in excess of what would have been obtained in an arms-length market situation.
8. Political conditionality has prompted much debate about its appropriateness and efficacy. See Sorensen 1993 for a range of views.
9. For good reviews of this thinking, see Healey and Robinson 1992; Van de Walle 1997; and Gordon 1996.
10. Mosley and Weeks 1993 provide a useful review of the methodological controversies swirling around the evaluation of Africa's adjustment programs until 1991. See Lipumba 1994; Sepehri 1994; Schatz 1994; Loxley 1995; and Gervais 1995b for critiques of the World Bank's methodology in a recent evaluation of adjustment in Africa (World Bank 1994).
11. The Human Development Index is a composite index based upon life expectancy at birth, educational attainment, and real GDP per capita.
12. An argument developed in chapter 6.
13. I am not suggesting that all African countries exhibited the same system. I am presenting a heuristic model that necessarily simplifies to capture what I take to be an important tendency. Each individual country will have its own characteristics; it is the task of the analyst to determine how closely an individual case fits this general model.
14. For a full exposition, see Sandbrook 1985; and Callaghy 1988.
15. Argentine Nobel Peace Prize winner Adolfo Pérez Esquivel coined the term "democratizing democracy" in relation to Latin America.

2   The Real World of African Democracy

1. This formulation is close to that of Diamond 1996.
2. Country reports of the International Foundation for Electoral Systems (IFES) were a crucial source of information on these external contributions. See Cooper, Hayward, and Lee 1992; Fischer and Kall 1994; Edgeworth et al. 1991; and Kuhn, Massicotte, and Owen 1992.
3. Although court orders obtained by the MMD in January and October 1991 progressively opened the government media to opposition voices. On the conduct of the election, see Chikulo 1993: 87–104; and Panter-Brick 1994: 235–41.
4. Data on these elections draws heavily on Wilfried Derksen, "Parliamentary and Presidential Elections around the World," www.universal.nl/users/derksen/election/home.htm.
5. Haggard and Kaufman 1992b: 343–47. Where, however, the polarization derives from ethnic or religious cleavages, it may lead to irreconcilable conflicts incongruent with democracy.
6. For a general analysis, see Widner 1997.
7. As one report (Edgeworth et al. 1991: 51) on Mali notes: "Among the government officials, party members, student groups, media representatives and associations with whom the team met, some had never experienced any kind of elections. Those who had participated in elections . . . had experienced a single party system in which no real choices existed, and in which the outcome was generally known in advance."
8. But this hollowing out of democratic institutions does not go uncontested: it generally meets strong resistance from various civil associations, political movements, and the media.
9. The following review draws heavily upon Amnesty International, *Annual Report*, 1997, 1998; and United States, Department of State, *Country Reports on Human Rights Practices*, 1997, 1998.
10. Yet we should not lose sight of the enormous variation in the circulation of daily newspapers. Ghana in 1985 had an average daily circulation of 37.3 copies per 1,000 of its population. This was vastly higher than the circulation per 1,000 in the other cases: Mali (0.5), Niger (0.8), Madagascar (5.6), Tanzania (9.7), and Zambia (17.6). Obviously, Ghana's relatively high level of literacy, urbanization, and economic development made a difference. See World Bank 1988a.
11. The following analyses are summarized from Committee to Protect Journalists 1997.

3   Democratization and Deadly Conflict

1. For a review of the competing explanations, see Sandbrook 1985, chap. 2.
2. For White (1995) these first two challenges constitute the agenda of a "democratic development state."
3. That is, the principle that only a plurality or majority vote of the relevant constituency is required to elect governors and pass legislation.
4. For an excellent study of how grassroots organizations have mobilized to resist environmental plundering, see Broad and Cavanagh 1993.

5.   For a case study of how factional relations undermine astute local environmental management, see Woodhouse's (1997) analysis of a collectively owned
Maasai ranch in southern Kenya.

4   Democratization and Market Reforms

1.   This model now seems out of reach even for the East Asian countries, since
rules negotiated through the World Trade Organization prohibit some forms
of state intervention in economic life.
2.   This interpretation draws heavily on Hutchful 1995.
3.   This viewpoint emerged in conversations with several representatives of the
World Bank and aid agencies. See also Grimm 1994.
4.   External shocks included two dramatic rises in the price of oil imports, declining international terms of trade, and soaring interest rates. Climatic shocks
refer to the devastating droughts of the 1970s and 1980s.
5.   Between 1975 and 1991, urban poverty in Zambia rose from 4 per cent to 50
per cent of total poverty. See White 1997: 73.
6.   This paragraph draws heavily on Kraus 1998, which provides a detailed survey
of external efforts to promote business influence in political decision-making
in Nigeria and Ghana.

5   Democratization and State Rehabilitation

1.   As Lewis (1994: 440) tersely observes in the case of Nigeria: "Prebendal strategies of political management directly contradict the requisites of productive
economic activity."
2.   Cf. Grafton and Rowlands 1996: 270–72.
3.   For the nature and development of the Economic Recovery Programs, see
Leechor 1994.
4.   Professional bodies, interest-based associations, and other voluntary organizations lost talented leaders to emigration, saw their financial and membership
bases dwindle, and suffered intimidation from the military regime.
5.   The independent press delighted in announcing new shipments of election
"goodies" as they arrived at Tema and were allegedly cleared through customs
by the NDC and its affiliates without the payment of import duties. See
Ghanaian Chronicle, April 25–28, 1996, June 6–9, 1996.
6.   Aside from higher producer prices, the government also restored bonuses to
cocoa farmers during the election year. According to one official of the cocoa
board this was the first time such bonuses had been paid since 1992.
7.   For good background information, see Hutchful 1997 and a series of investigative pieces by *The Statesman* [Ghana] based on interviews with anonymous
officers; see especially the issue of June 12, 1994. Note that *The Statesman* is
owned by Nana Akufo-Addo, a leader of the opposition NPP.
8.   By their nature, such reports cannot be verified.
9.   Confidential interview, National Commission for Civic Education, June 1994.
10. In 1994 and 1995 the outstanding loan to GPRTU totalled more than 171 million cedis. See Ghana 1996.

11. Donors withheld disbursements of $100–330 million each year from 1992 to 1995 (Economist Intelligence Unit 1996).
12. For a detailed analysis of party politics from 1951 to the formation of the PNDC in 1981, see Kraus 1986.
13. The rather clumsy elitist pronouncements of the NPP easily played to the NDC's advantage. A classic example occurred prior to the 1996 elections, when the NPP general secretary referred to residents of the Ayawaso Central constituency in Accra as "uneducated people who do not read newspapers" and accused them "of being in the low grade breed" (*Ghana Palaver*, Oct 7–8, 1997).
14. Between 1991 and early 1996 as many as seventy-two court cases were brought against journalists and media houses in Accra courts, often by the NDC chief whip and the deputy interior minister. See Gadzekpo 1996.
15. Information provided by the Comptroller and Accountant General's office in Accra in February 1997 from its computerized payroll system. The payroll list was "cleaned" after the 1996 elections.
16. In February 1997 the Finance Department had lacked a director of research for four years, and the Bank of Ghana for eight years.
17. Though it should be noted that exporters and importers we interviewed in 1997 were still far from satisfied with the state of affairs.
18. As Harris-White and White (1996: 4) observe, the impact of economic liberalization is likely to be, not the elimination of corruption, but its displacement from the state to the market sphere.
19. The few available studies of popular attitudes uniformly portray a public that expects their politicians to be self-aggrandizing and therefore expects to receive some tangible benefits in exchange for their support, electoral or otherwise. Political cynicism breeds at the same time a populist yearning that Rawlings initially satisfied. See Hayward 1972; Sandbrook and Arn 1977; Brown 1980; and Ninsin 1993a: 180–85.
20. This was a common theme in interviews with opposition leaders during four stints of fieldwork.

6   Closing the Circle

1. For evidence concerning the rural-urban distribution of poverty in the early 1990s compared to earlier surveys of household income, see World Bank 1995b.
2. The G7 includes the United States, Japan, Germany, France, the United Kingdom, Italy, and Canada. The G7 became the G8 with the addition of Russia.
3. Neo-liberal globalization refers to the project of constructing integrated and self-regulating global markets for goods, capital, technology, and skills.
4. South Africa may, in time, join Mauritius and Botswana among the "elect."
5. See, for example, Soros 1998 and Rodrik 1997, both of whom demonstrate that farsighted neo-liberals recognize the need for some reforms of the global economic order, especially to prevent heightened tensions between "winners" and "losers" from spiralling into social disintegration (conflict, crime, populist politics).
6. This paragraph draws heavily on Helleiner 1997: 78–81.

7. The Institute for International Economics is a think-tank in Washington, D.C., that has been a major intellectual force behind neo-liberal globalization.

8. Social-democratic globalization also obviously requires new governance mechanisms. Neo-liberal globalization, as an ideal, aspires to self-regulating global markets. In practice the transnational management that does exist, notably through the World Trade Organization (since 1995), the International Monetary Fund, and the co-ordination of advanced-country policies through the G7 and G8, reflects primarily the interests of the industrial countries. Social-democratic globalization demands governance institutions with a broader representation.

9. For a stimulating discussion of how trade rules might advance environmental concerns, see Esty 1994.

10. Cited in Van de Walle 1999: 98.

11. That is, a "third way" between neo-conservatism and traditional socialism. For Blair's view of the power of transnational capital, which cannot be resisted, see Blair 1996: 86.

12. For a graphic insider view of how the power of Wall Street influenced the key economic decision-makers around President Clinton, see the memoir of Clinton's secretary of labour, Robert Reich (1997).

13. Sadly, we now see that the catastrophe may have to be global in scope to impel a protective response to the destructive potential of self-regulating markets. Neither the financial collapse of East Asia and Russia (1997–99) nor the mounting evidence of disastrous global warming has aroused Western governments or their electorates from their stupor.

14. This is a view commonly espoused by those involved in this movement. See, for example, Wallgren 1998; and Wilson and Whitmore 1998.

15. See Korten 1996, ch.23; and Henderson 1996: 298–329. The term "global grassroots activists" is used by Henderson.

References

Abrahamsen, R. 1997. "The Victory of Popular Forces or Passive Revolution? A Neo-Gramscian Perspective on Democratization." *Journal of Modern African Studies* 35,1: 129–52.

Adekanye, J.B. 1995. "Structural Adjustment, Democratization and Rising Ethnic Tensions in Africa." *Development and Change* 26,2: 355–74.

African Development Bank, United Nations Development Programme (UNDP), and World Bank. 1990. *The Social Dimensions of Adjustment in Africa: A Policy Agenda*. Washington, D.C.: World Bank.

Ake, C. 1996. *Democracy and Development in Africa*. Washington, D.C.: Brookings Institution.

Allen, P.M. 1995. *Madagascar: Conflicts of Authority in the Great Island*. Boulder, Col.: Westview Press.

Ali, T. and R.O. Matthews. 1998a. "Civil War and Failed Efforts for Peace in the Sudan." In *Civil Wars in Africa: Their Roots and Resolution*, ed. T. Ali and R.O. Matthews. Montreal and Kingston: McGill-Queen's University Press.

———1998b. "Conclusions: Conflict, Resolution, and Building Peace." In *Civil Wars in Africa*, ed. T. Ali and R.O. Matthews. Montreal and Kingston: McGill-Queen's University Press.

Amissah, A.N.E. 1981. *The Contribution of the Courts to Government: A West African View*. Oxford: Oxford University Press.

Amnesty International. 1997. *Annual Report 1996*. www.amnesty.org/ailib/aireport/ar97/
———1998. *Annual Report 1997*. www.amnesty.org/ailib/aireport/ar98/

Amselle, J.L. 1992. "La corruption et le clientelisme au Mali et en Europe de l'Est." *Cahiers d'études africaines* 32: 629–42.

Ansah, P.A.V. 1991. "Blueprint for Freedom." *Index on Censorship* 20: 3–8.

Armstrong, R.P. 1996. *Ghana Country Assistance Review: A Study in Development Effectiveness*. World Bank Operations Evaluation Study. Washington, D.C.: World Bank.

Aron, J. 1996. "The Institutional Foundations of Growth." In *Africa Now: Peoples, Policies, Institutions*, ed. S. Ellis. London: James Currey.

Aryeetey, E. 1994. "Private Investment under Uncertainty in Ghana." *World Development* 22: 1211–21.

Asibuo, S. 1994. *A Study of Governance in Ghana under Decentralization*. Legon: School of Administration, University of Ghana. January.

Austin, D. 1964. *Politics in Ghana, 1946–1960*. London: Oxford University Press.

Ayee, J. 1995. "Civil Service Reform in Ghana: A Case Study in Contemporary Problems of Reform in Africa." Paper presented to Development Policy Management Forum, Addis Ababa, Ethiopia. December 4–5.

Azam, J.-P. 1994. "The Uncertain Distributional Impact of Structural Adjustment in Sub-Saharan Africa." In *Structural Adjustment and Beyond in Sub-Saharan Africa*, ed. R. Van der Hoeven and F. Van der Kraaij. London: James Currey.

Bangura, Y. 1994. "Economic Restructuring, Coping Strategies and Social Change: Implications for Institutional Development in Africa." Paper delivered to International Colloquium on New Directions in Development Economics, SAREC, Stockholm, Sweden. March 9–11.

Bangura, T. and P. Gibbon 1992. "Adjustment, Authoritarianism and Democracy: An Introduction to Some Conceptual and Empirical Issues." In *Authoritarianism, Democracy and Adjustment: The Politics of Economic Reform in Africa*, ed. P. Gibbon, Y. Bangura, and A. Ofstad. Uppsala, Sweden: Scandinavian Institute of African Studies.

Baregu, M. 1993. "The Economic Origins of Political Liberalization and Future Prospects." In *Economic Policy under a Multiparty System in Tanzania*, ed. M.S.D. Bagachwa and A.V.Y. Mbelle. Dar es Salaam, Tanzania: University of Dar es Salaam Press.

Barrett, C.B. 1998. "Immiserated Growth in Liberalized Agriculture." *World Development* 26,5: 743–53.

Bawumia, M. 1998. "Understanding the Rural-Urban Voting Patterns in the 1992 Presidential Elections: A Closer Look at the Distributional Patterns of Ghana's Structural Adjustment Programme." *Journal of Modern African Studies* 36,1: 47–70.

Bayart, J.-F. 1993. *The State in Africa: The Politics of the Belly*. London: Longman.

Baylies, C. and M. Szeftel. 1997. "The 1996 Zambian Elections: Still Awaiting Democratic Consolidation." *Review of African Political Economy* 71: 113–28.

Bendix, R. 1962. *Max Weber: An Intellectual Portrait*. Garden City, N.Y.: Doubleday.

Bhagwati, J. 1966. *The Economics of Underdeveloped Countries*. New York: McGraw-Hill.

Bienen, H. and J. Herbst. 1996. "The Relationship between Economic and Political Reform in Africa." *Comparative Politics* 29,1: 23–42.

Biersteker, T.J. 1995. "The 'Triumph' of Liberal Economic Ideas in the Developing World." In *Global Change, Regional Responses*, ed. B. Stallings. Cambridge: Cambridge University Press.

Blair, T. 1996. *New Britain*. Boulder, Col.: Westview Press.

Block, F. 1999. "Deconstructing Capitalism as a System." Paper delivered to "Approaches to Varieties of Capitalism" symposium, University of Manchester, England. March.

Bowen, M.L. 1992. "Beyond Reform: Adjustment and Political Power in Contemporary Mozambique." *Journal of Modern African Studies* 30: 255–79.

Bowman, L.W. 1991. *Mauritius: Democracy and Development in the Indian Ocean*. Boulder, Col.: Westview Press.

Bratton, M. 1994. "Economic Crisis and Political Realignment in Zambia." In *Economic Change and Political Liberalization in Sub-Saharan Africa*, ed. J. Widner. Baltimore: Johns Hopkins University Press.

———1998. "Second Elections in Africa." *Journal of Democracy* 9,13: 51–66.

Bratton, M. and N. Van de Walle. 1997. *Democratic Experiments in Africa: Regime Transitions in Comparative Perspective.* New York: Cambridge University Press.

Brautigam, D. 1999. "The 'Mauritius Miracle': Democracy, Institutions and Economic Policy." In *State, Conflict and Democracy in Africa,* ed. R. Joseph. Boulder, Col.: Lynne Rienner.

Bretton, H. 1966. *The Rise and Fall of Kwame Nkrumah.* London: Pall Mall.

Broad, R. 1994. "The Poor and the Environment: Friends or Foes?" *World Development* 22,6: 811–22.

Broad, R. and J. Cavanagh. 1993. *Plundering Paradise: The Struggle for the Environment in the Philippines.* Los Angeles: University of California Press.

Brown, A. 1999. "Democratization and Women's Empowerment in Tanzania." Ph.D. thesis. University of Toronto.

Brown, D. 1980. "The Political Response to Immiseration: A Case Study of Rural Ghana." *Génève-Afrique* 18: 57–64.

Brown, J. 1985. *Modern India: The Origins of an Asian Democracy.* Delhi: Oxford University Press.

Brownbridge, M. and A.F. Gockel. 1996. "The Impact of Financial Sector Policies on Banking in Ghana." Working Paper 38. Institute of Development Studies, Brighton, England. August.

Bush, K.D. 1996. "Beyond Bungee Cord Humanitarianism: Towards a Developmental Agenda for Peacebuilding." *Canadian Journal of Development Studies,* Special Issue: 75–92.

Calamitsis, E. 1999. "Adjustment and Growth in Sub-Saharan Africa: The Unfinished Agenda." *Finance and Development* 36,1: 6–9.

Callaghy, T.M. 1988. "The State and the Development of Capitalism in Africa." In *The Precarious Balance,* ed. D. Rothchild and N. Chazan. Boulder, Col.: Westview Press.

———1990. "Lost between State and Market: The Politics of Economic Adjustment in Ghana, Zambia and Nigeria." In *Economic Crisis and Policy Choice,* ed. J.M. Nelson. Princeton, N.J.: Princeton University Press.

———1995. "Africa: Back to the Future?" In *Economic Reform and Democracy,* ed. L. Diamond and M.F. Plattner. Baltimore: Johns Hopkins University Press.

Cammack, P. 1997. *Capitalism and Democracy in the Third World: The Doctrine for Political Development.* London: Leicester University Press.

Carnegie Commission on Preventing Deadly Conflict. 1997. *Preventing Deadly Conflict: Final Report.* New York: Carnegie Corporation. December.

Castaneda, J. 1993. *Utopia Unarmed: The Latin American Left after the Cold War.* New York: Alfred A. Knopf.

Centre for Economic Policy Analysis (CEPA). 1996. *Macroeconomic Review and Outlook.* Accra, Ghana.

Chabal, P. 1998. "A Few Considerations on Democracy in Africa." *International Affairs* 74,2: 289–303.

Charlick, R.B. 1991. *Niger: Personal Rule and Survival in the Sahel.* Boulder, Col.: Westview Press.

Charlick, R.B., L. Fox, S. Geller, P. Robinson, and T. West. 1994. *Improving Democratic Governance for Sustainable Development: An Assessment of Change and Continuity in Niger.* Washington, D.C.: Associates in Rural Development. October 9.

Chazan, N. 1983. *An Anatomy of Ghanaian Politics: Managing Political Recession,*

1969–1982. Boulder, Col.: Westview Press.

Chege, M. 1994. "Swapping Development Strategies: Kenya and Tanzania after Their Founding Fathers." In *Political Development and the New Realism in Sub-Saharan Africa,* ed. D.E. Apter and C.G. Rosberg. Charlottesville: University Press of Virginia.

————1995. "Sub-Saharan Africa: Underdevelopment's Last Stand." In *Global Change, Regional Response: The New International Context of Development,* ed. B. Stallings. Cambridge: Cambridge University Press.

Chikulo, B.C. 1993. "End of an Era: An Analysis of the 1991 Zambian Presidential and Parliamentary Elections." *Politikon* 20: 87–104.

Chirot, D. 1995. "National Liberation and Nationalist Nightmare: The Consequences of the End of Empires in the Twentieth Century." In *Markets, States and Democracy: The Political Economy of Post-Colonial Transformation,* ed. B. Crawford. Boulder, Col.: Westview Press.

Clark, A.F. 1995. "From Military Dictatorship to Democracy: The Democratization Process in Mali." *Journal of Third World Studies* 12,1: 201–22.

Cliffe, L. and R. Luckham. 1999. "Complex Political Emergencies and the State: Failure and the Fate of the State." *Third World Quarterly* 20,1: 27–50.

Committee to Protect Journalists. 1997. *Country Reports 1997.* www.cpj.org/countrystatus/1997

Conteh-Morgan, E. 1997. *Democratization in Africa: The Theory and Dynamics of Political Transition.* Westport, Conn.: Praeger.

Cooper, L., F. Hayward, and A. Lee. 1992. *Ghana: A Pre-Election Assessment Report.* Washington, D.C.: International Foundation for Electoral Systems.

Cranenburgh, O. van. 1996. "Tanzania's 1995 Multi-Party Elections: The Emerging Party System." *Party Politics* 2,4: 535–47.

Da Costa, P. 1995. "Out with the Old." *Africa Report* 40 (January–February): 48–51.

Dahl, R. 1971. *Polyarchy: Participation and Opposition.* New Haven: Yale University Press.

Decalo, S. 1992. "The Process, Prospects and Constraints of Democratization in Africa." *African Affairs* 91: 7–35.

de Nevers, R. 1993. "Democratization and Ethnic Conflict." *Survival* 35,2: 31–48.

de Soto, H. 1989. *The Other Path: The Invisible Revolution in the Third World.* London: I.B. Taurus.

Dia, M. 1993. *A Governance Approach to Civil Service Reform in Sub-Saharan Africa.* World Bank Technical Paper 225. Washington, D.C.

Diamond, L. 1996. "Is the Third Wave Over?" *Journal of Democracy* 7,3: 20–37.

————1997. *Prospects for Democratic Development in Africa.* Essays in Public Policy, Hoover Institution, Stanford University. Stanford, Cal.

Diamond, L. and M.F. Plattner. 1994. "Introduction." In *Nationalism, Ethnic Conflict and Democracy,* ed. L. Diamond and M.F. Plattner. Baltimore: Johns Hopkins University Press.

Diop, M. and M. Diouf. 1992. "Enjeux et contraintes politiques de la gestion municipale au Sénégal." *Revue canadienne des études africaines* 26: 1–23.

Donnelly, J. 1984. "Human Rights and Development." *World Politics* 36,1: 253–83.

Dornbusch, R. and S. Edwards. 1990. "Macroeconomic Populism." *Journal of Development Economics* 32: 247–77.

Duffield, M. 1994. "Complex Emergencies and the Crisis of Developmentalism." *Institute for Development Studies Bulletin* 25,5: 37–45.

Easterly, W. and C. Levine 1997. "Africa's Growth Tragedy: Policies and Ethnic Divisions." *Quarterly Journal of Economics* 112 (November).

The Economist (London). Various issues 1996–98.

Economist Intelligence Unit. 1996. *Ghana: Country Profile, 1996–97.*

Edgeworth, L., L. Lavoie, L. Masicotte, and H. Whittaker. 1991. *Mali: A Pre-Election Technical Assessment Report of Capabilities and Needs.* Washington, D.C.: International Foundation for Electoral Systems. July 8.

Ekins, P. 1992. *A New World Order: Grassroots Movements for Global Change.* London: Routledge.

Essuman-Johnson, A. 1993. "The Democratic Ethos and Internal Party Democracy: The Case of the Parties of the Fourth Republic." In *Political Parties and Democracy in Ghana's Fourth Republic*, ed. K. Ninsin and K. Drah. Accra, Ghana: Woeli Publishing.

Esty, D.C. 1994. *Greening the GATT.* Washington, D.C.: Institute for International Economics.

Fage, J.D. 1959. *Ghana: A Historical Interpretation.* Madison: University of Wisconsin Press.

Fairhead, J. and M. Leach. 1996. *Misreading the African Landscape: Society and Ecology in a Forest-Savanna Mosaic.* Cambridge: Cambridge University Press.

Fatton, R. 1987. *The Making of a Liberal Democracy.* Boulder, Col.: Lynne Rienner.

Fay, C. 1995. "La démocratie au Mali, ou le pouvoir en pature." *Cahiers d'études africaines* 35,1: 19–53.

Financial Times (London). 1996–99.

Fischer, J. and R. Kall. 1994. *Voter Identification and Registration in Ghana: A Technical Assessment.* Washington, D.C.: International Foundation for Electoral Systems. January 26.

Fox, L. and M. Covell. 1994. *An Assessment of Politics and Governance in Madagascar.* Washington, D.C.: Associates in Rural Development. April 24.

Friedmann, J. and H. Rangan, eds. 1993. *In Defense of Livelihood: Comparative Studies in Environmental Action.* West Hartford, Conn.: Kumarian Press.

Gadzekpo, A. 1996. "Lawsuits against the Press: Justice or Punishment?" *Media Monitor* (Accra, Ghana), July–September.

Garcia Marquez, G. 1970. *One Hundred Years of Solitude.* New York: Harper Perennial.

Gary, I. 1996. "Confrontation, Cooperation or Cooptation: NGOs and the Ghanaian State during Structural Adjustment." *Review of African Political Economy* 48: 149–68.

Geddes, B. 1995. "Challenging the Conventional Wisdom." In *Economic Reform and Democracy*, ed. L. Diamond and M.F. Plattner. Baltimore: Johns Hopkins University Press.

Geisler, G. 1993. "Fair? What Has Fairness Got to Do with It? Vagaries of Election Observations and Democratic Standards." *Journal of Modern African Studies* 31,4: 613–37.

Gervais, M. 1995a. "Structural Adjustment in Niger: Implementation Effects and Determining Political Factors." *Review of African Political Economy* 63: 27–42.

———1995b. "Ajustements: un débat stérile, des résultats tronqués et une conclusion biaisée." *Revue canadienne des études africaines* 29,2: 272–77.

Ghai, D. 1994. "Environment, Livelihood and Empowerment." In *Development and Environment: Sustaining People and Nature*, ed. D. Ghai. Oxford: Blackwell.

Ghai, D. and J.M. Vivian. 1992. *Grassroots Environmental Action: People's Participation in Sustainable Development*. London: Routledge.

Ghana, Republic of. 1996. *Report and Financial Statements of the Comptroller and Accountant-General on the Public Accounts of Ghana, Year Ending 31 Dec. 1995*. Accra: Ghana Publishing Corporation.

Ghana Palaver (Accra). 1996–97.

Ghanaian Chronicle (Accra). 1994–98.

Gordon, D.F. 1996. "Sustaining Economic Reform under Political Liberalization in Africa: Issues and Implications." *World Development* 24,9: 1527–37.

Grafton, R.O. and D. Rowlands. 1996. "Development Impeding Institutions: The Political Economy of Haiti." *Canadian Journal of Development Studies* 17,2: 261–77.

Graham, C. 1994. *Safety Nets, Politics and the Poor: Transitions to Market Economies*. Washington, D.C.: Brookings Institution.

Graham, Y. 1989. "From GTP to Assene: Aspects of Industrial Working Class Struggles." In *The State, Development and Politics in Ghana*, ed. E. Hansen and K. Ninsen. Dakar, Senegal: CODESRIA.

Graybeal, N. and L. Picard. 1991. "Internal Capacity and Overload in Guinea and Niger." *Journal of Modern African Studies* 29: 275–300.

Greider, W. 1997. *One World, Ready or Not: The Manic Logic of Global Capitalism*. New York: Simon and Schuster.

Green, D. 1995. "Ghana's 'Adjusted' Democracy." *Review of African Political Economy* 66: 577–85.

Green, R.H. 1987. *Ghana Country Study 1*. Helsinki: World Institute for Development Economics Research.

Gregory, P. 1996. "Dealing with Redundancies in Government Employment in Ghana." In *Rehabilitating Government: Pay and Employment Reform in Africa*, ed. D.L. Lindauer and B. Nunberg. Aldershot, England: Avebury.

Grimm, C. 1994. "Increasing Participation in the Context of African Political Liberalization: The Benin Budget Crisis of 1994 and Its Implications for Donors." Annual Meeting of the African Studies Association, Toronto. November 3–6.

Gros, J.-G. 1998. *Democratization in Late Twentieth Century Africa: Coping with Uncertainty*. Westport, Conn.: Greenwood Press.

Grosh, B. 1994. "Through the Structural Adjustment Minefield: Politics in an Era of Economic Liberalization." In *Economic Change and Political Liberalization in Sub-Saharan Africa*, ed. J. Widner. Baltimore: Johns Hopkins University Press.

Gulhati, R. and R. Nallari. 1990. *Successful Stabilization and Recovery in Mauritius*. EDI Policy Case Series no. 5. Washington, D.C.: World Bank.

Gunther, R. and A. Mughan. 1993. "Political Institutions and Cleavage Management." In *Do Institutions Matter?* ed. R.K. Weaver and B.A. Rockman. Washington, D.C.: Brookings Institution.

Gurdon, C.G. 1991. "The Economy of Sudan and Recent Strains." In *The Sudan after Nimeiri*, ed. P. Woodward. London: Routledge.

Gyimah-Boadi, E. 1994. "Associational Life, Civil Society, and Democratization in Ghana." In *Civil Society and the State in Africa*, ed. J.W. Harbeson, D. Rothchild, and N. Chazan. Boulder, Col.: Lynne Rienner.

———1996. "Civil Society in Africa." *Journal of Democracy* 7,2: 118–32.

———1997. "Ghana: The Challenges Ahead." *Journal of Democracy* 8,2: 78–91.

Haggard, S. and R. Kaufman. 1992a. "Institutions and Economic Adjustment." In

The Politics of Economic Adjustment, ed. S. Haggard and R. Kaufman. Princeton, N.J.: Princeton University Press.

———1992b. "Economic Adjustment and the Prospects for Democracy." In *The Politics of Economic Adjustment*, ed. S. Haggard and R. Kaufman. Princeton, N.J.: Princeton University Press.

Harris-White, B. and G. White. 1996. "Corruption, Liberalization and Democracy." *Institute of Development Studies Bulletin* 27,2: 1–5.

Harvey, C. 1996. "Constraints on Sustained Recovery from Economic Disaster in Africa." In *Constraints on the Success of Structural Adjustment Programmes in Africa*, ed. C. Harvey. New York: St. Martin's Press.

Haynes, J. 1993. "Sustainable Democracy in Ghana? Problems and Prospects." *Third World Quarterly* 14,3: 451–68.

———1995. "Ghana: From Personalist to Democratic Rule." In *Democracy and Political Change in Sub-Saharan Africa*, ed. J.A. Wiseman. London: Routledge.

Hayward, R.M. 1972. "Rural Attitudes and Expectations about National Government: Experiences in Selected Ghanaian Communities." *Rural Africana* 18: 40–58.

Healey, J. and M. Robinson. 1992. *Democracy, Governance, and Economic Policy: Sub-Saharan Africa in Comparative Perspective*. London: Overseas Development Institute.

Healey, J., R. Ketley, and M. Robinson. 1993. "Will Political Reform Bring about Improved Economic Management in Sub-Saharan Africa?" *Institute for Development Studies Bulletin* 24,1: 31–38.

Helleiner, G.K. 1994. "From Adjustment to Development in Sub-Saharan Africa: Consensus and Continuing Conflict." In *From Adjustment to Development in Africa*, ed. G.A. Cornia and G.K. Helleiner. New York: St. Martin's Press.

———1997. "External Constraints and Prospects." In *Toward Autonomous Development in Africa*, ed. R. Culpeper and C. McAskie. Ottawa: North-South Institute.

———1998. "External Conditionality, Local Ownership and Development." In *Transforming Development*, ed. J. Freedman. Toronto: University of Toronto Press.

Henderson, H. 1996. *Building a Win-Win World: Life beyond Global Economic Warfare*. San Francisco: Berett-Koehler.

Herbst, J. 1993. *The Politics of Reform in Ghana, 1982–1991*. Berkeley: University of California Press.

———1996/97. "Responding to State Failure in Africa." *International Security* 21,3: 120–44.

Hernández-Catá, C. 1999. "Sub-Saharan Africa: Economic Policy and Outlook for Growth." *Finance and Development* 36,1: 10–12.

Hibou, B. 1999. "The 'Social Capital' of the State as an Agent of Deception." In *The Criminalization of the State in Africa*, ed. J.-F. Bayart, S. Ellis, and B. Hibou. Oxford: James Currey.

Ho Won Jeong. 1998. "Economic Reforms and Democratic Transition in Ghana." *World Affairs* 160,4: 218–30.

Holm, J.D. and R.G. Morgan. 1985. "Coping with Drought in Botswana: An African Success." *Journal of Modern African Studies* 23,3: 463–82.

Holsti, K.J. 1999. "The Political Sources of Humanitarian Disasters." In *War and Displacement: The Origins of Humanitarian Emergencies*, vol. 1, *War, Hunger and Displacement: The Causes and Prevention of Humanitarian Emergencies*, ed. W.E.

Nafziger, R. Stewart, and R. Vayrynen. London: Oxford University Press.

Homer-Dixon, T. 1994. "Environmental Scarcities and Violent Conflict: Evidence from Cases." *International Security* 19,1: 1–25.

Horowitz, D. 1991. "Ethnic Conflict Management for Policymakers." In *Conflict and Peacemaking in Multiethnic Societies*, ed. J. Montville. New York: Lexington.

———1992. "Comparing Democratic Systems." In *Parliamentary vs. Presidential Government*, ed. A. Lijphart. Oxford: Oxford University Press.

———1994. "Democracy in Divided Societies." In *Nationalism, Ethnic Conflict and Democracy*, ed. L. Diamond and M.F. Plattner. Baltimore: Johns Hopkins University Press.

Hulme, M. and A. Trilsbach. 1991. "Rainfall Trends and Rural Changes in Sudan since Nimeiri." In *The Sudan after Nimeiri*, ed. P. Woodward. London: Routledge.

Hutchful, E. 1994. "'Smoke and Mirrors': The World Bank's Social Dimensions of Adjustment Programme." *Review of African Political Economy* 62: 669–84.

———1995. "Why Regimes Adjust: The World Bank Ponders Its Star Pupil." *Canadian Journal of African Studies* 29,2: 303–17.

———1997. "Military Policy and Reform in Ghana." *Journal of Modern African Studies* 35,2: 251–78.

Huntington, S. and J. Nelson. 1976. *No Easy Choice: Political Participation in Developing Countries*. Cambridge, Mass.: Harvard University Press.

Hyden, G. 1983. *No Shortcuts to Progress: African Development Management in Perspective*. London: Heinemann.

———1994. "Party, State and Civil Society: Control versus Openness." In *Beyond Socialism versus Capitalism in Kenya and Tanzania*, ed. J. Barkan. Boulder, Col.: Lynne Rienner.

Ibrahim, J. 1994. "Political Exclusion, Democratization and the Dynamics of Ethnicity in Niger Republic." *Africa Today* 41,3: 15–39.

———1997. "Expanding Nigerian Democratic Space." In *Expanding Democratic Space in Nigeria*, ed. J. Ibrahim. Dakar, Senegal: CODESRIA.

Ibrahim, J. and A. Niandou-Souley. 1996. "The Rise to Power of an Opposition Party: The MNSD in Niger Republic." *Politeia* 15,3: 32–50.

Ihonvbere, J.O. 1995. "From Movement to Government: The Movement for Multiparty Democracy and the Crisis of Democratic Consolidation in Zambia." *Canadian Journal of African Studies* 29: 1–25.

Institute of Statistical, Social and Economic Research (ISSER). 1996. *The State of the Ghanaian Economy in 1995*. Legon. July.

International Monetary Fund (IMF). 1991. *Ghana: Adjustment and Growth, 1983–91*. Occasional Paper 86. Washington, D.C. September.

———1996. *Ghana Selected Issues and Statistical Annex: Background Information to the Staff Report on the 1996 Article IV Consultation*. Washington, D.C. June 7.

International Peace Research Institute. 1997. *The State of War and Peace*. London: Penguin.

Jakobsen, M. 1996. "La paix et prosperité ou le chaos démocratique? Changements de régime et guerres civiles entre 1945 et 1992." *Internasjonal Politikk* 54,2: 237–52.

Jeffries, R. 1982. "Rawlings and the Political Economy of Underdevelopment in Ghana." *African Affairs* 131: 307–17.

Jeffries, R. and C. Thomas. 1993. "The Ghanaian Elections of 1992." *African Affairs* 92: 331–66.

Jonah, K. 1993. "Elections in the Ahanta West Constituency and Its Capital." Paper presented to Democratization and the 1992 Election in Ghana Conference, University of London. August 5–6.

Joseph, R. 1987. *Democracy and Prebendal Politics in Nigeria.* Cambridge: Cambridge University Press.

———1997. "Democratization in Africa after 1989: Comparative and Theoretical Issues." *Comparative Politics* 29,3: 363–82.

———, ed. 1999. *State, Conflict, and Democracy in Africa.* Boulder, Col.: Lynne Rienner.

Kabaya Katumbwa, J.-J. 1986. "La conception du pouvoir et de la démocratie en Afrique noire apres les indépendances." *Le mois en Afrique:* 23–38.

Kaiser, P.J. 1996. "Structural Adjustment and the Fragile Nation: The Demise of Social Unity in Tanzania." *Journal of Modern African Studies* 34,2: 227–37.

Kanbur, R. 1994. "Welfare Economics, Political Economy, and Policy Reform in Ghana." Policy Research Working Paper no. 1381. World Bank, Washington, D.C.

Kaplan, R.D. 1994. "The Coming Anarchy." *The Atlantic Monthly* 273,2: 44–76.

Kanté, M., H. Hologood, B. Lewis, and C. Coulibaly. 1994. *Governance in Democratic Mali: An Assessment of Transition and Consolidation and Guidelines for Near-Term Action.* Washington, D.C.: Associates in Rural Development. July.

Keen, D. 1994. *The Benefits of Famine: A Political Economy of Famine and Relief in Southwestern Sudan,* 1983–89. Princeton, N.J.: Princeton University Press.

Kennedy, P. 1994. "Political Barriers to African Capitalism." *Journal of Modern African Studies* 32,2: 191–213.

Khalid, M. 1990. *The Government They Deserve: The Role of the Elite in Sudan's Political Evolution.* London: Kegan Paul.

Kibreab, G. 1999. "The Environment, Sustainable Livelihoods, and Conflict." In *War and Displacement: The Origins of Humanitarian Emergencies,* vol. 1, *War, Hunger and Displacement: The Causes and Prevention of Humanitarian Emergencies,* ed. E.W. Nafziger, F. Stewart, and R. Vayrynen. London: Oxford University Press.

Killick, T. 1978. *Development Economics in Action: A Study of Economic Policies in Ghana.* London: Heinemann Educational Books.

———1995a. "Economic Inflexibility in Africa: Evidence and Causes." In *The Flexible Economy: Causes and Consequences of the Adaptability of National Economies,* ed. T. Killick. London: Routledge.

———1995b. "Structural Adjustment and Poverty Alleviation." *Development and Change* 26: 305–31.

Kimble, D. 1963. *A Political History of Ghana,* 1850–1928. London: Oxford University Press.

Kohli, A. 1993. "Democracy amid Economic Orthodoxy: Trends in Developing Countries." *Third World Quarterly* 14,4: 671–89.

———1997. "On Sources of Social and Political Conflicts in Follower Democracies." In *Democracy's Victory and Crisis,* ed. A. Hadenius. Cambridge: Cambridge University Press.

Korten, D.C. 1996. *When Corporations Rule the World.* West Hartford, Conn.: Kumarian Press.

Kraus, J. 1986. "Political Party Failures and Political Responses in Ghana." In *When Parties Fail,* ed. K. Lawson and P.H. Merkl. Princeton, N.J.: Princeton

University Press.

———1998. "Capital, Power and Business Associations in the African Political Economy: A Tale of Two Countries, Ghana and Nigeria." Unpublished paper, State University of New York, College at Fredonia.

Kuhn, W.S., L. Massicotte, and B. Owen. 1992. *Madagascar: A Pre-Election Assessment Report*. Washington, D.C.: International Foundation for Electoral Systems. March 30.

Lal, D. 1983. *The Poverty of Development Economics*. London: IEA Hobart.

Lall, S. and F. Stewart. 1996. "Trade and Industrial Policy in Africa." In *Agenda for Africa's Economic Renewal*, ed. B. Ndudu and N. Van de Walle. Washington, D.C.: Overseas Development Council.

Landell-Mills, P. 1992. "Governance, Cultural Change and Empowerment." *Journal of Modern African Studies* 30,4: 543–67.

Leach, M., R. Mearns, and I. Scoones. 1997. "Community-Based Sustainable Development: Consensus or Conflict?" *Institute of Development Studies Bulletin* 28,4: 1–3.

Leechor, C. 1994. "Ghana: Frontrunner in Adjustment." In *Adjustment in Africa: Lessons from Country Case Studies*, ed. I. Husain and R. Faruqee. Washington, D.C.: World Bank.

Leftwich, A. 1993. "Governance, Democracy and Development in the Third World." *Third World Quarterly* 14,3: 505–24.

Leith, J. and M. Lofchie. 1993. "The Political Economy of Structural Adjustment in Ghana." In *Political and Economic Interactions in Economic Policy Reform*, ed. R. Bates and A. Krueger. Oxford: Blackwell.

Lemarchand, R. 1992. "Africa's Troubled Transitions." *Journal of Democracy* 3,4: 98–109.

———1994. "Report of a Democracy/Governance Consultancy to Ghana: Local Government." Accra, Ghana: USAID. January.

Leslie, W.J. 1987. *The World Bank and Structural Transformation in Developing Countries: The Case of Zaire*. Boulder, Col.: Lynne Rienner.

LeVine, V.T. 1975. *Political Corruption: The Ghana Case*. Stanford, Cal.: Hoover Institution Press.

Lewis, P. 1994. "Economic Statism, Private Capital, and the Dilemmas of Accumulation in Nigeria." *World Development* 22: 437–51.

Lindauer, D., O. Meesook, and P. Suebsaeng. 1988. "Government Wage Policy in Africa." *World Bank Research Observer* 3,1.

Lijphart, A. 1977. *Democracy in Plural Societies*. New Haven, Conn.: Yale University Press.

———1991. "Constitutional Choices for New Democracies." *Journal of Democracy* 2,1: 72–84.

Lijphart, A. and C.H. Waisman. 1996. "The Design of Democracies and Markets: Generalizing across Regions." In *Institutional Design in New Democracies*, ed. A. Lijphart and C.H. Waisman. Boulder, Col.: Westview Press.

Linz, J. 1990. "The Perils of Presidentialism." *Journal of Democracy* 1: 51–69.

Lipumba, N.H.I. 1994. *Africa beyond Adjustment*. Washington, D.C.: Overseas Development Council.

Loxley, J. 1995. "A Review of Adjustment in Africa." *Canadian Journal of African Studies* 29,2: 266–71.

Lyons, T. 1997. "Ghana's Encouraging Elections: A Major Step Forward." *Journal of

Democracy 8,2: 65–77.

Mair, S. 1996. "Africa between Structural Adjustment, Democratisation and State Disintegration." *Aussenpolitik* 47,2: 175–85.

Mandela, N. 1995. *Long Walk to Freedom*. London: Abacus.

Marc, A., C. Graham, M. Schacter, and M. Schmidt. 1995. *Social Action Programs and Social Funds: A Review of Design and Implementation in Sub-Saharan Africa*. Discussion Paper 274. World Bank, Washington, D.C.

Martin, H.-P. and H. Schumann. 1997. *The Global Trap*. 2nd ed. London: Zed Books.

Mauro, P. 1997. "The Effects of Corruption on Growth, Investment and Government Expenditure: A Cross-Country Analysis." In *Corruption and the Global Economy*, ed. K.A. Elliott. Washington, D.C.: Institute for International Economics.

May, E. 1985. "Exchange Controls and Parallel Market Economies in Sub-Saharan Africa." *World Bank Staff Working Papers*, WPS711. Washington, D.C.

Mengisteab, K. 1995. "A Partnership of the State and the Market in African Development." In *Beyond Economic Liberalization in Africa*, ed. K. Mengisteab and I. Logan. London: Zed Books.

Mkandawire, T. 1996. "Stylizing Accumulation in African Countries and the Role of the State in Policy Making." In *New Directions in Development Economics*, ed. M. Lundahl and B.J. Ndulu. London: Routledge.

Mmuya, M. and A. Chaligha. 1993. *The Anticlimax in Kwahani, Zanzibar: Participation and Multipartyism in Tanzania*. Dar es Salaam, Tanzania: University of Dar es Salaam Press.

Moore, M. 1995. "Democracy and Development in Cross-National Perspective: A New Look at the Statistics." *Democratization* 2,2: 1–19.

Mosley, P., J. Harrigan, and J. Toye. 1991. *Aid and Power: The World Bank and Policy-Based Lending*, vol. 1. London: Routledge.

Mosley, P. and J. Weeks. 1993. "Has Recovery Begun? Africa's Adjustment in the 1980s Revisited." *World Development* 21: 1583–1606.

Munishi, G.K. 1989. "Bureaucratic Feudalism, Accountability and Development in the Third World: The Case of Tanzania." In *Public Service Accountability*, ed. J.G. Jabbra and O.P. Dwivedi. West Hartford, Conn.: Kumarian Press.

Nafziger, E.W. 1999. "The Economics of Complex Humanitarian Emergencies." In *War and Displacement: The Origins of Humanitarian Emergencies*, vol. 1, *War, Hunger and Displacement: The Causes and Prevention of Humanitarian Emergencies*, ed. E.W. Nafziger, F. Stewart, and R. Vayrynen. London: Oxford University Press.

———and R. Vayrynen. 1999. "The Wave of Emergencies of the Last Decade: Causes, Extent, Predictability and Response." In *War and Displacement: The Origins of Humanitarian Emergencies*, vol. 1, *War, Hunger and Displacement: The Causes and Prevention of Humanitarian Emergencies*, ed. E.W. Nafziger, F. Stewart, and R. Vayrynen. London: Oxford University Press.

National Capacity Building Assessment Group (NCBAG). 1996. *Report of a Study Prepared by the National Capacity Building Assessment Group*. Accra, Ghana. August.

New Patriotic Party. 1993. *The Stolen Verdict: Ghana, November 1992 Presidential Elections*. Accra, Ghana.

Ninsin, K.A. 1993a. "Some Problems in Ghana's Transition to Democratic Governance." *Africa Development* 18,2: 5–22.

———1993b. "The Electoral System, Elections and Democracy in Ghana." In

Political Parties and Democracy in Ghana's Fourth Republic, ed. K.A. Ninsin and K. Drah. Accra, Ghana: Woeli Publishing.

Nugent, P. 1996. *Big Men, Small Boys and Politics in Ghana: Power, Ideology and the Burden of History 1982–1994*. London: Pinter.

Nun, J. 1993. "Democracy and Modernization, Thirty Years Later." *Latin American Perspectives* 20,4: 7–27.

O'Donnell, G. 1994. "Delegative Democracy." *Journal of Democracy* 5,1: 55–69.

———1996. "Illusions about Consolidation." *Journal of Democracy* 7,2: 34–51.

Oquaye, M. 1995. "The Ghanaian Elections of 1992: A Dissenting View." *African Affairs* 94: 259–75.

Organization for Economic Cooperation and Development (OECD). 1999. *Development Cooperation Report 1999*. Paris.

Osaghae, E. 1999. "Democratization in Sub-Saharan Africa: Faltering Prospects, New Hopes." *Journal of Contemporary African Studies* 17,1: 5–28.

Ottaway, M. 1995. "Democratization in Collapsed States." In *Collapsed States: The Disintegration and Restoration of Legitimate Authority*, ed. I.W. Zartman. Boulder, Col.: Lynne Rienner.

———, ed. 1997. *Democracy in Africa: The Hard Road Ahead*. Boulder, Col.: Lynne Rienner.

Overseas Development Institute. 1996. *Adjustment in Africa: Lessons from Ghana*. ODI Briefing Paper. London. July.

Owusu, M. 1970. *Uses and Abuses of Political Power: A Case Study of Continuity and Change in the Politics of Ghana*. Chicago: University of Chicago Press.

———1996. "Tradition and Transformation: Democracy and the Politics of Popular Power in Ghana." *Journal of Modern African Studies* 34,2: 307–43.

Panter-Brick, K. 1994. "Prospects for Democracy in Zambia." *Government and Opposition* 29,2: 231–47.

Parson, J. 1984. *Botswana: Liberal Democracy and the Labor Reserve in Southern Africa*. Boulder, Col.: Westview Press.

Peter, C.M. 1997. "Incarcerating the Innocent: Preventive Detention in Tanzania." *Human Rights Quarterly* 19: 113–35.

Polanyi, Karl. 1944. *The Great Transformation: The Political and Economic Origins of Our Time*. Boston: Beacon Press.

Price, R. 1974. "Politics and Culture in Contemporary Ghana: The Big-Man, Small-Boy Syndrome." *Journal of African Studies* 1,2: 173–204.

———1984. "Neo-Colonialism and Ghana's Economic Decline: A Critical Assessment." *Canadian Journal of African Studies* 18,1: 163–93.

Przeworski, A., M. Alvarez, J.A. Cheibub, and F. Limongi. 1996. "What Makes Democracy Endure?" *Journal of Democracy* 7,1: 39–55.

Putnam, R.D. 1993. *Making Democracy Work: Civic Traditions in Modern Italy*. Princeton, N.J.: Princeton University Press.

Rajoelisoa, P. 1997. "Le referendum constitutional du 17 septembre et son suites." *Afrique Contemporaine* (sept.–mars): 50–58.

Ramaro, E. 1997. "Mali: Nouvelle Démocratie, Nouvelle Impatience." *Le Monde Diplomatique*. Paris: Le Monde. May.

Randall, V. 1993. "The Media and Democratisation in the Third World." *Third World Quarterly* 14,3: 625–45.

Rapoport, D.C. and Weinberg, L. 1997. "Elections and Violence." Paper delivered to Annual Meeting of the International Studies Association, Toronto. March 18.

Ratsimbaharison, A. 1997. "La démocratie Malagache: est-elle menacé?" *Gasikara.net* 1,2: 1–3. www.gasikara.net/main.html

"Recent Trends in FDI for the Developing World." 1992. *Finance and Development* 29,1: 50–51.

Reich, R. 1997. *Locked in the Cabinet*. New York: Alfred A. Knopf.

Reno, W. 1998a. "Humanitarian Emergencies and Warlord Economies in Liberia and Sierra Leone." Paper prepared for the UNU/WIDER Conference on War, Hunger, and Displacement, Stockholm. June 15–16.

————1998b. *Warlord Politics in African States*. Boulder, Col.: Lynne Rienner.

Reynolds, A. 1995. "Constitutional Engineering in Southern Africa." *Journal of Democracy* 6,2: 86–99.

Rimmer, D. 1992. *Staying Poor: Ghana's Political Economy 1950–1990*. Oxford: Pergamon.

Robinson, I. 1995. "Globalization and Democracy." *Dissent*, Summer: 373–80.

Robinson, W.I. 1996. *Promoting Polyarchy: Globalization, U.S. Intervention, and Hegemony*. Cambridge: Cambridge University Press.

Rodrik, D. 1997. *Has Globalization Gone Too Far?* Washington, D.C.: Institute for International Economics.

Rothchild, D. 1993. "Rawlings and the Engineering of Legitimacy in Ghana." Paper presented to Conference on Democratization and the 1992 Election in Ghana, University of London. August 5–6.

Sahn, D.E. 1994. "Economic Crisis and Policy Reform in Africa: Lessons Learned and Implications for Policy." In *Adjusting to Policy Failure in Africa*, ed. D. Sahn. Ithaca, N.Y.: Cornell University Press.

Sahn, D.E., P. Dorosh, and S. Younger. 1997. *Structural Adjustment Reconsidered: Economic Policy and Poverty in Africa*. New York: Cambridge University Press.

Salih, K.O. 1991. "The Sudan, 1985–89: The Fading Democracy." In *The Sudan after Nimeiri*, ed. P. Woodward. London: Routledge.

Sandbrook, R. 1985. *The Politics of Africa's Economic Stagnation*. Cambridge: Cambridge University Press.

————1991. "Economic Crisis, Structural Adjustment and the State in Sub-Saharan Africa." In *The IMF and the South*, ed. D. Ghai. London: Zed Books.

————1993. *The Politics of Africa's Economic Recovery*. Cambridge: Cambridge University Press.

Sandbrook, R. and J. Arn. 1977. *The Labouring Poor and Urban Class Formation: The Case of Greater Accra*. Occasional Monograph no. 12. Montreal: McGill University.

Saul, J. 1997. "Liberal Democracy versus Popular Democracy." *Review of African Political Economy* 73: 339–53.

Schatz, S. 1994. "Structural Adjustment in Africa: A Failing Grade So Far." *Journal of Modern African Studies* 22: 679–92.

————1996. "The World Bank's Fundamental Misconception on Africa." *Journal of Modern African Studies* 34,2: 239–47.

Schiavo-Campo, S. 1996. "Reforming the Civil Service." *Finance and Development* 33,3: 10–13.

Sepehri, A. 1994. "Back to the Future? A Critical Review of 'Adjustment in Africa.'" *Review of African Political Economy* 62: 559–68.

Sharfstein, D.J. 1995. "Radio Free Ghana." *Africa Report* 40,3: 46–48.

Shivji, I. 1990. "The Pitfalls in the Debate on Democracy." *CODESRIA Bulletin* 1: 12.

Simiyu, V.G. 1987. "The Democratic Myth in African Traditional Societies." In *Democratic Theory and Practice in Africa*, ed. W. O. Oyugi. Nairobi, Kenya: Heinemann.

Simutanyi, N. 1996. "The Politics of Structural Adjustment in Zambia." *Third World Quarterly* 17,4: 825–39.

Skalnes, T. 1995. *The Politics of Economic Reform in Zimbabwe*. London: Macmillan.

Smith, Z.K. 1997. "From Demons to Democrats: Mali's Student Movement, 1991–96." *Review of African Political Economy* 72: 249–63.

Sorensen, G. 1992. "Democracy, Dictatorship and Development: Consequences for Economic Development of Different Forms of Regime in the Third World." In *The Role of the State in the Development Processes*, ed. C. Auroi. London: Frank Cass.

———, ed. 1993. *Political Conditionality*. London: Frank Cass.

———1996. "Development as a Hobbesian Dilemma." *Third World Quarterly* 17,5: 903–16.

Soros, G. 1998. "Towards a Global Open Society." *Atlantic Monthly* 281,1: 20–24, 32.

The Statesman (Accra, Ghana). Occasional, 1993–97.

Stewart, F. 1991. "The Many Faces of Adjustment." *World Development* 19,12: 1847–64.

Stewart, F. and M. O'Sullivan. 1997. "Democracy, Conflict and Development—Three Cases." Paper delivered at the Conference on the Economics and the Political Economy of Development at the Turn of the Century, Taipei. August 1–2.

Stockholm International Peace Research Institute (SIPRI). 1998. *SIPRI Yearbook 1998*. London: Oxford University Press.

Swain, A. 1996. "Environmental Migration and Conflict Dynamics: Focus on Developing Regions." *Third World Quarterly* 17,5: 959–73.

Tangri, R. 1992. "The Politics of Government-Business Relations in Ghana." *Journal of Modern African Studies* 30,1: 97–111.

Teal, F. 1995. "Does 'Getting Prices Right' Work? Micro Evidence from Ghana." Working Paper 95–19. Centre for the Study of African Economies, Oxford University, Oxford.

Tobin, J. 1978. "A Proposal for International Monetary Reform." *Eastern Economic Journal* 3–4.

Toye, J. 1991. "Ghana." In *Aid and Power: The World Bank and Policy-based Lending*, vol. 2, ed. P. Mosley, J. Hannigan, and J. Toye. London: Routledge.

Trimberger, E.K. 1978. *Revolution from Above: Military Bureaucrats and Development in Japan, Turkey, Egypt and Peru*. New Brunswick, N.J.: Transaction Books.

Umbadda, S. 1989. "Economic Crisis in the Sudan: Impact and Response." Paper delivered at the UNRISD Conference on Economic Crisis and Third World Countries, Kingston, Jamaica. August 3–6.

United Nations Development Programme (UNDP). 1990. *Human Development Report 1990*. New York: Oxford University Press.

———1997. *Human Development Report 1997*. New York: Oxford University Press.

———1998. *Human Development Report 1998*. New York: Oxford University Press.

———1999. *Human Development Report 1999*. New York: Oxford University Press.

United States, Department of State. 1997. *Country Reports on Human Rights Practices for 1996*. www.usis.usemb.sc/human/

Van de Walle, N. 1995. "Crisis and Opportunity in Africa." In *Economic Reform and Democracy*, ed. L. Diamond and M.F. Plattner. Baltimore: Johns Hopkins

University Press.

———1997. "Economic Reform and the Consolidation of Democracy in Africa." In *Democracy in Africa: The Hard Road Ahead*, ed. M. Ottaway. Boulder, Col.: Lynne Rienner.

———1999. "Globalization and African Democracy." In *State, Conflict and Democracy in Africa*, ed. R. Joseph. Boulder, Col.: Lynne Rienner.

Vayrynen, R. 1999. "The Age of Humanitarian Emergencies." In *War and Displacement*, vol. 1, *War, Hunger and Displacement: The Causes and Prevention of Humanitarian Emergencies*, ed. W.E. Nafziger, R. Stewart, and R. Vayrynen. London: Oxford University Press.

Vengroff, R. 1993. "Governance and Transitions to Democracy: Political Parties and the Party System in Mali." *Journal of Modern African Studies* 31: 541–62.

Vivian, J.M. 1992. "Greening at the Grassroots: People's Participation in Sustainable Development." In *Grassroots Environmental Action*, ed. D. Ghai and J.M. Vivian. London: Routledge.

Wade, R. 1985. "The Market for Public Office: Why the Indian State Is Not Better at Development." *World Development* 13.

Waldron, S. 1997. "Sudan: Review Article." *African Studies Review* 40,1: 145–50.

Wallgren, T. 1998. "Political Semantics of 'Globalization': A Brief Note." *Development* 41,2: 30–32.

Wallis, J. 1999. "Understanding the Role of Leadership in Economic Policy Reform." *World Development* 27,1: 39–53.

Watts, M. 1991. "Entitlements or Empowerment? Famine and Starvation in Africa." *Review of African Political Economy* 51: 9–26.

Weber, M. 1968. *Economy and Society*, vol. 2, ed. G. Roth and C. Wittieh. Berkeley: University of California Press.

Welsh, D. 1993. "Domestic Politics and Ethnic Conflict." *Survival* 35,1: 63–80.

West, T., R. Charlick, M. Lofchie, and A.M. Tripp. 1994. *The Transition to Democratic Governance in Tanzania: An Assessment and Guidelines for Near-Term Action*. Washington, D.C.: Associates in Rural Development. March.

West Africa (London). 1993–96.

White, G. 1995. "Towards a Democratic Developmental State." *Institute for Development Studies Bulletin* 26,2: 27–36.

White, H. 1997. "Zambia in the 1990s as a Case of Adjustment in Africa." *African Development Review* 9,2: 56–87.

Widner, J.A. 1997. "Political Parties and Civil Societies in Sub-Saharan Africa." In *Democracy in Africa: The Hard Road Ahead*, ed. M. Ottaway. Boulder, Col.: Lynne Rienner.

Wilcox, D.I. 1982. "Black African States." In *Press Control around the World*, ed. J.L. Curry and J.R. Dassin. New York: Praeger.

Wilfried Derksen Web page, "Parliamentary and Presidential Elections around the World." www.universal.nl/users/derksen/election/home.htm

Williams, D. and T. Young. 1994. "Governance, the World Bank and Liberal Theory." *Political Studies* 42,1: 84–100.

Williamson, F. and S. Haggard. 1994. "The Political Conditions for Economic Reform." In *The Political Economy of Policy Reform*, ed. J. Williamson. Washington, D.C.: Institute for International Economics.

Wilson, M.G. and E. Whitmore. 1998. "The Transnationalization of Popular Movements: Social Policy Making from Below." *Canadian Journal of Development*

Studies 19,1: 7–36.

Wiseman, J.A. 1990. *Democracy in Black Africa: Survival and Revival.* New York: Paragon House.

———1992. "Early Post-Redemocratization Elections in Africa." *Electoral Studies* 11: 279–91.

———1996. *The New Struggle for Democracy in Africa.* Aldershot, England: Avebury.

Woodhouse, P. 1997. "Governance and Local Environmental Management in Africa." *Review of African Political Economy* 74: 535–47.

World Bank. 1981. *Accelerated Development in Sub-Saharan Africa.* Washington, D.C.

———1983. *World Development Report 1983.* New York: Oxford University Press.

———1988a. *Social Indicators of Development 1988.* Baltimore: Johns Hopkins University Press.

———1988b. *World Development Report 1988.* New York: Oxford University Press.

———1989. *Sub-Saharan Africa: From Crisis to Sustainable Growth.* Washington, D.C.

———1990. "Poverty." *World Development Report 1990.* New York: Oxford University Press.

———1992. *Governance and Development.* Washington, D.C.

———1994. *Adjustment in Africa: Reforms, Results and the Road Ahead.* New York: Oxford University Press.

———1995a. *African Development Indicators 1994–95.* Washington, D.C.

———1995b. *Ghana: Growth, Private Sector and Poverty Reduction.* World Bank, Country Economic Memorandum, Washington, D.C. May 15.

———1995c. *Strengthening the Effectiveness of Aid: Lessons for Donors.* Washington, D.C.

———1995d. *Zambia: Poverty Assessment,* vol. 1. Washington, D.C.

———1997. "The State in a Changing World." *World Development Report 1997.* New York: Oxford University Press.

———1999a. *African Development Indicators 1999.* Washington, D.C.

———1999b. *World Development Indicators 1999.* Washington, D.C.

World Commission on Environment and Development. 1987. *Our Common Future.* New York: Oxford University Press.

Yeats, A., A. Amjadi, U. Reineke, and F. Ng. 1996. "What Caused Sub-Saharan Africa's Marginalization in World Trade?" *Finance and Development* 33,4: 38–44.

Zolberg, A.R. 1992. "The Specter of Anarchy in Africa: African States Verging on Dissolution." *Dissent,* Summer: 303–11.

Index

capitalism, "political", 93
  attempts to transform, 82, 89–90, 94
  nature of, 17–9, 76, 78
  See also markets; rent-seeking
Castaneda, Jorge, 147
Catholic Standard (Ghana), 42
Central African Republic, 7
Chad, 8, 49, 53, 61
Christian Council of Ghana, 109
Chama Cha Mapenduzi (CCM -
  Revolutionary Party), 27, 85
chambers of commerce, 88
Chile, 76
Chiluba, Frederick, 32, 34, 39, 45, 69,
  79–80
Chissano, Joaquim, 80–1
Civic United Front (CUF - Tanzania),
  29, 34
civil associations. *See* non-governmental
  organizations; movements
Civil Defence Organization (CDO -
  Ghana), 110
civil servants. *See* public employees
civil service, 126
  causes of decline, 75, 77, 91–2
  and democratization, 97–8
  and neo-patrimonial rule, 18, 53, 91,
  92–3
  reform of, 12, 16, 67, 77, 92–4,
  123–4
  weakness of, 12, 136
  See also capacity-building;
  governance; individual countries;
  state reform
civil society, 53, 72, 93, 95, 126
  See also media; movements; non-
  governmental organizations
civil war, 1, 4, 72
  and defence spending, 135
  and democratization, 51
  and ethnicity, 7, 49–50
  and famine, 55
  See also complex political emergencies; individual countries
class formation, 82–3, 85, 86–90, 128
clientelism, 127
  and democratization, 23, 76, 93
  and national unity, 93
  nature of, 18, 104, 110, 114

and political parties, 35, 107, 110–1
and safety nets, 134
and structural adjustment, 75,
  89–90, 100
  See also individual countries, neo-
  patrimonialism, rent-seeking
climate change, 54, 147
Clinton, Bill, 139, 144
cocoa economy, 127
Cold War, 4, 6
colonialism, 1, 9, 127–8. *See also*
  individual countries
Commercial Farmers Union
  (Zimbabwe), 88
Committees for the Defence of the
  Revolution (Ghana), 109, 110, 111
Commonwealth Observer Team, 29,
  105
"complex political emergencies"
  and democratization, 7–10, 59–71,
  72
  roots of, 2, 51–5, 71–2
  Sudan case, 56–9
  See also civil wars; state decay/decline
Confederation of Zimbabwe Industries,
  87–8
Congo (Brazzaville), 7
Congo (Zaire), 4, 7, 8, 53, 61
consociational democracy, 61
Convention People's Party (CPP -
  Ghana), 101, 114, 118
corporations, transnational, 69, 70, 86,
  143–4, 146
Council of Independent Business
  Associations (CIBA - Ghana), 112–3,
  121
corruption
  consequences of, 83
  and democratization, 60, 64, 67, 68,
  76, 97–9
  extent of, 53, 89, 92
  and neo-patrimonialism, 91, 104–7
  privatization of, 125
  See also clientelism; individual
  countries; rent-seeking
coup. *See* individual countries; military

Daily Graphic (Ghana), 43
Danquah-Busia tradition (Ghana), 36,